Praise for Living in the Tension

Living in the Tension explores the complex tension between spiritual practice and social action with thoughtfulness, nuance, and clarity. The book's many examples, questions, and useful suggestions will challenge your thinking and inspire your activism and are sure to provoke important conversations that we all need to have to participate effectively and sustainably in multiracial organizing for racial justice.

> **Paul Kivel** – educator, activist and author *Uprooting Racism* and *Living in the Shadow of the Cross.* www.paulkivel.com

Our faith traditions have long played a vital role in speaking to the moral and social issues of the day, from the suffragist and abolitionist movements to the civil rights movement. Many communities of faith and faith leaders sense a yearning as well as a need to reinvigorate their role and provide a language that can speak to our deepest values and connect to contemporary issues. Shelly Tochluk invites you into welcome conversation about how we can reawaken our deepest moral traditions to promote inclusion, equity, and address fundamental questions of belonging that embrace our diversity and complexity. Her book will be helpful for all of us dealing with spirituality, race and social justice.

> **john a powell** – director, Haas Institute for a Fair and Inclusive Society, UC Berkeley; author, *Racing to Justice: Transforming Our Conceptions of Self and Other to Build an Inclusive Society*

With grace, poignancy and careful precision *Living in the Tension* makes it clear that racial justice work requires spirituality and spirituality requires racial justice work. In these beautiful and wise pages, white allies who have long-labored for the dream of beloved community will find new approaches to the dilemmas that can stymie effective spiritual activism. For those who are just coming awake to their complicity in white privilege and are eager to work for racial justice, this book offers inspiration and reliable guidance. Tochluk's personal candor carries us with her as she comes to deeper understandings of what is required to hold a both/and approach to otherwise intractable tensions. Her broad-ranging scholarship and her hands on experience are a winning combination, making this book a must-read for whites devoted to participating responsibly in the work of racial justice.

Rebecca Parker – President Emerita and Professor Emerita, Starr King School for the Ministry

In *Living in the Tension: The Quest for Spiritualized Racial Justice,* Shelly Tochluk has taken the bold step of connecting two thought communities — social justice and spirituality — that are often skeptical of each other. In doing so, she asks social justice activists to dig more deeply into the personal motivations for our work and the spiritual community to be very clear about our need to be held accountable to those who aren't in the same privileged groups in which we live our lives. Through personal stories and suggested exercises, Tochluk has provided a gift to those us who want to live in the shared space of a spiritual racial justice community.

Frances E. Kendall – author of *Understanding White Privilege: Creating Pathways to Authentic Pathways Across Race*

Exploring and transforming what is totally contradictory to everything you have been taught about societal "norms" requires great courage. Shelly Tochluk not only has courage, she also is steeped in generosity. She freely shares the wisdom she has garnered with so many people who are also dealing with the paradoxical nature of justice and spirituality. Ms. Tochluk allows us to benefit from her deep inquiry into difference, sameness, spirituality and justice, which inform a quest into the nature of what it means to become fully human. Thank you Shelly!

Shakti Butler, Ph.D. – producer/director, *Cracking the Codes: The System of Racial Inequity, Mirrors of Privilege: Making Whiteness Visible,* and *The Way Home* and *Light in the Shadows*

With this courageous and provocative book, Shelly Tochluk invites us to dive deeply into the shadows of our American psyche, illuminating a path toward the kind of hard-won racial awareness that is so desperately needed in the world today. The contents herein both challenge and inspire. Like pre-operative saline solution, this soul-searching work flushes the deepest wounds of our culture, preparing them, and us, for closer examination, and, ultimately perhaps, healing.

Christopher Henrikson – founder/executive director, Street Poets Inc.

Living in The Tension is a multi-directional approach to one of the major issues we face in the world today and particularly in the United States: racism. It offers a way of unraveling the layers of cultural confusion, it gives language to identify and properly understand the constraints embedded in the culture for many generations. By sharing her explorations into the issue with us in her writing, Shelly Tochluk provides us with a great resource so we can be supported in our own exploration of the issue. Many of the great revolutions over the last three centuries have failed miserably because at the core the individuals that were leading them did not complete the internal work necessary to support and carry out the change in the world espoused by the ideology. This is an example of an individual's personal exploration journey and, should it be mirrored by those in major positions of leadership, we will have a chance to make a much needed change in the communities we live in and in the world at large.

Miguel Rivera – director, Western Gate Roots and Wings Foundation

Shelly has done it again: as in *Witnessing Whiteness,* when she explored the complexities involved in broaching the topic of race, both within public and ourselves, Shelly has taken the time to slow down and recognize the essential question of the day. How do we live a balanced moral life? Using a thoughtful blend of research and narrative, Shelly creates space for her reader to consider the possibilities and the pitfalls of responding to that question in 21st century U.S. culture. It's aimed at those engaged in social justice work, but it will resonate with anyone and everyone who wants to do the right thing in the world.

Ayres Stiles-Hall – director, Office of Community and Equity, Concord Academy

Living in the Tension

Living in the Tension

The Quest for a Spiritualized Racial Justice

Shelly Tochluk

Crandall, Dostie & Douglass Books, Inc.
Roselle, New Jersey

Published by Crandall, Dostie & Douglass Books, Inc.
245 West 4th Avenue, Roselle, NJ 07203-1135
(908) 241-5439 www.cddbooks.com

ISBN 978-1-934390-03-0

Library of Congress Cataloging-in-Publication Data

Names: Tochluk, Shelly, 1971- author.
Title: Living in the tension : the quest for a spiritualized racial justice / Shelly Tochluk.
Description: Roselle, New Jersey : Crandall, Dostie & Douglass Books, Inc., [2016] | Includes bibliographical references and index.
Identifiers: LCCN 2015050699 | ISBN 9781934390030 (alk. paper)
Subjects: LCSH: Racism--United States. | Racism--Religious aspects. | Social justice--United States. | Social justice--Religious aspects. | United States--Race relations.
Classification: LCC E184.A1 T627 2016 | DDC 305.800973--dc23 LC record available at http://lccn.loc.gov/2015050699

For all my relations

Table of Contents

Acknowledgments

Numerous individuals offered essential and valuable critical insight and encouragement during the writing of this work and deserve much thanks. Mentors who allowed me to interview them include Orland Bishop and Miguel Rivera. Those who read initial drafts and guided my thinking include: Vance Aniebo, Michele Dumont, Susanne Owen, Christine Saxman, Ayres Stiles-Hall, Jamie Utt, and Sr. Kieran Vaughan. Shakti Butler, Francie Kendall, Paul Kivel, Rebecca Parker, and john a. powell generously read later drafts and provided words of encouragement. George Tinker, although never offering his approval, provided unambiguous critiques that prompted me to correct many errors. My editor, Bonnie Berman Cushing, and publisher, Jeff Hitchcock, believed in this work enough to bring it into existence. Thanks to all of you.

I am honored to share this journey with additional members of my racial justice community who shape my thinking and, by extension, shaped this work: Beth Applegate, Diane Burbie, Jenna Chandler-Ward, Robin DiAngelo, Hamid Khan, Jorge Zeballos, and members of my AWARE-LA family, specifically Jason David, Clare Fox, Matt Harper, James Hilman, Matt Killian, Ariana Manov, Andrea Nickerson, Sylvia Raskin, Ariane White, and Vitaly.

Essential have been additional members of my ShadeTree community who bore witness to my struggles: Akil Bell, Salvador Macias, Pasqual Torres, Fabian Montes, Matt Sawaya, Seth Weiner, Alex Keeve, and Julie Chavez. To others within community circles who inspire me, I am grateful for your influence: Max Diamond, Chris Henrikson, Tony LoRe, Michael Meade, Amanda Perez, and Luis and Trini Rodriquez.

Finally, to my parents, Cathy and Larry Tochluk, and friends, particularly Aisha Blanchard-Young and Salina Gray, your unwavering support has made a world of difference.

Introduction

While at a family gathering nearly two decades ago, I challenged a conversation between my father and a family friend, both white men in their late forties. That evening, these men spoke of their common wish to retire to Mexico, where life would be considerably cheaper. I initially sat in stunned silence, having just recently awakened to the horrific exploitation of land and human labor inherent to the U.S. capitalist system, its relationship with past and present racism, and my complicity as a white woman, regardless of my conscious intent. I eventually joined in the discussion, but was hopelessly inarticulate. My efforts to convey the seriousness of what I considered misguided and damaging plans were received as the naïve ramblings of youth. Out of frustration, my final contribution was a softly-stated lament that "I just think there needs to be more love in the world."

The inadequacy I felt in that moment was transformative, spurring me to develop a deeper understanding of social, economic, and political issues. I wanted to be understood more than ever before, for my voice to be strong and clear. I wanted my elders to recognize the dehumanization and violence inherent in our society and make different choices. Expanding outward, and extending over subsequent years, I sought to influence the "hearts and minds" of people who do not recognize the destruction and suffering caused by oppressive systems and relationships.

Fast forward to March 2014, when I witnessed john a. powell, legal scholar and professor at the University of California at Berkeley, deliver a keynote speech at a conference. He spoke about what it means to be fully human and the need to recognize our interconnections, bring spirituality back into the public space, and understand that our private experience affects social/political/economic life. His lecture paralleled much of what I was thinking and writing about, and it inspired me to read one of his earlier published articles. This reading brought my long-ago conversation at my family's gathering to mind. In the article titled, *Does Living a Spiritually Engaged Life Mandate Us to Be Actively Engaged in Issues of Social Justice?*,[1] john a. powell argues that there is a kind of surplus suffering in the world which is caused by a lack of love, lived out through our social and economic systems and institutional arrangements (p. 35). I immediately looked for the date of publication and was struck that his inspiration to write about the need for increased love in the world was not so far removed from the moment when I made my desperate declaration.

Reading this article and recalling my earlier inspiration was critical. There is an expanding wave of energy and a growing movement of people calling for humanity to recognize that spiritual development and social care and action are intertwined. They are bound together by the inspiration to love. This book is in service of this energetic push.

An essential first step is recognizing that social justice advocacy and spiritual traditions each have particular orienting principles. Over the past decade I have attempted to live out the values of both spiritual and advocacy perspectives. A few essential tenets of my spirituality include:

- Humanity is connected to all living beings; we are all one.

- Equilibrium between the outer (action) and inner (meditative) paths is desirable.

- The movements of spirit and soul are distinct, and both require attention.

Essential tenets of my social justice advocacy include:

- All people are injured by racism, sexism, classism, homophobia, etc.

- Non-violent living requires the unraveling of one's relationship to privilege and oppression.

- Supporting collective action to end individual and systemic oppression is a social responsibility and a part of being fully human.

Although the principles appear compatible, tensions arise when trying to live out their associated values, strategies, and approaches. Seeming contradictions and internal turmoil are most pronounced when considering issues of race, racial identity, and racial justice.

Over the years, one thing has remained constant; meeting the expectations set forth by both spiritual and racial justice circles is easier said than done. Staying in the dialogue, however, and working to find a path through the challenge is essential for collective well-being and social transformation. It is a necessary part of riding the wave. For this reason, this book explores the paradoxical tensions that accompany an attempt to remain true to both spiritually focused and racial justice focused principles at the same time.

Tensions between Spirituality and Racial Justice Advocacy

In an effort to provide context regarding the issues explored, the next few pages describe the personal crisis/initiation that took place during my mid-twenties which resulted in a simultaneous investigation of my relationship to race and spirituality. This initiation began while I was a Masters-level graduate student working part-time for a violence intervention project in an urban elementary school. The first trigger occurred when a significant romantic relationship ended. Nothing in my plan had accounted for the possibility that life would not turn out as expected. Having grown up 15 minutes from Disneyland, I had thoroughly absorbed the fantasy of a life lived happily ever after.

While struggling to make sense of this most unexpected break up, a roommate began asking questions about my religious beliefs because her sister had recently joined a questionable Christian denomination with a cult-like system of rules for its members. She was greatly concerned about her sister's psychological well-being and safety. We sat together and she asked questions like: What does it mean to be Christian? Do you think people who don't believe in Jesus will go to hell? What about good people having bad things happen to them? Is that part of God's plan?

Answers to these questions quickly revealed that I did not follow the mainstream interpretation of Christian scripture, although I would have answered in the affirmative if someone had asked me if I were Christian. I said things like, "Well, I think life and consciousness are too complex for us to only get one shot at it on Earth." "It seems cruel that all those who aren't Christian are going to a place called hell. I'm sure that's not really how it works." Conversations continued, with me struggling for words, but at each turn realizing that I had no consciously thought-through answers.

Hearing my own answers to my roommate, I was conflicted in a new way. I had never considered that perhaps my silent dismissal of church doctrine meant that I was not really a Christian in the way that term is generally understood. Until this time, my absence of spiritual guidance had not posed a problem, as I had never before needed a ground upon which to draw wisdom to engage difficulty. Suddenly, I found myself lacking.

Realizing within the same month that my entire life's plan had been built around a Disneyland-type fantasy and that I had no good answers to support my roommate through a crisis, I was ripe for an awakening. As minor as these two events may be in the large scheme of life's potential crises, my internal sense of self was teetering. It was at that point that an African American colleague named Vance Aniebo began to provide insights that upended my remaining assurances.

Simply and bluntly, Vance informed me that I did not know what the hell was going on around me. I was ignorant of the way race and class dynamics were playing out within the violence intervention project where we both worked. He said my race and class standing had rendered me unable to understand the lives of those with whom I was working. My lack of insight was not only offensive, but dangerous. This was not a message I wanted to hear; resistance came easily and swiftly. In *Witnessing Whiteness,* I describe more fully my initial and protracted defensiveness at being told I was essentially "unconscious" about my life.[2] One brief exchange demonstrates how basic the issues were:

Vance said, "You don't even know what's up with Damian."

"What?" I replied. Damian was a sweet, five-year old boy with an infectious grin. I knew he had witnessed familial and community violence to be eligible for the program. I gave him a hug every day upon his entry to the classroom.

Vance said something to the effect of, "But what you don't recognize is that every day, when you pull him close to you to give him a hug, your actions aren't experienced as innocently as you intend. His older brother has porn on most nights, Damian watches it; he's been sexualized really early. He's completely conscious of you pulling him toward your breasts, but you are not."

"What? No! Really? How do you know? Are you sure?" I questioned.

Thus began a slow dismantling of all I thought was true about my life, my experiences, and how I interpreted the world around me. Just as I had to learn how to bend down at my knees to give a more appropriate hug to Damian, *everything* in my life had to be reevaluated for a potentially necessary change. Religion, my relationships, actions, and assumptions, my purpose in life, and effects of race and class were all fodder for question. Vance became a mentor and teacher. Our time together supported my development psychologically, socially, and spiritually. We spent countless evenings discussing spiritually oriented readings he received from the Aquarian Spiritual Center in Los Angeles. Through text and conversation, he challenged me to expand my thinking.

This mentorship relationship with Vance allowed me to (1) become aware of race and class privilege, its concrete and very real individual and institutional effects and (2) be introduced to two spiritually oriented groups vastly different than any I had known existed. (Descriptions of those groups and my time with them can be found in an accompanying essay, *Grounding*.)[3]

Initially, the challenges to my worldview took a toll. I was in turmoil. I would not have admitted it at the time; my pride was too great to allow myself to feel the internal distress. In terms of the race issues, it was like a battle of wills on most occasions; I was fighting with my mentor. Yet, spiritually, much of what I was learning resonated so strongly that it kept me in the relationship. As time progressed, my relationships with family and old friends became increasingly challenged and tense. I was changing, radically.

Ultimately, these changes resulted in a complete shift in my life's trajectory. Within a year and a half I was a fifth grade teacher at that same elementary school, earning a teaching credential and struggling to come to grips with the race and class issues that faculty of color around me mentioned regularly. Vance and his close friendship circle were part of a spiritual study group at the Aquarian Spiritual Center and they were also members of an organization called Shade Tree, a spiritually oriented youth mentoring non-profit. Because I lived in a central location, I played host to Shade Tree's meetings and dialogues. For several years they met weekly in my apartment, with me primarily listening and learning. Through this group's weekly meetings, rituals, programs, and dialogue events, I was exposed to regular conversations on how to provide sanctuary space for, and host the destinies of, youth whose gifts were not recognized. The youth mentors at that time were primarily African American and Latino.

Within a few years of my initial crisis, my academic focus also shifted and clarified. No longer did the status of attending a top-tier doctoral program hold appeal. Neither did a mainstream approach to psychology. My interest now tended toward the psychology of the soul and the power of the unconscious, recognizing that this was a pathway that honored the connection between psyche and spirit. The spiritual study I had undertaken with Vance had been transformative; this new orientation felt like a continuation of that work. I enrolled in a doctoral program in Depth Psychology.

I entered the program with a fire in my belly, searching for the language necessary to convince my white community that a tragic mistake was being made in devaluing the lives of youth of color in the inner city. Prompting my white community into action to support healing efforts was my goal. However, by the time I neared the dissertation phase of the program, I was convinced that no language would be sufficiently penetrating until the veil of whiteness was lifted. Therefore, I launched into an investigation of what it meant to be white and how it affected cross-race relationship building. I was, in part, searching for my own way through confusion. The result of that work became the foundation for *Witnessing Whiteness*.

My confidence in the value of focusing on white racial identity increased over those years. I joined a white racial justice organization,

AWARE-LA (Alliance of White Anti-racists Everywhere – Los Angeles), and was inspired by the members' thoughtful analysis of how both consciousness-raising and political action are required for the dismantling of racism. During this time period, Shade Tree was my primary home for spiritual connection.

As I moved forward on these two parallel tracks, significant confusion ensued. On one track was my increasing dedication to racial justice advocacy. This included becoming aligned with a multiracial collection of people calling for attention to the differential impacts of racism and privilege. On the other track was my spiritually oriented home base, Shade Tree, which was invested in ameliorating the effects of injustice on youth and highlighting our interconnections. Some of my closest friends in Shade Tree, African American, Latino, and white, did not connect with my focus on racial identity. Conversations with my Shade Tree friends primarily focused on how to approach social justice through universal and collective healing efforts. At the same time, some of my experiences in racial justice events felt emotionally and spiritually destructive, as though only one aspect of my total self was being seen. In cyclical fashion I struggled, feeling conflicted and unsure which "side" was right.

The more I participated in wider circles, both of spiritually oriented people and racial justice advocates, the more I heard two commonly uttered judgments. Each criticized the other for what were interpreted to be unhelpful and/or unhealthy approaches that justified keeping distance and foregoing efforts to appreciate and (perhaps participate in) the other's activities. What I heard from spiritually oriented people:

> People focused on politics and social justice activism are angry, wounded, unhealthy individuals who sabotage their own efforts by using antagonistic and divisive language, including terms like oppression, privilege, and supremacy.

On the other hand, many racial justice advocates said something like the following about spiritually oriented people:

> People focused on their spirituality as part of their personal growth are trying to escape into transcendence or a false "kumbaya" experience and deny their ongoing role in continuing personal and institutional racism, privilege, and the reinforce-

ment of an unjust status quo that operates through interlocking systems of oppression.

Although, deep down, I knew that the racial justice focus supported the spiritual sense of connection with others, and vice versa, that awareness did not provide for a clear pathway between these two polarized positions. It is this experience of being pulled between opposing ideologies that led to the identification of the six primary tensions explored in this book.

Primary Tensions Revealed

Each of the book chapters tackles one tension-filled theme. The essential questions regarding each topic include: What happens if one of the "sides" of this tension is ignored? How can both sides cultivate strategies and approaches that allow spirituality and social justice efforts to support one another?

Chapter 1: Transcendence and Race Consciousness considers the following: What are the effects of focusing *exclusively* on spirituality, seeking to transcend the matters of the social world? Alternatively, what occurs when people focus *exclusively* on race issues and fail to attend to people's full humanity, spirit, and/or the movements of soul? This chapter explores a way of understanding race, spirit, and soul that supports navigation between the spiritual wish to "rise above" and the soul work needed "on the ground."

Chapter 2: Self-Acceptance and Self-Improvement explores the tension arising between the psycho-spiritual ideal that *"I am good enough just as I am"* and the social justice view that *"dismantling internal superiority is life-long work and I will always need to improve."* This exploration invites a self-reflective look at the psychology underlying healing societal disconnections, the symptoms of being a bystander, shame responses, and constant striving. It also asks readers to consider how shame resilience, compassion, and empathy increase self-acceptance and the ability to extend love to one's community in the service of social justice.

Chapter 3: Personal Healing and Political Action treats the tension between messages regarding the value of focusing attention toward *healing the self* and those emphasizing *taking part in political action*. This discussion includes how spiritual people seemingly rejecting individualism as part of their healing process are, nonetheless, often influenced by it in ways that disrupt participation in racial justice efforts. The chapter also explores how political organizing efforts may feel divisive and reactionary, appear to reject the role of personal agency, and lead to value judgments regarding different types of organizing and change efforts.

Chapter 4: Common Humanity and Group Differences explores questions that arise even when there is agreement that racism has negatively affected many people and healing is needed. The primary tension is whether the better course of action is to focus attention toward the *present* and *common humanity* or keep an eye trained on the *past* and *racial group differences*. Some questions include: Are there meaningful racial differences? How does paying attention to those differences help resolve ancestral wounds? Also discussed are ways people can be exhausted by storytelling across difference, get stuck in past trauma, and be treated stereotypically when they are assumed to be either ignorant or enlightened regarding issues of race. A final discussion involves imagining what group soul work might entail and how people may begin a healing process.

Chapter 5: Belonging and Appropriation tackles the sticky question of how racial privilege and power intersect with one's spiritual path. Included is a detailed discussion of what spiritual appropriation is and the harm it does. The focus is on the relationship between spiritual seekers and Native American traditions as a primary case study, although readers are asked to consider how the same themes and issues apply to the appropriation of Eastern religions or other Indigenous practices. The chapter concludes with an offering of steps that may support spiritual seekers in maintaining their spiritual sensibilities while avoiding damaging forms of appropriation.

Chapter 6: Inner Truth and Accountability considers what it means to use one's "authentic voice" or recognize a deep "truth" while trying to be accountable to racial justice efforts. This is necessary because a message delivered within racial justice circles is that people granted social privileges within a society cannot trust that their thinking is free from embedded assumptions and prejudices. Their "voice" may, therefore, be considered fundamentally suspect. This chapter describes a number of situations where misalignment occurs and ends with some approaches that support people in self-checking their perspective and building relationships across difference.

The Purpose of This Book

This book is meant to contribute to a complex conversation. I hope it helps to unravel why the judgments about spiritually focused people and racial justice advocates emerge, where the truth in the judgments exists, and where points of mutual understanding are viable. Questions are raised in the context of both personal narrative and theoretical analysis so that readers may consider these questions in their own way and through dialogue within their own relationships and communities. The information presented and questions posed can hopefully support the building of stronger connections and collaborations across spiritual and racial justice oriented people. There is a vast potential of untapped power to be released if activists and spiritual people of various backgrounds build bridges between their differing principles and expectations.

Theoretical Foundations

For years I wrestled with how to simultaneously live out the principles of my spirituality and racial justice advocacy, turning to friends and colleagues for support when grappling with specific situations. These conversations were generally validating, insofar as my confusion was met with identification and understanding. Once affirmed, I began a search for what prominent theorists have written on the topic.

A first concern was whether or not there would be support for my growing belief that there is an essential connection between one's spiritual development and racial justice advocacy. Support for this perspective came from reading *At the Root of this Longing: Reconciling a Spiritual Hunger and a Feminist Thirst*,[4] by Carol Lee Flinders. This book provides an illustration of one individual's negotiations between feminism and spiritual practice in a way that paralleled my negotiation between racial justice advocacy and spirituality.

Just as many spiritual practices are historically linked to racial oppression, structured spiritual/religious practices have been thoroughly infused with patriarchal values and strictures in ways that have been at the core of women's suffering for centuries. Flinders describes coming to awareness of the contradictions between what was being asked of her via her spiritual practice and feeling pulled in the opposite direction by a burgeoning feminism. For example, she notes that contemplative spiritual practices value silence as part of meditation, prayer, hosting the presence of the sacred, and reserving *prana,* the Hindu term for "breath" and "vitality." While nothing is inherently wrong with silence, patriarchy throughout the world's cultures has operated to silence women.

As many women today turn to spiritual traditions in search of an unfolding/growth process to heal from disconnections between body, mind, spirit, self and other, dissonance can occur when the feminist-inspired, empowered drive to express oneself and regain voice is met with a spiritual tradition that asks for silence. In other words, although engaging in a tradition that values silence may be part of a "spiritual unfolding," this practice collides with the "political emancipation" many women also need. Both the spiritual unfolding (through quiet contemplation) and the political emancipation (through use of one's voice) are important. Neither may be complete on its own. Flinders concludes that, "feminism and spirituality may actually *require* each other."[5]

The suggestion that neither spiritual development nor justice work are complete on their own parallels my sense that white people's psycho-spiritual unfolding and racial justice advocacy may also require one another. To note one connection, racism, like patriarchy, has historically been justified and perpetuated through religion. The ways crusades, missionaries, interpretations of spiritual text, and various attempts at conversion have both propelled and justified white supremacy resulting in the injury and subjugation of entire groups of people are well-documented. The image of the white-skinned, blue-eyed Jesus Christ is one example.

What also deserves focus is how many white, Western individuals, including me, turn toward Eastern or Indigenous spiritual traditions. For many, at least part of the motivation is similar to that of
women seeking the type of spiritual unfolding mentioned above: a
desire to heal from disconnections of the modern world that are related to a Western, Christian worldview. It is important to question
how race and racism play out when white individuals turn to forms
of religiosity/spirituality that do not follow the mainstream Christian
perspective. It is important to ask, what harm is done when white
people focus on spiritual development, but lack an awareness regarding underlying racial dynamics? Does the consistent perpetuation of
unintended harm upon others (due to a lack of awareness of race)
detract from the ability to claim a high level of spiritual insight? As I
believe the answer is yes, it is important to consider how a transformative, psychological healing process via a spiritual practice might *require* the development of a racial justice practice, and vice versa.

If my concern were only about my personal growth and increasing the effectiveness of my advocacy efforts, the theoretical connections made above would suffice. However, this line of question has
implications for social movements. Leela Fernandes, in *Transforming
Feminist Practice,* highlights how social movements require a spiritual
foundation. She suggests that,

> ...movements for social justice are sacred endeavors. Further-
> more, I suggest that movements for social or political transfor-
> mation have faltered not because of the impossibility of
> realizing their visions of social justice, but because such trans-
> formations cannot be complete unless they are explicitly and
> inextricably linked to a deeper form of spiritual transformation
> on a mass basis....if movements for social justice are to be
> fully transformative, they must be based on an understanding
> of the connections between the spiritual and the material
> realms.[6]

Of particular concern is how power hierarchies are often reproduced
when progressive social movements do not value the interconnections
between the spiritual and material.[7] A potential solution is found
within approaches of many women of color, such as Gloria Anzaldúa
and Jacqui Alexander, who call for a "spiritual activism" that "works

to transform all structures of hierarchy and exclusion and is based on a spiritualized understanding of ourselves both as individuals and as part of a larger interconnected world."[8] The call for a "spiritualizing feminism" is akin to a spiritualizing racial justice advocacy.[9]

This idea of marrying the spiritual and racial justice dimensions does, however, require a belief that "healing" is an important part of social justice and that psycho-spiritual growth incorporates, and extends beyond, one's personal well-being. In *Consciousness-in-Action: Toward an Integral Psychology of Liberation and Transformation,*[10] Raúl Quiñones-Rosado outlines a framework for personal and collective transformation that is inclusive of mental, emotional, physical, social, and spiritual aspects.[11] He explains the path that led him to develop this holistic framework of human development and well-being by describing his study of both psychological systems and spiritual traditions and its effect on his understanding of both well-being and social change.

Of primary concern is the question, "What is the root cause of humanity's current state of limited well-being and development?" Quiñones-Rosado reinforces that he is speaking of "all humankind" and then suggests that, "humanity *in general* — individuals, groups, communities, and societies across the planet — does not enjoy a state of advanced or optimal well-being." He names the root cause of this limited well-being *oppression,* defining oppression as "the system of differential power that privileges certain identity groups over, and at the expense of, others."[12] His position is that unless social, economic, and political systems are just, personal and collective efforts at psychological or spiritual well-being remain limited.

A lack of just systems impacts not only disadvantaged, subordinated groups who are, and who traditionally have been, treated unfairly or inequitably. Unjust systems affect people with privileged status as well. Quiñones-Rosado writes that after spending much time focused on how oppression related to his subordinated positions, he turned attention toward areas in which he enjoyed privileged status. For example, as a man, he benefits from being male within a patriarchal society. He thus paid attention to the ways he receives privileges based on one social identity (gender) along with recognition of disadvantages based on another (race/ethnicity). What he learned was how

challenging it can be to "unlearn" the assumptions and behaviors en-
gendered when part of an advantaged group.

Quiñones-Rosado then reveals that as he, "explored internalized
superiority and inferiority and how we are all socialized in oppression's insidious ideology, I truly understood that *oppression really does
negatively impact us all!"* (emphasis in the original).[13] This puts
Quiñones-Rosado in line with Freire, educational leader and author
of *Pedagogy of the Oppressed,*[14] who has always been clear that oppression damages both the oppressed and oppressors (albeit in different
ways, with differential impacts and severity), and that all people require some type of liberation.[15] The work required for liberation may
be different, depending upon one's position within subordinated or
dominant groups, but, in either case, a liberated consciousness is necessary for well-being.

The fact that I experience much advantage due to my race
(white) and class status (middle-class) does not stop my spiritual life
from being affected by injustice around me. On the contrary, my well-
being and the well-being of my community depends upon myself and
others unlearning and resisting the ways we oppressively interact with
the world, both in interpersonal interactions and through unjust economic, political, and social systems.

A final point involves the movement past *either/or* thinking and
an embrace of a *both/and* approach. The *both/and* approach is encouraged by an expanding group of people who appreciate that life pres-
ents us with many "interdependent opposites" to navigate.[16] The
term "interdependent opposites" refers to a set (or pair) of aspects
of our lives that are each essential, and yet provide paradoxical tension because each has different requirements. To offer one example, I
am simultaneously a unique individual with personal needs and a
member of a faculty group on my campus. If I only consider my *individual* needs, I am liable to act selfishly and make decisions that do
not satisfy the needs of my faculty group. On the other hand, only
considering my faculty *group's* needs and ignoring my own would
eventually impact my well-being, causing me to be overworked and
resentful. Thus, I may either act narcissistically or as a people pleaser
without healthy boundaries if I do not function in a balanced way
that values (and attends to) *both* individual *and* group needs.[17]

There are a myriad of such paradoxical interdependent opposites, also called "polarities," experienced on a daily basis, and it is useful to identify the pros and cons of each side. This allows each side to become a resource.[18] This book describes some spiritual and racial justice principles as "interdependent opposites" or "polarities" since they are both considered essential, and yet they sometimes have seemingly contradictory requirements. The attempt throughout is to imagine how to maximize the benefits of both while minimizing the problems that arise when there is a singular focus on either one.[19]

Depth psychologists and many spiritually oriented people seek a solution that is quite similar. It is understood that consciousness is created through alternating between opposites.[20] Yet, how to navigate between two aspects, or energies, is viewed in a variety of ways. For example, a Jungian psychologist will speak of the "transcendent function" that offers a synthesis, rather than the balancing of a back and forth flow.[21] Either way, there is a core belief that links the approaches: "To move into a position of synthesis, we must be willing to see the good in an opponent's position and to realize that each one only has a partial view."[22] The ability to transcend, synthesize, locate a middle way, third space,[23] or balance polarities (whatever term is chosen) is made possible by taking a step back to get a different perspective, reducing the ego investment in a particular position, and allowing for a connecting, or new, truth to emerge.

This is what Quiñones-Rosado does within his framework and what I hope this book will do. He allows for integration of concepts and ideas that have traditionally been seen by many as separate and/or antagonistic to one another. Seeking to create a bridge between what appears to be a competing focus on *liberation* within social justice groups against a focus on *personal transformation* within psychological/spiritual groups, he explains that,

> …while liberation could be characterized as the struggle against oppression, transformation could be characterized as the movement toward a future vision. Yet, from the perspective of this integral framework, liberation and transformation are not approaches in opposition to each other. Instead, they are complementary forces for change. Both liberation and transformation

approaches are essential to the developmental process of integral well-being, and as such, they are bound to, and contained within, each other.[24]

This *both/and* orientation as a way to locate connections between spirituality and a racial justice practice is explored throughout each chapter.

Out of these various influences emerges a set of tenets that might be considered part of a spiritualized social justice:

- All people are connected and in the same socio-political boat; thus, my healing is bound to yours, and no one is truly free unless all are free.

- Albeit with differential impacts and severity, all have been injured by oppression; thus, tending to the historic wounds and continuing trauma requires people to work toward healing through individual and collective efforts.

- Being born into a socio-political group is part of one's fate during a given lifetime; thus, fulfilling one's destiny requires the discovery of how one's racial group placement can be a part of increasing individual and collective consciousness.

- All people deserve compassion, respect, and a level of care while doing the work of unraveling their relationship to privilege and oppression and healing from its effects.

Clarifying Terms

"Spiritual" and **"Psycho-spiritual"** - The term "spiritual" is used in a broad sense and does not refer to the specific beliefs or practices of a particular religion or spiritual path, nor is the term used to create distance from those who locate their sense of spirit within an organized religion or spiritual tradition. There is no belief system or practice recommended in answer to the questions raised in the chapters. With that said, my core set of sacred principles derives essential wisdom from a combination of various esoteric streams of the world's major religions and is associated with what is called "the Ageless Wisdom tradition."[25] It incorporates Theosophy, Occult Philosophy, Rosicrucian and Gnostic systems, the Mystery Schools, and various Indigenous religions that experience direct relationship with spirit(s) and the divine. It is a mystical type of spirituality[26] and could be considered influenced by New Age ideas.

In addition, my academic study allows me to see how theoretical traditions, such as depth and liberation psychologies, are also aligned with the aforementioned spiritual and/or religious traditions.[27] In this way, my grounding allows the mystical and magical to meet and to relate to the intellectual and psychological, leading me to frequently combine the two as I discuss people who hold a "psycho-spiritual" orientation.

"Social Justice" and **"Racial Justice"** - Both the terms "social justice" and "racial justice" are used throughout the text.[28] The term "racial justice" is used when speaking about the community of people focusing specifically (but not exclusively) on issues of race. This is a broad group of people I refer to as my "racial justice community" and it includes those who attend or join workshops, conferences, events, political organizations, and community organizing efforts dedicated to dismantling individual and systemic racism and white privilege.

The term "social justice" is used when speaking about advocates who focus on any type of structured inequity within society. This choice is made with the understanding that it is likely that the confusions and dissonance I face when trying to reconcile my racial justice practice with my spiritual principles are, in some ways, parallel processes with the work against other types of oppression, such as classism, sexism, heterosexism, etc. or any number of particular policy issues, such as police brutality, environmental justice, immigration, etc. In this way, some points of discussion may be relevant to environmental activists, feminists, LGBTQQI activists, community organizers, etc., when negotiating issues within their own networks and considering outreach efforts to local, spiritually oriented people.

When focusing on one form of oppression, it is important to note that any effort toward justice also requires an understanding of Kimberlé Crenshaw's concept of "intersectionality."[29] This is because once one commits to investigating and dismantling advantages associated with one's social position, an investigation of the other areas becomes an essential part of developing a full social justice practice. The term "intersectionality" describes how each person occupies many different social positions in society at one time and that these positions are related; they intersect. They each have their own implications for how a person experiences the world; the implications are intertwined and cannot be separated out. As a person's social justice practice evolves, it involves paying attention to each social position in order to create a fuller picture of the ways in which the person may experience both advantages and disadvantages.

I have experienced numerous advantages. The only social position that places me in a "target" position (where the historical power position has been disadvantaged), is being part of the group "female." Women have been subject to patriarchy and sexism for centuries; the vestiges remain visible within U.S. culture and institutions in various ways. For me, attending to intersectionality means recognizing that there are some areas where being female affects me adversely. Yet, these same experiences have also been modified by my racial position (white) and my class standing (middle class). My race and class help me fit into a society that recognizes me as familiar and part of the "norm." My visual appearance and manner do not prompt people within most institutions to fear that I will disrupt their status quo. These are just a couple of examples in a long list of ways I receive advantages due to my race and class, benefits that are called "privileges" in social justice communities.

Admittedly, there were moments when I questioned whether or not my current position as operating outside the Christian faith might put me into a target category, as a non-Christian. However, being raised attending a Lutheran church shaped me in ways that continue to allow me to participate fluidly with society's cultural norms related to religion. I still fit in, if I so choose. Although I find myself relatively annoyed that my current spiritual practices are often dismissed or a subject of mockery, this cannot be equated with experiencing systematic disadvantage or oppression. The role that race plays in how my spiritual practice is viewed is a subject addressed within a later chapter.

Influences and Contributors

The whole of this effort has been shaped by the myriad influences that make me who I am today, all those I have learned from, both white and people of color. The ideas put forward were not written in isolation, but are a result of deep conversations with a multiracial collection of colleagues. In working to hold myself to standards of both my spiritual and racial justice communities, every aspect of this work was reviewed by long-term colleagues (some white, some people of color) from the communities with whom I consider myself in mutually accountable relationships.

This book would not exist without the spiritual and racial justice communities of which I have been a part. The pulls and tugs I have experienced while trying to live up to expectations and bring my full self to the table have been invaluable. They have given me the insight and the courage to articulate the tensions, connections, and the hope which accompanies me on my quest to live out a spiritualized racial justice advocacy.

CHAPTER 1

Transcendence and Race Consciousness

The word "indaba" is Zulu and refers to a group coming together to talk about something important.[1] For many years, the Shade Tree community, a spiritually oriented youth mentoring non-profit based in Los Angeles, hosted indaba events that brought together an extended network of diverse individuals from throughout Southern California. Those attending for the first time witnessed the immediacy of deep sharing and connection across race, class, and gender and often took note of these indabas as a "different" kind of gathering. Drums played. Water was poured on the ground as part of an opening ritual to set the intention. Orland Bishop, African-American founder of Shade Tree, Black Gnostic Studies teacher, and initiate of the Zulu tradition by High Sanusi Healer Vusamazulu Credo Mutwa, invited the "deep talk" conversations to begin.[2]

"Sawubona", Orland would say to the group. The word "sawubona" is Zulu, and means "we see you." Orland describes the word as returning to a time when people were able to see each other in a fuller, deeper way.[3] He describes the word as acknowledging that one's eyes are connected to the ancestral and divine realms. When he says "we see you," he is talking about bearing witness to the depth of a person's fate and the promise of his or her destiny. The word implies that not only does he intend to see the fullness of the person before him, but he commits to participating in a conversation about shared existence.

According to Orland, seeing/sawubona is an obligation. It is an obligation for each person to recognize and be willing to give to another person what is needed in that moment for life to be enhanced. He says,

> For me "seeing" now represents the question, how do I have to be in order for you to be free? Because I think our present civilization has taken away freedom from human beings, not because one culture oppressed another, but because we lost the imagination of what sight meant, of what these inner capacities really mean. So, for me, it's important to re-establish the question, "how do I have to be as a human being for someone else to be free?" …We can't do it out of self-interest. Freedom can't be pursued out of self-interest. Freedom must be a mutual gift from one human being to another recognizing that if I limit one person's freedom I limit my own.[4]

Considering that one's humanity rests on a freedom that obligates each person to one another in a spirit of mutual seeing and giving uplifts and inspires.

These indaba sessions were the most connecting and inspiring moments I had ever experienced. They felt racially transcendent. A common statement heard in those events was that race no longer mattered. Both white and people of color used the terms "post-racial" and "colorblind." The bridges built at these events across diverse lines of race and class were a hopeful image of how U.S. society could move toward peace and healing.

As the years passed and my understanding of social justice issues clarified, I became increasingly troubled. Evident within the call of sawubona (we see you) is that, if one is truly open to meeting people's needs, then all manner of social, racial, economic, and political issues require attention. Recognizing that each person has a transcending spirit, or mind, as well as collectively transcendent moments does not mean that people are excused from exploring how social identities, such as race, class, or gender, impact people and affect their lived experience in different ways.[5] It also does not mean that those impacts go away because of singular experiences, such as an indaba. The transcendent moments were wonderful, but they do not replace an obligation to pay attention to the consequences of racial identity. Over time, I became increasingly concerned that the majority of people in the crowd did not hold this *both/and* vision.

This experience illustrates a fundamental tension. People oriented toward spirituality often express:

> I don't buy into the idea of different races. Focusing on my oneness with spirit and all spirit beings supports me in moving beyond the categories we place on ourselves. This helps me detach from ideas and experiences that would otherwise bring pain and negativity. This is part of developing consciousness, growing, and evolving.

On the other hand, people oriented toward racial justice tend to express:

> Being race conscious involves recognizing that although race is not real, it has real impacts. Paying attention to race allows me to better recognize how society's systems injure people. It also lets me see how my unconscious thoughts and behaviors negatively affect people. Only by becoming aware of how race affects people will I be able to work against ongoing personal and institutional racism.

The tension between valuing transcendence versus race consciousness is important to explore because the exclusive focus on either has troublesome consequences.

❖ What has been your experience with these two orientations? Do they appear opposed? Have you focused on one or the other at some points in your life?

❖ How does your spiritual community, if you are a part of one, handle these ideas?

———————

Transcendence

Nothing others do is because of you.
What others say and do is a projection of their own dream.
When you are immune to the opinions and actions of others,
you won't be the victim of needless suffering.

———

The Four Agreements, by Don Miguel Ruiz

Live quietly in the moment
and see the beauty of all before you.
The future will take care of itself.

———

Yogananda

These quotes hold deep truths. They can be comforting and inspiring; they support the creation of a level of detachment that brings a valuable perspective. They can inspire the desire to spend the fullness of one's days in generosity and love, letting life unfold without worry and concern and enjoying the beauty of the world.

The attitude expressed also does nothing to counteract the U.S. conditioning most white people receive to avoid investigating the effects of racial identity. In fact, U.S. culture as a whole, and some mainstream spiritual traditions, advocate movement past race, whether via efforts to be colorblind, transcendent, or post-racial. For this reason, the idea that one should pay increased attention to race contradicts many people's deeply held and cherished beliefs. The goal of moving beyond the false concept of race is important. Yet, it is also important to recognize the downside of the transcendent view.

What deserves attention are a set of tensions that, when left unrecognized, lead to hurtful and oppressive patterns; these patterns occur when people devalue race consciousness.[6] Most spiritual traditions have some related concepts that support the issues outlined below.

Tension

Our individual consciousness affects the level of suffering we experience.	**— AND —**	Systemic injustice creates suffering in U.S. society, regardless of individual consciousness.

Examples drawn from a book by Eckhart Tolle, *A New Earth: Awakening to Your Life's Purpose* illustrates how an important spiritual idea can be taken in the wrong direction.[7] Eckhart Tolle is a German-born Canadian resident who shot to fame after his first book, *The Power of Now,* became a #1 bestseller when it was recommended by Oprah in 2000. When read without the lens of race or privilege, Tolle's third book, *A New Earth,* is inspiring and calls readers to take stock of how people form ego attachments in ways that produce suffering. It speaks to the evolution of consciousness, inner development, and how people are collectively creating a new, awakened earth.

Tolle suggests that seeing oneself as a victim results in self-pity, resentment, and anger.[8] He goes on to say that surrendering to one's circumstances and moving past ego reduces outer resistance.[9] Holding onto a long-standing resentment, or grievance, contaminates present emotional stability.[10] Telling personal tales of victimhood, outrage, slights, and offenses can be used to garner sympathy and attention from others in ways that result in attachment to one's sad stories.[11] And, when challenged by an event in the present, seeing oneself as a victim calls up energy from past pains, which are then amplified through emotional reactivity.[12] Tolle's fundamental message in *A New Earth* is not the primary problem that concerns me.

The concern is that Tolle's message can be used by spiritual people to see suffering as an individual issue, resulting in offers of advice or judgment regarding how others should respond to unjust treatment. Taking Tolle's message and applying it to what others "ought" to do to decrease their own pain and anger is a misapplication.[13] If I, as a white person, take from Tolle's message an attitude that people of color should release themselves from feeling the effects of pain and injury born from racism, then I am judging people of color for how they handle experiences I do not fully understand and of which I may be complicit in some way.

That is, if I as a white, spiritually oriented person feel people of color should release their attachment to injury without considering how I am part of the cause of their pain, then I avoid facing my continuing participation in structural racism and fail to recognize how race impacts people differently. It reveals that the "suggestion" as to how people of color can "grow" may be a defensive maneuver coming from my racially privileged position. This same critique applies to any person protected by privilege suggesting to others experiencing discrimination how they ought to handle their outrage. Unfortunately, blaming others for their pain, using the principles Tolle describes, is common.

Part of the tension faced here is the paradoxical message Tolle delivers; *suffering is caused by the ego, and suffering also breaks ego down.* Tolle explains, "suffering has a noble purpose: the evolution of consciousness and the burning up of the ego." By this, Tolle is referring to a reduction, a lessening, of the ego. For this reason, Tolle invites readers to "suffer consciously" and see the "man on the cross" as an archetypal image for the value of yielding to suffering. He concludes by saying that "the truth is that you need to say yes to suffering before you can transcend it."[14] By this logic, suffering is caused by the ego *and* one can use that suffering to enhance learning as part of a personal evolution.

If I apply this message to myself, then submitting to the pain of developing a white racial consciousness is akin to entering an initiatory fire of transformation. I would be able to say "yes" to the suffering that results from identifying as a white person connected to a history of colonization, genocide, and slavery that set in motion systems and attitudes that continue to benefit white people and do damage to people of color. This personal work would enhance consciousness and help disentangle the false concept called "race" and its effects.

On the other hand, if I do not apply Tolle's message to myself in the way just described, I am more likely to suggest that Tolle's "conscious suffering" message is one people of color ought to accept in order to deal with the challenges they face. Unfortunately, this orientation is common and implies that people of color should see the suffering they experience due to individual and institutional racism as part of their divine task, as a way to further their personal evolution of consciousness. In addition, it conveys the view that people of color are in control of how much pain they experience and that the regularly occurring injustices and aggressions should be interpreted as a valuable pathway toward ego reduction. Focusing my attention in this way would allow me to see myself as unrelated to people of color's pain, and may even lead to the belief that people of color should consciously and willingly accept their suffering in order to achieve enlightenment and relief.[15]

This is not to suggest that people of color cannot find great agency and peace through Tolle's suggestions and insights. However, each person's primary job is to concentrate on his or her own spiritual development, resisting the ego-influenced drive to suggest how others should grow and heal. The truth is that there are a myriad of small and large offenses, slights, and structural inequities that do not press upon me on a daily basis but which do affect people of color. If I do not explore how I benefit from these differential experiences, I will not be sufficiently aware of my true motivations in wanting others to embrace Tolle's message.

Some insight into this comes from Dick Anthony and Bruce Ecker's analysis of how the spiritual concept of detachment (which, they assert, may be an aspect of genuine transcendence) can manifest itself as "the ego defense mechanisms of dissociation and repression, the splitting-off and 'burial' of uncomfortable thoughts and feelings."[16] The authors suggest that some people use the idea of karmic law (those who suffer do so because they have merited or chosen their conditions) to justify indifference to people's suffering. In other words, believing that transcending pain is part of a person's self-selected and self-created karmic education means there is no obligation to help relieve people' social conditions.

The primary concern is that, as a white person, mistaking an unconscious desire to avoid grappling with race for spiritual transcendence can result in seeing suffering as an individual issue unrelated to social systems. This can lead to unwittingly blaming others for their suffering, resulting in unintended or implied messages such as:

- I will not take your concerns about how I might be acting racist seriously.

- Therefore, I will neither reflect on my behavior nor consider how my racial privilege acts as a shield, protecting me from experiencing what you do.

- Therefore, I will continue acting in ways you find injurious.

The only way to avoid sending these messages is by being race conscious.

❧ How does your own spiritual and/or philosophical worldview conceive of suffering?

❧ Whose responsibility is it to relieve societal suffering?

❧ How does your relationship to racial identity impact your view of suffering?

Tension

Transcending race is a necessary part of humanity's evolution and growth.	**AND**	Transcending race in this lifetime is impossible because racism has been absorbed into the unconscious and structured into the fabric of society.

Imagine the following situation. A woman of color suggests to a white co-worker that the way she speaks to their clients is racially problematic and full of assumptions. The white co-worker calmly replies to the person of color that the situation is not a racial issue, assuring her colleague of color that she is colorblind and treats everyone equally and with openness. The person of color reacts with frustration.

How is this situation to be interpreted? The white colleague, if drawing on Tolle's messages about the value of reducing ego identification, may consider the person of color too attached to her identification with race. When discussing how the "collective American pain-body" affects all parties, perpetrators and victims alike, Tolle suggests:

> It doesn't really matter what proportion of your pain-body belongs to your nation or race and what proportion is personal. In either case, you can only go beyond it by taking responsibility for your inner state now. Even if blame seems more than justified, as long as you blame others, you keep feeding the pain-body with your thoughts and remain trapped in your ego.[17]

Without the recognition that Tolle invites *all of us* to look at how racial history affects ourselves as part of a growth process, an easy misinterpretation is that the woman of color, in her frustration, is too strongly identified with her ego.[18] Missed is how the white co-worker is at least equally, if not more so, identified with, and influenced by, her ego and its defenses. Due to the white woman's ability to live without being reminded of her race every day, she may remain unaware of how she mistreats people in her immediate environment by enacting daily slights, called "microaggressions,"[19] toward people of color.

Unfortunately, all too often, spiritual people who believe issues of race can be transcended within this lifetime via ego reduction consider those who continue to demonstrate intense frustration about racism as "less evolved." The consideration of who is more evolved than another leads down a useless path. Everyone has pain and everyone is ego-identified on some level. U.S. racial history has left everyone traumatized to varying degrees. But, when Tolle suggests that the only "perpetrator of evil on the planet" is human unconsciousness, this includes a lack of consciousness regarding the effects of one's racial positioning.[20] Electing to bypass racial awareness for the sake of a hoped-for transcendence undercuts a necessary aspect of per-

sonal growth and expansion of consciousness. This is because becoming race conscious helps one avoid unconsciously participating in
aggressions, adding to others' pain, and helping to maintain an unjust
society through ignorance and silence. Even when missteps and microaggressions occur, being race conscious can help one to respond
openly and authentically when offered critical feedback. These are
signs of spiritual awareness and health.

As a final note on this issue, Tolle quotes Ram Dass as having
said, "If you think you are so enlightened, go and spend a week
with your parents."[21] He offers this as a test for one's ability to stay
emotionally calm and present to an emotional trigger, like family
dynamics. Another trigger is race. A good test of one's current state
of transcendence, particularly for white people, may be by facing
personal and systemic racism while staying authentically present,
open, and unreactive.

Recognizing how one is responsible for wounding others is
not easy. It requires an acceptance that one is not nearly as "autonomous" as desired and that it is nearly impossible to avoid complicity with unconscious prejudices and structural racism.[22] The
effects of whiteness and its depth of influence are emotionally
challenging, often painful, and take a great deal of effort to confront.[23] And yet, it is a suffering that can help diminish the aspects
of ego that are shaped by racial socialization. It avoids what is commonly critiqued as a "spiritual bypass" and stops the delivery of the
following, implied messages:

- I do not believe there are significant differences in how we experience the world, and even if there are, we can control our
  reactions to our experiences.

- I cannot understand why your racial background is so meaningful to you.

- I don't believe that racial privilege exists. Race will stop being
  an issue as soon as we stop paying attention to it, and so I see
  no reason to spend energy talking about it.

All these messages become unavoidable when a colorblind or
racially transcendent attitude leads to the belief that one is more
consciously evolved than another.

❖ To what degree have you seen a version of the "I'm more evolved" dynamic play out in your community?

❖ Do your beliefs support you in seeing race as significant and a valuable part of your evolution as a human being?

Tension

Concentrating on positivity breeds positivity.	**—** **AND** **—**	Concentrating exclusively on positivity can reduce recognition of privilege and inequity.

Another tension related to a focus on transcendence is that spiritual people concentrating on seeing only the positive often do not spend much time investigating issues of societal inequity and power. The result is a lack of awareness about how people are perceived and treated differently and how this often benefits white people. When someone remains unaware of the various ways that he or she is treated differently than others, this often leads to attitudes, speech, and actions that get in the way of hosting the spirit of sawubona (we see you). A person cannot truly see others if there is an inability to appreciate how those individuals might be experiencing society differently. To address this lack of awareness of white privilege, a brief introduction to how societal advantages are experienced seems warranted.

Peggy McIntosh's *Unpacking the Invisible Knapsack,* first published in the early 1980s, is the first stop for most people on the road toward understanding how living as a white person in the U.S. has different consequences than for people of color.[24] It includes a list of things that the author realized she did not have to worry about simply because she is white. It is a revealing list, one that only seems obvious to most white people *after* reading the article. There are many updated and varied resources available that fully explain these concepts.[25] Resources are important because learning to identify how white people receive advantages in society (whether sought after or not) is a real challenge for most white people. It is like the fish in a fishbowl becoming aware of the surrounding water. Or, it is like a right-handed person coming to recognize how instruments, like scissors or auditorium-seating desks on college campuses, are made for right-handed people.[26]

The benefits of being part of what is considered the norm initially seem subtle and inconsequential to people who have been recipients. For people of color who have experienced the flip side, they are hardly subtle. They are, in fact, highly impactful and damaging. People of color have written extensively about this.[27]

There are three levels of advantages to consider: personal, social, and systemic. For the most part, personal advantages are experienced unconsciously. One example is the ability to believe that "I am not white, I am a human being" without society regularly challenging that view.[28] The result of being told throughout life that I am an individual is that I can easily attribute anything good that happens to me as due to my skill or hard work. I also assume that others do the same for themselves. I am able to consider my experiences as "universal" or "normal," and when I think of race I think of "others," not me.[29] By extension, being part of the dominant race culture allows me to easily dismiss and disbelieve people of color's accounts of racism without it resulting in obvious negative consequences to my life.

Societal factors also bestow advantages to white people regardless of an individual's conscious intent or interest in benefiting from the inequity. In many cases, there is no chance to refuse to accept society's unequal treatment. For example, my body is part of social space and how people react to it is not under my control.[30] I cannot control people feeling less afraid of me because of my white skin. I cannot control people giving me the benefit of the doubt that I will be smart, capable, honest, and likely to fit in. I rarely have to worry about whether my race will cause me to be unsafe or treated poorly and, if I am concerned, I can generally choose to avoid going to those places with little negative impact on my life. The fact that I receive the benefit of the doubt on each of the above named points highlights the related reality that people of color are often assumed to be less safe, less intelligent, less capable, less honest, and less likely to fit in. Research evidence suggests that people of color are denied equal employment and housing opportunities, and this is likely related to the assumptions named above.[31] My life is made easier without my awareness,[32] while people of color are often treated poorly through no fault of their own.

Benefits offered to white people are also experienced through systems, policies, and institutions. Store clerks never follow me in stores to ensure I am not shoplifting, nor do police stop me when I drive through a well-to-do neighborhood. My home culture is well represented at my place of work, and receiving a promotion does not require me to significantly shift my language, dress, or manner to suit those in power. My family benefited from the GI Bill when people of color were disallowed its benefits, and the wealth that has accrued will be passed on to me. This wealth allows my family to weather economic downturns more easily. That wealth accrual also supported my attending graduate school. My doctoral studies in depth psychology then built upon a tradition understood to have gone through a "whitening" process as psychoanalytic practitioners assimilated to the U.S. culture. This resulted in depth psychology in the U.S. exhibiting a narrow view that does not consider racial or cultural issues sufficiently.[33] My graduate studies, therefore, reinforced the white, individualistic worldview of the culture in which I was raised. All of these things are true for me because U.S. society's systems, immigration policies, and legal judgments were premised on the maintenance of the U.S. as a nation designed for white people.

Choosing to concentrate solely on ideas that generate a feeling of "positivity" allows one to remain ignorant of how white privilege differentially affects our lives and those of people of color. Conversely, courageously facing the uncomfortable truth of white privilege allows for a deeper understanding of others' lived reality, a fuller embrace of the principle of sawubona (we see you), and a more active role in social justice advocacy.

❖ What does the concept of "white privilege" mean to you?

❖ How can one simultaneously attend to issues of societal advantage and work toward a life that sees through the false construct of race?

After considering how focusing exclusively on spiritual enlightenment or transcendence can allow racism to continue unchecked, the next section considers tensions that arise when there is a focus only on race consciousness. What happens if one spends too little time recognizing the spirit enlivening one another and the world? How does a lack of attention toward the psycho-spiritual undermine efforts at dismantling racism?

Race Consciousness

It is commonly understood that as soon as an object or idea becomes meaningful (salient) it is more readily observed. As soon as I bought a Honda Civic, I began to see them everywhere. It was as though they flooded the Los Angeles' freeways where they had never before been seen. Deciding to focus my dissertation work on whiteness meant the topic was *highly* salient for me. Everything was filtered through the lens of race. People of color figured prominently in my life, and their voices played in my mind. During that time, I co-produced a multicultural women's retreat that drew heavily on Indigenous principles and ritual processes to address cross-race bridge building. It was during this time that I had a memorable dream and had the opportunity to have it analyzed by a well-respected depth psychologist during a Dream Tending workshop.[34]

The contents of the dream went something like this: As I walked along a country road, I was approached by two African-appearing women wearing traditional garb and head wraps. One of the women said she would accompany me back to my home. The second woman, carrying a basket, said the growth of our charge was not yet complete, and she would return to the village where it could continue to develop. That "charge" was a partially developed fetus lying unwrapped in the basket on a bed of cloth. It was understood that I had a deep connection to this tiny being and was part of its ongoing development. The first woman and I returned to my living room. There, a set of women were gathered in community, planning and sharing, collaborating on a project. The African-appearing woman observed for a time and then, nodding her approval that the project under discussion was headed in the right direction and was good work.

My day-world consciousness had already made connections and meaning. I interpreted this as a reinforcement that the multiracial work was good, that the work was supported, and that somehow, the work had a future currently in development. Sitting face to face with the individual conducting the workshop session, he asked about moments where he had seen subtle, but physical, responses while I narrated the dream. His questions focused on the emotions underlying the dream events instead of on the events themselves. The answers revealed my deep need for validation from people of color.

Then, the workshop leader asked about the color of the women's eyes. Without stopping to think, I understood their eyes had been bright blue. My immediate recognition was that my race-focused consciousness had easily perceived the portions of the women's outer appearance which satisfied my need for race-based validation (skin color and garb). The way I interpret this today is that these beings represented a more spiritual element. Reducing the meaning of the dream as simply receiving validation from people of color was a symptom of my insecurity. I was actively seeking validation from people of color in my day-world life. So, of course, my psyche clothed these spirit beings in garments of skin and cloth that I would best receive.

This made me wonder, how else does a focused attention on race sometimes miss the presence of the spiritual or the universally human? What unresolved tensions arise during these moments? How do the problems resulting from these unresolved tensions undermine social justice efforts?

Reflecting on my experience with racial justice communities, there are a few important things to take into account. One is that there are many, many people working on racial justice issues who have a spiritual sensibility. Most of these individuals report their dedication to racial justice as being part of a spiritual, religious, or at least humanistic, practice. They already tend to carry a *both/and* orientation to some degree. And yet, there are three frequently unresolved tensions prevalent and damaging enough to describe. Although the three tensions described below are not foundational to the basic principles of racial justice, the problems born from them are common and have a relationship to the effectiveness of advocacy efforts.

Tension

Narrowly focusing on race breeds a myopic view.	—— *AND* ——	Since race is so often avoided, it is an essential issue to address whenever possible.

An old Japanese proverb says, "When all you have is a hammer, everything looks like a nail." This is an important caution for those who take up advocacy work with passion. Those invested in social justice are challenged to consistently raise awareness among friends and family. When white people take racial justice work seriously, there is often a desire to take every opportunity available to educate others about the impacts of race-based privilege and then encourage active work to dismantle or change unjust systems. Choosing to let a conversation slide is itself interpreted as an enactment of privilege.

During my early years coming to awareness about privilege, I raised the issue almost every time I spoke with one of my white friends, including moments when she turned to me for emotional support. During those conversations I showed up like a hammer and reduced my friend to a nail. My inspired and impassioned focus on race often stopped me from seeing what she needed. Ignoring what she found most emotionally evocative and painful allowed a feeling of disconnection to grow between us. I became a less than supportive friend as well as a less than effective advocate for racial justice. An unwavering and distancing focus on race squashed any future opportunity to engage her in a productive conversation about race. The insistence on focusing on race during each conversation was a result of my need to feel like a consistent advocate. A healthier approach would have allowed for the recognition that not every moment is the right one for a conversation on race.

Many versions of this story exist wherein a person invested in racial justice only sees the race dynamics in a situation when those issues may not be the most essential. It is a frequent lament that racial justice advocates sometimes focus so much on the desire to address racism and privilege that the immediate, emotional needs of people are missed. This is not to suggest that the racial dynamics are not relevant and should not be discussed eventually, only that people can sometimes fail to recognize the best time and place for the issues to be raised. The concern is not only for the health of relationships, but also for what it means for advocacy. We cannot afford to alienate potential allies.

❧ Have you ever focused so much on an issue that was meaningful to you that you failed to recognize the needs of someone close to you? What was the result?

❧ Have you ever unwittingly pushed people away because they were not ready to hear your insistent analysis about race or some other issue?

❧ How might those situations have been avoided if, in those moments, you had a stronger focus on the full humanity of the person with whom you were speaking?

Tension

Every human deserves care, love, and positive regard while seeking to raise consciousness.	——— **AND** ———	Developing race consciousness can be painful.

The first time I heard the phrase "sledgehammer tactics," it was used by someone explaining to me why she would not participate in a cross-race dialogue group. She expressed her strong reactions against antiracism workshops as they had been practiced in the late '80s and '90s wherein facilitators held the attitude that making participants feel guilty meant something good had happened. More than that, the sense was that white people had experienced a coddled existence for far too long and that the best way to move forward and right historic wrongs was to induce pain. Respect for the courage it takes to confront the effects of societal advantages and internalized racism was nowhere in evidence. This colleague was concerned that this dynamic was still too present within racial justice circles.

There are attitudes among some racial justice advocates that encourage the use of harsh approaches. They tend to arise from the following beliefs:

- "White people need to feel the pain of people of color so they will understand."

- "A focus on healing promotes 'navel gazing' in white people."

- "White people are too invested in seeing themselves as good people."

These attitudes can provoke interactions that leave people feeling confused, guilty, shamed, and mistreated. They reinforce fear, disconnection, insecurity, and silence.

Most people who attend educational conferences are not in favor of harsh tactics, however, and some of the veterans within racial justice circles have responded to my questions about this

Sledgehammer justice

subject with a curious look, suggesting they believe these tactics are no longer prevalent. Research of activists' views supports the belief that attitudes have shifted.[35] However, there are many more people doing grass-roots work, both veterans and newcomers, who nod their heads and agree that harsh tactics continue to be used regularly and in destructive ways. They acknowledge that feeling pain may be inherent to the process of uncovering internalized racism, but they are troubled by the underlying intention of instilling shame that informs their tone and results in disconnection.

A memorable example of this occurred during a lecture by a nationally renowned author when the speaker joked about white people "having no heart." Many white attendees responded by commenting about their desire not to be white and also to "get tougher" and "hit" other white people harder with the author's message. On another occasion, a speaker angrily told white people that, because they occupy land stolen from Native peoples, they have no right to live in the U.S. The conversations that followed among many white people new to racial justice revealed how they were emotionally paralyzed by those statements. They correctly perceived that the message they heard told them that if they could not give up ownership or occupation of U.S. land that they would continue to be a problem. This message left them feeling that any attempt towards racial justice by whites was fruitless, as they would never be able to correct the primary injustice named by the speaker.

The outcomes of these tactics are not always predictable, however. There have been moments when extremely harsh experiences I perceived as ignoring my core humanity also provided me an opening to understand something important. For example, being publicly challenged in a very harsh way about the way I blew past someone walking slowly within a crowded space became an important moment for me in recognizing how my relationship to time, and timeliness, can result in me unconsciously, and literally, stepping on the toes of others. The angry tone of voice and embarrassment of the moment may have felt inappropriate at the time, but it was an unforgettable and visceral experience that continues to remind me to this day to slow down. In this way, even this analysis is best held with a *both/and* attitude. Momentary use of the sledgehammer may or may not provide important learning opportunities. We cannot always predict the impact our words and actions will have in advance.

And yet, it is important to name a couple of beliefs which discourage the use of sledgehammer tactics:

- "All people have been injured by racism."

- "All people deserve to experience a level of care, compassion, and respect while doing the work of unraveling their relationship to privilege and internalized oppression."

These beliefs tend to result in exchanges that offer a less threatening entry to racial justice work and are aligned with a "whole person" approach. They reinforce risk-taking, connection, and a sense of hope amid difficulty and challenge.

The intention to respect everyone's full humanity is widely held among people invested in racial justice. And yet, consistently treating people non-oppressively and respectfully is easier said than done. Although all people need a caring environment in which to explore how they receive societal advantages, there are moments when speech can emerge out of frustration and land with destructive force. Aggressive speech can emerge from any of us given the right circumstances.

The important issue to highlight is that there is a risk of pushing people away from transforming oppressive systems and policies when the focus on race and privilege limits the ability to see people's humanity. This is true whether this is done as a consciously-determined strategy or unwittingly in moments when emotionally triggered.

❖ How does this issue relate to your learning experiences?

❖ In what ways have you been encouraged or discouraged from using harsh tactics with people?

Tension

Spiritual development allows one to hold the tension of contradiction and varied perspectives.	**———** **AND** **———**	Clear and consistent messages among allies are important when working on issues of social justice.

Effective efforts for racial justice require continued exploration into how emotional triggers disrupt the ability to hear other's perspectives non-reactively. A spiritual or humanistic approach centered in the knowledge that all people are potential allies, even if their perspectives currently belie a privileged position, may be helpful. It involves the principle of: *Engaging everyone with respect and openness as part of retaining/regaining one's own humanity*. Without this attitude it becomes easier to dismiss people as soon as their arguments or suggestions appear offensive or problematic.

As part of the research for this essay, I read *The American Soul: Rediscovering the Wisdom of the Founders* by Jacob Needleman.[36] The book caught my attention because it draws on deep spiritual understandings and is concerned with the collective consciousness, national evolution, and destiny of the U.S. One major section title, "Crimes of America," made me hopeful that this book would offer an analysis that avoided uncritically lauding our country's founders. Ever since learning our true history, I have questioned whether these individuals were redeemable, given how they handled slavery, the Constitution's determination of Black people as counting as three-fifths of a person, and the genocide of Native Americans.

Most chapters of Needleman's book offered ideas that resonated with my spiritual and psychological perspective. I appreciated the book's aim, "to rediscover in the American vision the transcendent ideas that can bring and keep people together, both as individuals and in collectivities, for the purpose of serving the good."[37] How the author suggests readers go about this, however, challenged me. Needleman suggests U.S. citizens should re-mythologize key historical figures to represent American ideals. These are

Benjamin Franklin, Thomas Jefferson, George Washington, and Abraham Lincoln. Figures such as Frederick Douglass and Hiawatha appear as symbols, but they are introduced to express the need for honest reflection on the history of slavery and genocide. While beautifully conveyed, the chapters on Douglass and Native American culture remain as symbols of the United States' crimes and, therefore, secondary to its ideals. In relegating these figures only to a consideration of America's crimes, Needleman also ignores the contributions of Native American thought to the country's founding principles.[38]

I wanted to throw the book against the wall on numerous occasions. My sense is that Needleman has either not been exposed to or taken up a serious exploration of white privilege. Many points within the text appeared to speak primarily to white people without acknowledgement that race plays a significant role in how the work will be read and experienced. For example, references to how the "Indian was destroyed"[39] is reminiscent of a recent report documenting how a Native American tribal people's petition to a court was dismissed because the tribe was considered extinct.[40] The judge read that ruling while the tribal representatives stood in the courtroom. Stop to imagine that for a moment — a group of people being denied a petition based on the judgment that they, as a people, no longer exist.

A second example is in Needleman's suggestions that the world needs the new "inner America" he proposes as a guardian of hope, bringer of truth, and preserver of world order. This is disconcerting as it sets up global humanity as needing the growth of the American soul.[41] This primacy, self-importance, and exceptionalism of the U.S. is troubling and is a product of unrecognized privilege.

While reading, it was a challenge to stay present to the multiplicity of voices and see where truth might also lie within Needleman's perspective. During this process, ringing in my ears were the implications arising from this quote by Jung:

> The present day shows with appalling clarity how little able people are to let the other man's argument count, although this capacity is a fundamental and indispensable condition for

any human community. Everyone who proposes to come to
terms with himself must reckon with this basic problem. For,
to the degree that he does not admit the validity of the other
person, he denies the "other" within himself the right to exist
– and vice versa. <u>The capacity for inner dialogue is a touch-
stone for outer objectivity.</u>[42]

As I struggled to remain open, what became clear is that Jacob
Needleman is an accomplished thinker. There is value in his orientation, particularly in the various virtues he describes. There may be
something worthwhile to build upon. A different set of historical
figures that represent gender and racial diversity, for example, could
potentially symbolize the virtues suggested.

     In the end, the point to highlight is that it is fairly common
for people invested in social justice to express complete disap-
proval and dismissal of individuals who offer perspectives contrary
to their own. There are many moments where dedicated advocates
for justice take risks to make connections that end up sounding
problematic to other advocates. If the people in those moments
are rejected, spoken of as though they are not the solid ally one
thought they were, the message it sends to potential allies is that
there is only one way to see the world and if they don't, there is no
room for them in the overall effort.[43] Resisting this pattern is an
important key to building a larger, more inclusive movement for
justice.

❧ What allows you to stay engaged with someone who offers
   ideas that differ from your own?

❧ How do you engage in discussion in a way that holds up the
   person's humanity and allows for dialogue to bring in new
   ideas or a resolution of conflict?

The Search for Balance

     This section honors the search for the *both/and* of *transcendence*
and *race consciousness* as it highlights a connecting tie that links the
movement toward transcendence with soul growth and racial identity.

The hope is that this perspective will support those who are invested in a spiritualized racial justice.

The link at the heart of this discussion is the *soul*. To be sure, the terms *spirit* and *soul* are often collapsed together and used interchangeably. However, it is valuable to tease the concepts apart, explore different definitions of both, and note that one's perspective about these concepts has psychological and behavioral ramifications. Michael Meade, author, mythologist, and storyteller, offers a helpful distinction between *spirit* and *soul* that can influence one's relationship to issues of race.

Meade conceives of *spirit* as that which moves up, aspires, reaches towards the heavens, and seeks wholeness, beauty, symmetry, and transcendence. He conceives of *soul,* on the other hand, as that which descends into the depths, the darkness, the earth, the shadow, the mud, and the messiness of life. Spirit is uplifting, and soul is grounding.

In his book, *Fate and Destiny: The Two Agreements of the Soul,* Meade pulls together threads from ancient tales that connect with Ageless Wisdom, a concept defined by Corrine McLaughlin and Gordon Davidson.[44]

> The soul is another kind of body, a subtle body that partakes of both spirituality and physicality. As the third element in the trinity of existence, soul fills the space between spirit and matter, it grounds the spirit while animating the body and helping to refine the senses…
>
> Soul is the connecting principle of life, the "both-and" factor, the unifying third between any opposing forces….when life becomes more polarized than it need be and things become more divided than they should be, it is the way of the soul that is missing and needed to heal the divisions and make things whole again…
>
> For our soul instinctively knows where and how we should sink our feet into the mud of creation and grow our roots down. Spirit may seek peak experiences and the heavenly heights; but soul would have us incarnate fully and would help us to grow deep roots that allow the spirit of our life to branch out.[45]

Meade also discusses the differential investments of spirit and soul as he writes,

> In contrast to the tendency of spirit to unify under a single idea or singular image of the divine, the soul thrives on diversity and multiplicity…

> The conversation with the divine leads the soul of the seeker to an immersion in the dramas and delights of life on earth….On one hand we must know what it means to be alive in the human drama that alternates between love and loss. On the other hand there is a longing to know the divine and serve something that transcends all of that.[46]

In this view spirit seeks to serve the transcendent, while soul allows one to become increasingly conscious of what it means to be part of human experience. Neither spirit nor soul is more important than the other.

Unfortunately, many who look toward spirituality and healing practices in modern culture do so in a way that neglects soul. For the sake of transcending the pain and difficulty experienced within U.S. society, many people aspire to leave the physical world behind rather than take the initiatory step of engaging it more fully in order to be part of its transformation. This has tremendous implications for social justice.

It also has personal ramifications. Although there is no doubt that paying attention to race is a descent into a muddy mess, focusing on transcendence can leave one striving for the heavens without sufficient attention to the soul's work on the ground within earthly life. Bringing transcendental aspirations into harmony with the needs of the soul by becoming fully immersed in socially-oriented issues, such as race, is valuable. As a white person, it is important that I spend time attending to the still-evolving social world. This allows me to "recognize the complexity and weight of the current existence of white racism, to attempt to understand the ways in which [I] perpetuate racism, and to begin to think about the incredible difficulty in undoing it."[47] It might feel like drowning in the swirling waters of life, as the waters that surround this task are deep and powerful, and the initial relationship to issues of race may reflect more trauma than delight. But entering the difficulty is part of the earthly drama the soul requires.

For those who do not find value in Meade's conception of spirit and soul, other traditions create linkages between how to awaken to a deeper level of consciousness while also attending to earthly, political life. Readers might consider their own tradition as providing these linkages. Another example might be Tolle's language focusing on releasing ego and attachment to form. He offers the following:

> Being at one with what is doesn't mean you no longer initiate change or become incapable of taking action. But the motivation to take action comes from a deeper level, not from egoic wanting or fearing. Inner alignment with the present moment opens your consciousness and brings it into alignment with the whole, of which the present moment is an integral part.[48]

This suggests that becoming awakened supports the ability to swim in the swirling waters of earthly life without drowning, thus allowing for a conscious role in resolving worldly issues. Tolle describes "awakened doing" as "the alignment of your outer purpose — what you do — with your inner purpose — awakening and staying awake."[49] Tolle explains:

> Through awakened doing, you become one with the outgoing purpose of the universe. Consciousness flows through you into this world. It flows into your thoughts and inspires them. It flows into what you do and guides and empowers it.[50]

The action taken when awake, when not fueled by conditioned unconsciousness, helps to bring healing to the social world.

Engaged Buddhism also offers supportive concepts as it combines a focus on a person's inner experience and/or psychological health with attention toward the social, economic, and political realities that play a role in the person's experiences. Thich Nhat Hahn suggests that transformation of that which causes affliction is part of liberation.[51] The idea is that "Buddhism's original focus on personal liberation from the suffering arising from cycles of birth, old age, sickness, and death now requires a focus on social liberation."[52]

With significant critique leveled at Western concepts of development, this approach counters a focus on the individual and instead suggests a focus on "dependent co-arising" which stresses "the interdependence of personal, communal, and ecological liberation. Here the fulfillment of one's own true nature entails a turning away from seeing a separate 'me' and 'mine' and turning to the realization of the potential of others."[53] This is reminiscent of the meaning of sawubona. We see you, your fate, and your destiny, and we obligate ourselves to be partners in that process. In this view, disregarding others through inattention and inaction diminishes the shared world.

When it comes to doing the soul work of engaging racial justice, it is also essential to have a healthy racial identity. However, creating a deeply considered and authentic racial identity can be challenging. It requires an honest exploration of one's relationship to the history of U.S. racism, white supremacy, and its lingering effects. It also requires one to take responsibility for how race currently manifests in one's life and psyche. The benefit of this work is that it allows for a self-understanding that leaves nothing out. Identifying as a white person invested in advocacy can be a re-creation of self, as it rejects the idea of identity as "fixed" and re-imagines a new and radical way of being white.[54]

Admittedly, suggesting the need for white people to create an explicitly anti-racist identity around being a white person invested in racial justice strikes many as odd, unnecessary, presumptuous, or flat out wrong. Its value and import did not become apparent in my life until after attending a dialogue group for white people interested in dismantling racism, AWARE-LA. This grassroots, all-volunteer organization, active for more than 12 years, has been the vehicle for much of my growth. If the members of this white, racial justice community focused solely on race, privilege, and political issues, however, its approach would not have been balanced enough for me to stay engaged.

One of the first things that became apparent was that its core models recognize that everyone is damaged by racism and everyone needs a healing process that allows people to be fully human in the world.[55] This is the basis for white people's role in racial justice. I am not dedicated to racial justice simply because it is the right thing to do, and I am not active solely to support others. The group taught me that racial justice work is part of my own soul's work. Working toward social justice is part of me rebuilding my humanity after our culture has done so much to strip it away through racist conditioning. Many white activists also approach racial justice with this understanding.[56]

Believing that oppression wounds everyone, the organization's Saturday Dialogues offer a place where white people can support each other to heal from experiences as perpetrators, bystanders, and witnesses to racial trauma.[57] For example, a young college student attending a meeting for the first time shared her struggles to understand the perspective of her roommate, a person of color. She admitted being new to issues of privilege, and her sincerity was evident. Feedback from her friends and family was simply that the roommate was being mean and overly critical. They did not encourage her to take her roommate's concerns seriously. The sense of relief on this young woman's face as meeting participants offered her advice regarding how to stay present to her roommate's ideas while simultaneously holding herself as a valuable person is part of the reason I continue to attend after so many years.

This young woman left feeling uplifted, strengthened, renewed, and ready to engage further with the challenging feedback she would continue to receive from her roommate. She left with a readiness to be more accountable to issues of race. I tell this story because white people need one another for this kind of support to sustain a commitment to racial justice, and these meetings only exist because those of us who attend identify as being both white and committed to racial justice. We take responsibility for what white identity means for our lives as we validate our need to stick with the hard work of uncovering power and privilege and maintain our sense of self as worthy of love. Seeing ourselves for who we are as racial beings does not have to take away from our complex, multiple identities. We attempt to hold the *both/and*.

A spirit of *transcendence* and a dedication to *race consciousness* each has its own benefits and shadows. We are more likely to collectively take up the effort to become racially conscious if we appreciate each other's humanity and engage with compassion. The hope is that a strong, healthy community can uphold a spiritual orientation while also be skillful at challenging internal, interpersonal, and structural racism. Making this vision a reality, though, requires recognizing that doing active work on the ground, the soul's work, is part of living out a spiritual path. A story from Rabbi Avi Weiss captures the issue perfectly. He once told of a sign he keeps on his desk. It includes a conversation between two people. Person one says to person two, "Sometimes I feel like asking God, how come there is so much sickness and poverty and racism in this world." Person two says to person one, "Then why don't you ask God that question?" And person one responds, "Because I'm afraid that God is going to ask me the same question."[58]

CHAPTER 2

Self-Acceptance and Self-Improvement

A number of years ago, while attending a meeting that called together a broad network of people invested in restorative justice, a woman approached me after brief introductions concluded. Having mentioned my investment in dealing with white racial identity, she shared her story with me. This white woman explained how she had been part of a reality TV program focused on cross-race exchanges. From her narrative it is clear that the producers sought to cast individuals who would heighten the drama — and therefore ratings — by having some white individuals involved who knew very little about how their racial background and culture affect their behavior. The results were predictable, and this woman's ignorance about issues of race was exposed. She was also severely shamed in a very public way, to the degree that a significant familial relationship ended, she had to relocate, and she essentially went into hiding for quite some time.

I asked her what this experience taught her about race and racial identity. She articulated that the major lesson learned was about the need for self-acceptance in the face of challenge. Her sense of having been publicly humiliated continued to shape her response to the events. The thought of delving further into racial identity in order to better understand how the situation unfolded ran completely counter to her primary imperative — to recover and maintain her sense of self as a valuable, whole human being.

Humans have some common universal needs. These include acceptance, connection, empathy, and healing.[1] A healthy sense of self-esteem, self-respect, and/or self-acceptance allows people to have faith in their abilities and the confidence to participate in society.[2] One's sense of self is of primary value and is likely to be defended when challenged. On the other hand, outright resistance to critical feedback in order to protect a sense of self can lead to a lack of growth and a dismissal of concerns raised by others. A tension arises when people are singularly focused on either *self-acceptance* or *self-improvement*.

Many people oriented toward psycho-spiritual healing and growth express:

> My healing/spiritual practice of self-care includes observing what comes up for me without judgment. Self-acceptance means being unattached to the ideas of the mind and not getting caught in the message that I am deficient. I am a whole, complete being as I am. The idea that I have to do something to "fix" myself brings negativity.

The guiding principle is *"I accept myself as I am."*

This is in contrast to many oriented toward racial justice who tend to state:

> Investigating how privilege and oppression operate in our thoughts and actions is life-long work. We must continually be open to learning how we are acting out of internalized superiority and work to combat it, since we often can't identify it ourselves. Being an advocate for racial justice means I admit, and learn from, mistakes. White people who "take a break" from social justice efforts are enacting privilege.

The guiding principle is that *"I will always need to improve."*

For those invested primarily in psycho-spiritual healing, messages delivered from activist groups often seem unhealthy. On the other hand, for those invested primarily in racial justice, messages delivered from a spiritual community may be considered excuses that allow racism to continue.

Although this divide exists, it may be addressed by a *both/and* orientation involving approaching psycho-spiritual healing and racial justice efforts in ways that attempt to maximize the benefits of both self-acceptance *and* self-improvement. However, finding a healthy balance between the two values is a great challenge. The primary tensions addressed in this chapter are framed by these questions: What happens if a focus on self-acceptance discounts one's relationship to issues of race? Conversely, what happens if a focus on self-improvement diminishes the capacity to fully accept oneself? What are the implications for racial justice? How is the inner resilience necessary to healthfully live out the *both/and* of self-acceptance and self-improvement fostered?

Self-Acceptance

Since conversations about race regularly bring up uncomfortable thoughts and feelings, they can feel contrary to an approach to life dedicated to positivity and healing. For many, it is hard to accept that a necessary aspect of healing includes uncovering and grappling with issues of race.[3] Three related tensions frequently deter people focused on self-acceptance from including self-inquiry about race as part of their healing process.

Tension

A core human need is to have positive self-regard.	**AND**	Accepting that one has unconscious, embedded racism challenges the preferred "idealized self."

People who focus on self-acceptance often do so as part of an effort to generate, or nurture, a positive sense of self. When this is the case, being asked to accept that one is part of, or complicit with, ongoing individual and systemic racism poses a significant psychological challenge, as it calls one's self-concept into question.

I recall my own inner tension when initially trying to accept that I enact racism (do something bad) while at the same time trying to accept myself as I am (considering myself a good person). This inner struggle occurs because of the basic human need to feel accepted; being racist is unacceptable. Psychological theory teaches that *cognitive dissonance* occurs when people try to hold two competing ideas in mind at the same time. Accepting that I am both good *and* complicit with racism is hard to do. However, it is hard to do only as long as being complicit with racism is interpreted as meaning that I am a racist, and therefore, bad.

Many advocates try to deal with this difficulty by using language that distinguishes what people *do* versus who they *are*. Yet, for a person hearing the critique, it is common to interpret, "that thing you *did* was racist," as meaning "you *are* a racist." This is especially true if other people in prior confrontations made the two seem synonymous.

The cognitive dissonance that results leads to a sense of being misunderstood or attacked. In those moments, the core self as a valuable human being feels challenged. Researchers note that when someone lays an "unwanted identity" on a person that does not resonate, in this case, being considered a racist, it feels like an undermining of the "ideal" self. Whether or not I am actually being called a racist, it feels *implied*. The internal reaction is the same whether the message is implied or stated directly.[4] That does not feel good and the uncomfortable sensation gets translated into anger, anxiety, or shame.

When this sense of "mistaken identity" arises and emotions are engaged, there is an immediate wish to explain all the ways the situation has been misperceived and what was really meant by what was done or said. Common responses in these moments often include "How can you think that about me? You know me better than that. I don't have a racist bone in my body." These defensive responses are generally interpreted as a denial, a lie, or a fantasy by white racial justice advocates and people of color.[5]

Part of the problem in these situations is that all the stereotypes of what it means to be a racist are called to mind.[6] Since being racist is associated with images of the KKK, skinheads, and lynching, being linked to racism in any way automatically generates a horrific image for many people. Tolle speaks of what happens psychologically during these moments when he writes:

> When I defend my opinions (thoughts), I feel and act as if I were defending my very self. Unconsciously, I feel and act as if I were fighting for survival and so my emotions will reflect this unconscious belief. They become turbulent. I am upset, angry, defensive, or aggressive. I need to win at all cost lest I become annihilated.[7]

The perception of being called a racist can engage an all-out defensive struggle to retain one's sense of self. As psychologist Abraham Maslow's hierarchy of needs suggests, the need for sufficient positive self-regard must be met before a focus on critical thinking and problem solving is possible.[8] Only when there is an internal or external understanding that the core self can survive the situation whole and intact will the ability to thoughtfully engage return.

Coping with the unsettling emotions and reducing defensiveness in order to appropriately listen to critical feedback can be a big challenge. When first starting down this road, some wise mentors suggested not focusing on the labeling of "racist" and, instead, concentrating on the behavior or attitude that needed to change. This has been helpful in attempts to hold on to a spiritual sense of self as a good person while also accepting the need for change.

One story illustrates a particularly unsettling moment for me. Several years ago I was a guest on a radio program wherein the host asked me to admit to being a white supremacist. According to the host's logic, I am part of an ongoing system that benefits me as a white person. Simply living within our system, contributing to it and benefiting from it through daily activities, supports the system. This system, by its very nature, oppresses people of color. Thankfully, having studied how racism in the U.S. continues to function, I understood the truthfulness in the overall critique. Therefore, agreeing with the host about my complicity was not as difficult as it otherwise would have been. My complicity will be real as long as I use money and am not living absolutely and fully "off the grid." What this meant, however, is that, according to the way the host framed the discussion, I was a white supremacist. Understanding his ultimate point, I took a deep breath, followed his use of language, and admitted on the air for all to hear that I am a white supremacist, despite the dissonance it stirred in me.

What helped me get through that challenging moment without the need to self-defend or resist his framing was the effort to see the deeper message and not become caught up in the term used. It was necessary to depersonalize the charge being made, be present to the overall situation, and recognize that my ego was having an internal re-action. When authors write of the "embedded white racist self"[9] and ask white readers "How does it feel to be a problem?" a way through the immediate internal resistance is to focus on the core message de-livered underneath the ego-threatening language.[10] It helps to recog-nize that all people are affected in some way by the racism that washes over U.S. society via media and other social messages and that white people, in particular, are beneficiaries of it, regardless of their beliefs or desires. It also helps to believe that healing and growth is aided by these authors' efforts to reveal how the "social matrix of whiteness" functions.[11]

❧ If someone says you are something you consider offensive, how do you react?

❧ What helps you stay open to the core message being deliv-ered?

Tension

Self-critique can induce shame and a desire to avoid further reflection.	**AND**	Healthy self-critique al-lows for productive re-sponses regarding complicity with racism.

Many people who focus on self-acceptance as part of a psycho-spiritual healing process do so as a reaction against persistent and de-structive internal self-critique. The work of Brené Brown, a shame researcher, sheds light on this issue, although her research indicates that this concern likely affects far more women than men, given societal conditioning.[12]

Brown offers a strong argument that most people in the U.S. have not considered the role of shame deeply enough. She considers shame a taboo topic, a "silent epidemic."[13] It is quite possible that avoiding shame might have a lot to do with why many people resist conversations and critical feedback about race. Internal resistance might generate thoughts like: "I self-criticize enough all by myself, thank you very much. I don't need more criticism from anyone else."

Exploring how this might be true requires an explanation of Brown's key ideas. First, she refers to shame as "the fear of disconnection — the fear of being perceived as flawed and unworthy of acceptance or belonging."[14] She explains how people confuse shame with self-esteem, and this may have something to do with why many people do not identify their experiences as shame-filled. Brown writes:

> We <u>feel</u> shame. We think self-esteem. Our self-esteem is based on how we see ourselves — our strengths and limitations —. over time. It is how we think of ourselves. Shame is an emotion. It is how we feel when we have certain experiences. When we are in shame, we don't see the big picture; we don't accurately think about our strengths and limitations. We just feel alone, exposed and deeply flawed.[15]

It is altogether possible to *think* self-acceptance, but *feel* shame.

❖ What happens to you internally when criticized or after making a mistake?

❖ In those moments, is there is an internal rush of anxiety? Does it feel like the brain's mechanisms are both racing and frozen at the same time? Does a fight or flight response make critical thinking challenging?

––––––––––

An emotional process of working through shame occurs regularly for many people, not only in situations that are about race. Feelings of shame can easily overwhelm and, subsequently, undermine the ability to stay present to a conversation. It is important to recognize that feelings of shame may be independent of race issues. At the same time, feelings of shame are bound to surface — and potentially intensify —— any time race is involved.

Brown offers a more precise use of vocabulary to get at the heart of this issue. She notes that guilt is commonly confused with shame. The distinction is that guilt is what is experienced when feeling bad about something *done* and shame is feeling bad about one's *self*.[16] Brown discusses issues of shame and guilt related to privilege to help clarify why many white people shrink back when asked to discuss advantages conferred by race:

> So often I find that our feelings of unearned privilege kill empathy. By unearned privilege I mean the privileges afforded us simply because we are white or straight or members of certain groups. We get stuck in what I call privilege shame. This is very different from privilege guilt (or white guilt). It's appropriate to feel guilt over forwarding a racist e-mail or telling a hurtful joke. Guilt can motivate change. Guilt helps us reconcile our choices with our values.
>
> Shame doesn't help. If we feel shamed because we don't know how to relate to someone who is different or connect with someone who faces unfair discrimination, we get stuck. If we think, "I'm a bad person because I can't relate to her" or "I'm a bad person because I have this and these people don't" — we get paralyzed. For me, I've come to a place in my life where unlearning prejudice is more important than avoiding situations where I might be accused of saying or doing the wrong thing. I've learned that it is better for me to accept the fact that I struggle with many of the same learned biases that other people do. This has allowed me to spend my energy unlearning and changing my prejudices rather than proving that I don't have any.[17]

Having never before considered such a thing as "privilege shame," I am now certain that it affected me deeply in my early years learning about racial justice and it manifested in many of my actions and reactions as I sought to create a racial justice practice.

Brown is not alone in suggesting that shame is not healthy. Most activists believe white people should find ways to look at issues of privilege that do not inspire shame, as it tends to undermine attempts at actions for justice. Brown finishes the section on privilege shame with a note regarding how detrimental shame can be on relationships and how dealing with it openly supports healing:

> When we are honest about our struggles, we are much less likely to get stuck in shame. **This is critical because shame diminishes our capacity to practice empathy.** Ultimately, feeling shame about privilege actually perpetuates racism, sexism, heterosexism, classism, ageism, etc. I don't have to know "exactly how you feel" — I just have to touch a part of my life that opens me up to hearing your experience. If I can touch that place, I stay out of judgment and I can reach out with empathy. This is where both personal and social healing can begin.[18]

Part of what makes Brown's approach so useful is that it holds the *both/and* of self-acceptance and self-improvement when dealing with privilege, which might allow people to enter conversations about race with less need to self-defend.

❖ Do you think that avoidance of shame might underlie the attempt to avoid recognizing privilege?

❖ How can people tackle conversations about race without triggering a shame response?

Tension

People seek out psycho-spiritual healing to decrease emotional pain.	**AND**	White people are generally unaware of their need to understand and heal from racism.

A psycho-spiritual healing orientation often leads to the following beliefs:

> I am engaged in a healing process focused on what is immedi-
> ately present to my environment. It is not authentic for me to
> focus on race, as it is not my primary pain.
>
> Modern society is unhealthy on many levels, and my healing
> and spiritual practices support me in trying to heal from that
> dis-ease. My healing will naturally result in increased connec-
> tions with others. So, I'm already attending to racism in my
> own way.

Both of these positions make sense. It is hard to commit to a healing process for a pain that is not perceived. It is even harder when
convinced that another medicine is already taking care of the problem. Because so many white people may be disconnected from their
collective racial wounds, the call to attend to those wounds does not
resonate.

It is likely that the entire U.S. population has been, and continues to be, wounded in some way by the historic and continuing
racism in the U.S., whether consciously felt or not. Mary Watkins
and Helene Shulman highlight four different positions one can have
within a traumatic event: victim, perpetrator, witness, or bystander.
The bystander position is explored here, as this is the one that is
least commonly discussed and the one that is likely at the core of
many white people's current experience.

Watkins and Shulman suggest that, when people live their lives
"surrounded by people suffering chronic stress, poverty, or marginal-
ization that has developed over centuries, dissociative strategies will
allow the shutting out of feelings of empathy and connectedness."[19]
This is the situation regarding race in the U.S. — most white people
have become dissociated bystanders. There has been a shutdown of
the human feelings that should naturally arise when confronted by
images of ongoing violence and discrimination. The images and stories are overwhelming and saturating, and the shutdown is unconscious. This psychic shutdown is what allows people to live in
complicity with societal injustices without feeling internal dissonance.

Part of the challenge people face regarding this issue is that, although victims of oppression are generally clear about how their circumstances need to change, the psychological damage resulting from

being a bystander is not as easily recognized.[20] The situation is likened to a "chronic illness" that people do not know affects them. Another challenge is that one's family, work, and interpersonal relationships can be disrupted if one really begins to see the connections between a bystander status and psychological damage.[21] Yet, remaining unconscious to this damage is dangerous to self and society.

Watkins and Shulman describe a set of twelve symptoms related to socially sanctioned bystander behaviors. Offered below are five that are most pertinent for discussions on race (see notes for the full list).[22] As each is named and described, consider two questions: In what ways do these symptoms describe your experience? How have you seen them play out?

1. The severing of the self

This describes psychological boundaries that develop within bystanders in a culture that values individualism. Strong divisions between self and other, leading toward isolation from one's neighbors, anonymity, and a distorted sense of living "outside the web of interdependence" result.[23] This severing allows people to feel distance from the racism and damage occurring within U.S. society. The spiritual sense of feeling "connected to all" is compromised. The results are statements like the following: "It seems wrong for me to focus on race issues when it is not something that affects me."

2. Fear of oneself

This concept suggests that a bystander will disown personal attributes seen as inferior and project them onto others. Other people, therefore, hold all these "split-off feelings."[24] I am good and *they* are bad, because seeing what is negative within me is too scary. The projection occurs unconsciously. When this defense mechanism is active, a person cannot see in him or herself what is distasteful, while others are held in judgment. This is the defensive finger-pointing that protects a bystander from seeing what might unconsciously lurk within, and it leads to statements like, "I'm not a racist, but you are acting like one right now."

3. The empty self

The self of the bystander is disconnected, insecure, has experienced "losses of community, tradition, and shared meaning," and results from the adoption of a worldview that cuts one off from others.[25] It is a product of the modern world and people affected by it struggle to fill a void. It is related to a culture oriented to "individual transcendence rather than to community salvation; to isolated relationships rather than to community activism; to an individualistic mysticism rather than to political change."[26] Ultimately, feeling disconnected leaves one with a feeling of emptiness. Personal healing efforts are never enough because there is a never-ending space within that wants to be filled. The "empty self" causes a bystander to stay focused on him or herself in an attempt to fill that hollow space.

4. Psychic numbing

This refers to the "closing down of feelings" that interrupts the bystander's ability to identify with others. It is related to the "anaesthetized heart, the heart that has no reaction to what it faces."[27] It explains a tendency to focus on personal thoughts and pains while faced with others who are suffering greatly, and how, too often, there is a failure to hear or act on what could support them. It prompts the avoidance of "questions and situations that induce feelings of impotence and inadequacy."[28] This psychic numbing is what keeps the bystander intellectualizing racism in ways that inhibit the feelings of urgency and personal connection necessary to take action.

5. The obsessive-compulsive rehearsal of violence

This concept highlights desensitization to violence and how U.S. culture provides daily doses of murder and death through TV, film, video games, and news. "There is a vicious connection between bystanding and the normalization of violence. The less one interrupts violence and injustice, the more others, and perhaps even oneself, will end up in its sites [*sic*]."[29] U.S. society is so thoroughly infused with images of violence perpetrated against people of color that many people barely blink when hearing of people shot and killed. This is what allows for the quick changing of a news channel when hearing of another police abuse scandal or person released after 20 years of incarceration for a crime he or she did not commit. This normalization of violence, and subsequent lack of reactivity, allows a bystander to remain passive and fail to take action to create a safer community for all.

The symptoms of being a bystander correlate with a culture of dissociation in which people fail to both respond to one another with empathy and compassion as well as take action to work toward systemic change. A close look reveals how the symptoms bred from being a bystander collectively protect people from truly witnessing the horror of how vestiges of racism still play out in U.S. society, shield people from seeing themselves as part of the problem, and allow the status quo to continue as is. These are not the characteristics of a healthy and whole self.

Addressing these symptoms requires an opening of the heart so one can respond to people's pain and perspective.[30] It also requires accepting one's whole self *and* engaging in active efforts against racism. This *both/and* position may be liberating, even if daunting.

❖ What is your reaction to the symptoms of being a bystander?

❖ How might these symptoms and their possible causes hold people back from paying attention to race issues?

Self-Improvement

For every positive, there is its shadow. As important as self-improvement is, there are adverse consequences if the drive to improve is not balanced by an acceptance of the self. The following sections explore what can go wrong when there is too little time spent appreciating and working on the psycho-spiritual need for self-acceptance. Ultimately, without a balance between self-improvement and self-acceptance, efforts at engaging others are often not effective.

The work of Brené Brown reveals the concrete, specific relationship between psychological health and racial justice advocacy.[31] Brown describes three strategies of disconnection commonly used to avoid facing shame. They are *moving against, moving away,* and *mov-*

ing toward.[32] Discussion of each of the three strategies provides insight into how a constant striving to be seen favorably underlies many people's shame responses. Three common tensions are explored below in relationship to the challenges white people invested in racial justice may have when lacking a sufficiently strong sense of self-acceptance.

Tension

Loving one's self is an essential first step in connecting with, and extending love to, another.		Accepting one's self and racial position is hard to do when feeling shameful about complicity with racism.

White people invested in racial justice need to work within the white community to end unconsciousness around race privilege.[33] Yet, white people who struggle to accept what white skin means on a personal level often have difficulty supporting others with white skin who enter racial justice work. The lack of self-acceptance can lead many to: feel uncomfortable in predominantly white spaces, avoid people who are reminiscent of a former "unaware self," and use "sledgehammer tactics."

A brief story illustrates what commonly occurs. Years ago, when waiting to be interviewed for the doctoral program at Pacifica Graduate Institute, my heart raced and palms sweated profusely after entering a room filled with white students and faculty. At that time, I was steeped in the knowledge of how much change I needed as a white person. It was also clear to me how every white person around me needed to change. In my mind's eye, that room filled with white people was a hotbed of dysfunction. I did not accept myself, and therefore, I could not accept other white people. My simmering self-recrimination and anger bled into my perception of others and the way I conveyed information to other white people about race was often less than kind and did not take individual differences into account.

According to Brown, this kind of reaction is an attempt to disconnect and get out of a shame response. It is part of the "moving against" strategy and it involves "trying to gain power over others by being aggressive, and by using shame to fight shame."[34] Since a lack of self-acceptance makes it impossible to empathize with other people, building and maintaining trusted relationships is extraordinarily difficult. The result is ineffective efforts at influencing others to engage in conversations on race.

The issue is not simply about failing to bring other people into social justice work. Also important to consider is how trust and relationship building can be undermined in response to self-recrimination, an insecure sense of self, and competitiveness.[35] Within racial justice circles it is common knowledge that competition to be the "best white ally in the room" can run rampant. This type of competitive behavior is often about showing oneself as knowledgeable as a salve for the pain bred from self-judgment.

To offer an example about how subtle these behaviors can be, a few years ago a very well-known, long-established, and highly respected white activist approached me after a workshop to offer advice about ways to stay "in my heart space." The message was offered in front of a mixed-race group of her colleagues, in a crowded elevator, where all could hear. She offered to help me sometime in the future, if I was willing. My face flushed and moments later, we all emerged from the elevator and went in our respective directions. Although couched in concern, her words rang with judgment and a patronizing tone. Although my response to her centered on being grateful for her interest in helping me, I felt humiliated and pushed away rather than supported.

Almost two years after that experience, the woman who approached me that day called. She asked if I remembered the encounter. I said I did. She then apologized and explained how her self-judgment and the competition it bred had been part of that interaction. She told me how clear it was to her that her own lack of self-acceptance had been the prompt for her to approach me as she did that day. In that moment she demonstrated healthfully moving away from shame. She also became a model of the kind of self-reflective, open, and vulnerable racial justice advocate I strive to become.

♣ Have you ever experienced this "moving against" strategy?

♣ How have you been shamed by others?

♣ How might you sometimes shame people when you are really trying to make yourself feel better?

The "moving away" strategy is another type of response to shame that unwittingly shames others. This strategy kills many wonderful opportunities for advocacy. According to Brown, when we use the "moving away" strategy, this response results in "withdrawing, hiding, silencing ourselves, and keeping secrets."[36] This response is also related to an inability to love oneself sufficiently.

Once, while visiting with an old high school friend during the time period when I was most uncomfortable in my white skin, simply sitting in a restaurant proved challenging. It was disconcerting to recognize that there were no people of color visible except the busboys. My anxiety about the situation and negative internal speech (feeling shamefully complicit by being a patron) made me unable to talk about issues of privilege effectively with this old friend. I stammered, felt uneasy, and we lost touch soon afterward. This scenario reoccurred many times with different friends. Using the moving away strategy caused me to disconnect from those who do not already understand race in the way that I do, impeding my opportunity to become influential in their perception and thinking.

There is another way that self-recrimination can lead to paralysis or silence. Judging oneself as less intelligent, well-spoken, or valuable than another can get in the way of using one's voice against racism. I recall my first efforts at blogging. For inspiration, I had read one of Tim Wise's blog posts. The self-inflicted shame response it prompted propelled me into a self-critical dialogue that ended with me asking myself: "What is the point of me writing anything when his words are so clear? Who do I think I am anyway?"

I closed my computer and walked away. The next day I offered a post reflecting on the experience.[37] The post named how white people's insecurity and self-pity can derail a movement and stop people from using their voices against racism. I used my experience of walking away from the computer for a night to make a broad comment about white people who have the privilege to step away from race and my need to challenge that privilege.

After reading Brown's research, I now see that experience and my response differently. It is actually an excellent example of someone using shame to combat shame. I had beaten myself up with judgment about the privilege to stay silent. I then turned around and offered a shame-filled judgment against any reader who has felt similarly insecure and taken a momentary step back.

A healthier, more authentic message to deliver would have been the following: "I felt insecure about myself after reading Tim's blog post. Using that experience to beat myself up almost stopped me from offering my voice. Sharing my insecurity, fear, and vulnerability is not only okay, but it may be essential if people are going to use their voices against racism in a way that does not damage other people." This would have increased connections and offered a more supportive prompt for action.

Discussing these experiences is important because, as Brown suggests, to really understand the depth of how shame works, one needs to not only understand what experiencing shame feels like, but "we need to understand when and why we are most likely to engage in shaming behaviors toward others, how we can develop our resilience to shame and how we can consciously make the effort not to shame others."[38] Brown also talks about how people can feel shame just by hearing people talk about their own shame. When another person's story is reminiscent of something one is ashamed of one can then "blame them as a way to protect [oneself] from feeling uncomfortable."[39] It is as simple as responding to someone with the phrases: "Yeah, that doesn't seem so smart!" or "Wow, I can't believe you did that!" These are responses that shame people at the precise moment when they would benefit most from a compassionate response of identification. Effectively engaging in dialogues on identity and privilege would be increased through continued exploration of these issues.

❖ In what ways do you use the "moving away" strategy? What feelings and sensations do you experience in your body in those moments?

❖ Do you ever use words that hurt others through sarcasm? When is it most likely to occur? What is the result?

Tension

A lack of self-acceptance leads to an unhealthy need to gain validation from others.	— **AND** —	Seeking feedback from others allows for more effective work toward justice and equity.

An important value for people invested in social justice is consistently improving the capacity to work in solidarity with others. However, a key to this ability is ensuring that self-judgment does not override the ability to accept oneself. A lack of sufficient self-acceptance leads toward an unhealthy search for validation from others.

Brown writes that trying to get out of a shame response by using the "moving toward" strategy results in "seeking to appease and please."[40] This is the response that best characterizes my early experiences coming to grips with privilege. My grounding had been shaken so badly that acting "like me" was a real problem. Acting "normally" had been revealed as filled with racist assumptions and behaviors. Therefore, I could not trust myself. This made me susceptible to feelings of insecurity. Any experience that made me feel inadequate quickly resulted in my calling a friend of color for reassurance. This pattern wore on my friends of color and they did, in time, tell me to seek out white people to provide me with the support I sought.

This initial phase involved desperate attempts to please people of color in the room by being a model of the "white ally." What I sought to avoid was being the "bad white" who remains silent while people of color share their emotions. I also knew that, when sharing my emotions, I would cry. This provoked the fear of becoming a classic cliché — a white woman who allows her emotion to take center stage at the expense of people of color. No part of me wanted to risk prompting someone to take care of me, as that would also be a manifestation of privilege. To counteract this, I often attempted to offer the keenest insight possible so that people of color would see me as a valuable ally. This needy approach fooled no one and my attempts usually fell flat. The core of the problem was that I did not feel secure enough about myself to act authentically. The fear of not being a "good enough ally" caused me to try too hard to play a role. This undermined my ability to be present and fully engaged.

❖ In what ways have you tried to please someone in a way that was not healthy?

❖ Have you experienced this pattern on the part of others? What were the results?

Tension

A balanced life that allows for self-care supports long-term, sustained striving.	—— *AND* ——	The quest to end injustice is urgent and requires consistent striving.

The term "gremlin" is used in popular psychology as a user-friendly way of talking about internal shadows. *Taming Your Gremlin,* by Rick Carson, provides an easy-to-read introduction.[41] Working with gremlins is an introspective approach that asks people to see what takes hold of their psyche during emotionally evocative moments that prompts them to control and belittle self and others. As I consider how self-judgment undermines me, one particular gremlin stands out above all others.

This gremlin was revealed during a meditation that invited the inhabitants of my psyche to emerge. The process involved engaging in dialogue with whatever figure arose in my mind and asking it what it wanted. What emerged was an image of me on a stationary bike, pumping the pedals as hard as possible, with a female standing before me commanding "faster, faster, faster." The gremlin was wearing the Superman "S" symbol on her t-shirt.

This is how I lived my life, feeling pressured to do more, more, more, faster and faster. Taking a racial justice stance only contributed to the urgency of the voice within. A message often received within activist circles is that "if you're comfortable, you're doing it wrong." Dismantling racism is a time sensitive proposition, as people's lives are negatively impacted every day. White people who say they are "too busy" or "too tired" or need to "take a break" are considered to be acting out of their privilege. This prompted me to judge myself harshly on a regular basis. I could never be a good enough person because I could never do enough. This was neither healthy nor sustainable. Thankfully, this message about the value of a sustainable approach was one I heard delivered by a group of community organizers, and it served as a counterweight to the Superwoman standing over me, telling me to pedal ever harder.

It is only now, looking through the lens of shame, that I see how the dominant culture has taught me to strive for success at all times, resulting in frequent exaggerated emotional responses that leave me defensive and unable to think clearly. This reaction continues to occur when facilitating group conversations. It remains a very real and present challenge, even with my growing awareness of my inner Superwoman and her toxic effect on my life and racial justice efforts.

In recounting the story of this gremlin, the work of Michael Meade comes to mind. He talks about families having characteristic ways of "avoiding, denying, or glossing over the very issues that need to be faced and cleaned up and healed." Ignoring those issues allows them to "become a toxic inner lead that can be poisonous."[42] Expanding this perspective, my gremlin is not mine alone; it may affect how I limp along in the world, but it may reflect a cultural limp as well. U.S. culture affects many people in similar ways. Meade also states that "healing begins when the patient announces the nature of the suffering."[43] Brown also recognizes the societal need for this announcement. She quotes one of her teachers, Harriet Lerner, who states: "Although the connections are not always obvious, personal change is inseparable from social and political change."[44]

❖ In what ways can you relate to never feeling that your efforts are enough?

❖ How might shame underlie the way you move in the world?

❖ What is the gremlin that affects you most?

The Search for Balance

Valuing *both* self-acceptance *and* self-improvement does not automatically shield a person from struggling to navigate the tension between the two. It is challenging to balance the need for self-care and a positive self-image with the commitment to being self-reflective and open to critical feedback. Striking a balance is essential, however, because becoming resilient when in emotionally evocative situations allows for more meaningful connections with others.[45]

Developing authentic connections also requires the ability to offer empathy and compassion, both for self and others. This is not an easy task. Brown notes that only when people have accepted their own human struggles will they have the ability to extend compassion to others who express their shame, pain, and difficulties.[46] Only when people have accepted themselves as imperfect will they have the ability to extend compassion and empathy to themselves as well.[47]

For some people, a step toward resisting shaming others may involve letting go of unachievable expectations. Brown's book, *The Gifts of Imperfection*, reveals that perfectionism undermines social justice work (as well as psychological and spiritual health).[48] She recognizes that distinguishing between healthy self-improvement and perfectionism is critical and offers a useful set of descriptions of perfectionism to aid in making that distinction. They include *the wish to be perceived as perfect* and *allowing judgment from others to reinforce the belief that I am not perfect enough*. She also offers some essential clarification points. First, perfectionism is not the same thing as striving to be your best. Second, perfectionism is not self-improvement.[49] In order to combat perfectionism, Brown encourages more of the "good enough as we are" orientation while also valuing that we must continue to improve.

Brown is not alone in recognizing the value in allowing oneself to be seen as flawed, vulnerable, and fully human. There are many who speak of their scars and inadequacies so that others might gain courage to give up their self-concept as being unstained by racism's psychic effects. In response to an essay by Rebecca Parker in *Soul Work: Anti-racist Theologies in Dialogue,*[50] Susan Suchocki Brown says, "without the willingness to become vulnerable, open, and exposed to my lack of consciousness, my brokenness, and my alienation, I risk a spiritual incompleteness that leaves me…less present to life, more cut off, and less creative and loving."[51]

These models of vulnerability are important. What Brené Brown teaches is that being a perfectionist does not require a person to consciously want to be perfect. For example, I know fully well that I am not and will never be perfect. But that does not stop me from wanting to be *perceived* as perfect. I may know that perfectionism is damaging, but it does not stop me from experiencing strong, emotional reactions any time my imperfections are noticed by others. Brown offers an exercise that serves as a "gut check" to see how ready each of us is to live a life with unmet expectations for ourselves.[52] She calls it the "Life Shuffle."

First, pick ten *important* expectations you hold that are, in this case, related to social justice. For example, I might write:

1. I will intervene when a person in my workplace says something racist, sexist, homophobic, etc.

2. I will listen with openness and without reactivity when someone tells me I exhibit racism, classism, heterosexism, etc.

3. I will be compassionate with people while trying to increase their awareness about privilege.

Now write *your* list of ten personal expectations on index cards, one per card. Once you have brainstormed your list and written them out on cards, flip them over. Shuffle the deck of ten cards. Pick five to discard. Five are going to work out, and five will not. How prepared are you to have achieved only five of those goals?

Brown's exercise suggests that having limited success does not imply insufficient striving, but instead, human beings are bound to err. Accepting that some efforts won't be engaged perfectly does not in any way suggest an abandonment of effort. Accepting inescapable humanness simply allows for continued striving while holding sufficient self-esteem.

The importance of this activity is recognizing that each person has an internal process around accepting moments of mistake, failure, or missed opportunities. Self-judgment and the search for external validation may need to be reduced. Allowing for personal imperfections can help create sustainable social justice practices that do not get derailed by shame responses.

Another issue to consider involves how to remain present and open during critical conversations about race that challenge one's self-concept. Holding the view that these moments are opportunities for spiritual and soul growth can help. However, it is also useful to have some cognitive and practical strategies that support the reduction of emotional reactivity. These can help one stay effectively engaged and extend empathy and compassion to all involved. The following are ten approaches that may be useful.

Stop debating and explore people's feelings

This is particularly important when listening to accounts of people's direct experience of racism. Questioning the accuracy of a person of color's experience never helps. Too often, people of color are not believed. Too often, it is a white person who dismisses the person of color's narrative. Too often, people of color's stories are altogether accurate. Too often, the anger felt by people of color over their dismissal is interpreted by white people as "playing the race card" or having a "chip on their shoulder." Many people of color have developed a heightened sensitivity to this pattern,[53] which is a completely understandable response. The best course of action is to listen to and explore people's feelings. One can learn a lot when listening with a whole heart and allowing the inner debater to take a rest.

Recognize the value of perception

Recognize that the suggestion to another that what he or she is experiencing is only "perception" involves a great amount of shaming and blaming. Brown speaks of the danger of blaming people in such a way. She writes, "Some pop psychologists preach that 'There's no such thing as reality, just perception.' Not only is this inaccurate, it's dangerous. Racism is real."[54] She then suggests that instead of dismissing someone's concerns, one can ask questions such as, "How can I help?" or "Is there some way I can support you?"

Allow for differential emotional reactions

Brown teaches that "we can each experience embarrassment, guilt, or shame over the same situation. It just depends on where we are in our lives."[55] This is important because when interacting with another person, internal guideposts and perspective on how one might feel personally in that situation might not allow for a true understanding of what is occurring for the other individual. Assumptions based on personal tendencies may lead to incorrect judgments of others and block the ability to extend empathy and compassion. For example, something one person might find mildly embarrassing could be extremely shaming for another. Responding with supportive questions instead of advice born of judgment can help tease out what is prompting another into his or her position.

Gloria Anzaldúa writes about the value of looking for the unconscious feelings that lie at the root of an expressed emotion. For example, beneath anger may be fear. Compassionate questioning that reveals the underlying emotion can help locate common bonds between people and mediate polarized conversations.[56]

Be vulnerable

Dominant U.S. culture does not appreciate vulnerability. Showing fear and pain to another is often perceived as weakness. Few are immune to these social influences. The effort to hide one's inner mess from being seen by others can prompt actions that are not authentic. No one is fooled. The statements, "I am feeling unsure right now," or "I need a minute to process this," help. They are honest, and when people recognize there is an authentic struggle happening, people are more likely to feel connected.[57] When feeling confused, upset, or anxious, it is better to say it with humility than to try hiding it with defensive speech or shutting down the conversation altogether.

Brown's research indicates that men are even less socially rewarded for showing vulnerability than women. In fact, they may be emotionally punished for it.[58] Therefore, the approach offered here may sound easy coming from a woman, since men often do not receive the same type of validating responses to their sharing. In fact, men's struggles to demonstrate vulnerability may be akin to women's struggles with issues of perfectionism.

Be aware of emotional reactivity

One's sense of self may be tested each time unsolicited, critical feedback is offered about how race might influence one's behavior or thinking. Despite knowing that taking personal offense is unhelpful, the ego often goes into survival mode, resulting in a fight or flight response. The ego turns the situation into a threat, and those participating in it, the enemy.[59] On a good day I might have enough inner strength to nod and say thank you for the feedback, even if there is emotional upset raging within. I consider it spiritual progress when I do not actively flee that kind of situation. Healing from racial trauma requires acceptance of these situations and the ability to recognize emotional reactions in the moment. This is essential because the more reactivity reigns, the more disconnection is felt.[60] Conversely, the more one is aware of one's internal state, the more one can act authentically and remain connected.[61]

Sit in the transformative fire of emotion

Authentic cross-race dialogues often involve emotional reactions. The emotion may come from pent up pain from prior experiences or out of frustration, hurt, and anger at what is occurring in that very moment. Either way, conflict-avoidant people like me will want to escape anytime intense emotions rise. Yet, relationship-building across race requires white people to accept and engage with the rage of people of color.[62] I cannot expect people whose ancestors experienced centuries of abuse to speak of their ongoing pain in calm, soft tones. Nor can I expect people who experience themselves and their children battling discrimination to speak without passion and anger.

Ultimately, it does not matter whether I feel deserving of the heat or anger. As a white woman, in that moment I might be standing in for all of the white people who have injured this person and his or her family for decades. I may look like those who did harm. I may have attitudes reminiscent of those who did harm. My statements might have touched a painful nerve. It helps to remember that learning from whatever is occurring in the moment will help me engage with someone else's wound in a way that does not compound the injury and, instead, aids to heal it. The heat may be unpleasant, but when lovingly tended, the emotional fire can burn feelings down to their elements, and from the ash something new can emerge.

Allow the ego to be diminished

The ability to stay present in a challenging moment and sit in the heat of conflict and the expression of anger is a powerful capacity. Tolle offers some important advice on how to do this. He speaks about how the ego is "more interested in self-preservation than in the truth" when feeling threatened by blaming, criticizing, or the sense of being mistreated.[63] The ego then seeks to regain itself through dysfunctional responses. He goes on to suggest:

> A powerful spiritual practice is consciously to allow the diminishment of the ego when it happens without attempting to restore it....When you are seemingly diminished in some way and remain in absolute nonreaction, not just externally but also internally, you realize that nothing real has been diminished, that through becoming "less" you become more.[64]

This is different than simply "not taking it personally" in a way that resists any personal connection to the issues. That reaction commonly leads to a dismissal of the issues raised. Instead, consciously allowing the ego to be challenged without trying to rebuild it with defensiveness allows a person to more freely imagine how the experience has something to offer.

Operating with this level of freedom supports the interaction in ways that heighten consciousness for all involved.[65] It becomes possible to consider how some of the intensity may be caused by experiences unrelated to oneself, thus allowing one to accept the role of "stand in." This capacity can open up space and time for one to recognize the parts of the message that offer important insights into what can be done differently in the future to avoid future injuries.

Recognize expectations held for others

Sometimes expectations of others are shaped by privilege and ignorance. Most of my experiences with people across race involve authentic sharing, caring, and compassion, but, unfortunately, that is not always the case. Often enough, people with whom I interact are frustrated by common patterns others have exhibited before either of us even enter the room. My behavior can inadvertently increase their frustration or anger. *Expecting* everyone to approach me with empathy and compassion is not helpful. Recognizing that my privilege may cause me to be insensitive to what others are going through helps me extend a listening ear and stay in the transformative fire.

Many people invested in social justice recognize the urgency of this work. Out of this sense of urgency, people can demand faster change from those new to inequity or privilege issues than is reasonable, resulting in disconnection. Gary Smith writes of this when speaking to his Unitarian Universalist community:

> I have sometimes felt as if I am dealing with colleagues who are not walking with me but are instead sitting over in "Stage Five" shaking their heads at my cluelessness. This "Journey Toward Wholeness" effort could do with a little less self-righteousness and a little more companioning. I want to do the right thing. My world is opening. I am increasingly finding colleagues who know how to companion.[66]

He recognizes that the racial justice journey was "never meant to be safe," and yet he is calling for it to be supported with compassionate connection, not judgment.

Recognize the gift of critical feedback

It helps to recognize extremely hard to hear feedback as a gift.[67] It is an opportunity to learn something about oneself. Bearing witness to someone's story allows for self-reflection upon one's own. This can provide opportunities for maturation and growth.[68] Of course, this only happens if one is able to remain calm and humble.[69]

Michael Meade tells the story of a seeker who asked a spiritual teacher "for a practice that would help open his life to wisdom." He was told to give money to any person who insulted him. He should do this for three years and then return. The man was a somewhat abrasive person, and so he received a lot of criticism and paid out a lot of money. After the three years ended, he returned to his teacher who told him it was time to learn some wisdom. He was sent to a city where a holy man sat before the city gates, launching insults at all who passed. When the seeker arrived and the insult yelled at him by the gate keeper hit its mark, he laughed. The gate keeper asked why he was laughing, and the seeker replied "for three years I have been paying for this kind of thing in hopes of finding wisdom and now you give it to me for free." The gate keeper then bid the seeker to enter the city, saying "It is all yours."[70]

What a beautiful practice — to train oneself to see the value in critical feedback. It allows the critique to be accepted with humor and with the recognition that hearing unflattering things about ourselves is not a diminishment, but rather an opportunity to grow.

Mine for gold

Imagine for a moment that one is able to bring one's full and nonreactive presence to a challenging situation, seeing it as a moment of gift giving. What happens if the feedback conveyed does not resonate or the message seems misperceived or illogical? Then one can mine for gold. Something golden is there and it is essential to stay in the moment long enough to find it. For example, references to George Yancy's writing appear throughout this book.[71] Yancy's analysis is strong, and his message clear. He has many valuable insights to share. Initially, I found his language too direct and abrasive. It was necessary for me to fight my defensiveness in order to keep reading. I am so glad I did. Putting down the text and simply moving on to another author who wrote more reassuringly to white readers would have resulted in a missed opportunity to check myself and find the gold.

❖ Have you ever utilized any of these strategies when navigating through difficult conversations?

❖ What other approaches have you found valuable?

Michael Meade's words are useful as a conclusion:

> All true paths include dark stretches that expose the afflictions within us, but also make their healing possible. Limping our limp means accepting how we stumble inside our lives. When seen from the other end of life, our affliction is a sacred wound secretly connected to the hidden gold.[72]

No one is perfect. All must navigate the challenge of balancing between self-acceptance and self-improvement. Practicing the various strategies described fosters resilience and the capacity to engage ourselves and others with compassion and empathy. We can foster deeper connections to others while developing our capacity for self-examination, self-improvement, and self-acceptance.

CHAPTER 3

Personal Healing and
Political Action

One afternoon, while my parallel paths of racial and spiritual consciousness were newly unfolding, I sat on my apartment balcony with my mentor. We were discussing how I related to people and my ability (or inability) to recognize how my behaviors and attitudes affected others. That afternoon my worldview shifted. As I looked across the street at the apartments, trees, cars, people walking by, and clouds overhead, I envisioned a grid of parallel and intersecting lines, as though everything was enveloped in a single sheet of graph paper. My mentor, I, and the balcony were also part of this grid. The gridlines extended seamlessly from one object to another, and movement in one created movement in all.

This vision was a personal revelation. It impacts the way I interpret events around the world as well as those in my immediate surroundings. It is an image of the Earth as an interconnected, living system of which humanity is but one part.[1] The vision incorporates the Earth's natural processes, interspecies relationships, and need for balance. It links me to all those I know and do not know, all I perceive and do not perceive, all that is animate and inanimate. It makes me responsible in the world in a very deep way.[2] This is an image of interconnectedness and interdependence.

This view of the world is one many spiritual people share. It supports the goals of raising consciousness, doing no harm, and contributing positively to the world. Yet, this image does little to alter the policies and institutional systems that contribute to and maintain injustice.

There is a tension between the need to focus on one's personal psycho-spiritual growth process and the importance of political action to support societal change. Many spiritually oriented people face this tension when asked to address issues of race. People oriented toward psycho-spiritual healing often express:

> I am working to heal from the disconnections of the modern world. Since we are all interconnected, I contribute to the world positively when I am centered and can balance the needs of self and other, feminine and masculine principles, body and mind, and spirit and earth. Working on my personal growth is how I do the most good.

The message is *"I am the change I want to see in the world."*

This is in contrast to people focused on racial justice who tend to state:

> Working together to change the unjust policies and practices in effect today is essential. To do this, we need to know how institutional racism affects people's lives. This requires moving beyond a focus on personal consciousness-raising to taking action to change the systems that negatively impact people's lives.

The message is, *"political action and institutional change efforts are needed because personal consciousness-raising does not create sufficient policy shifts."*

Balancing this tension requires a *both/and* approach. Both sides offer important contributions. On one hand, concentrating on personal psycho-spiritual development may increase the ability to withstand the emotional struggles inherent in racial justice work. Even minor personal gains in the right direction can help maintain one's striving and active investment over time. Without this sense of personal agency, one can feel lost under the weight and complexity of the collective work needed to alter entrenched, unjust systems. At the same time, actively working in alliance with many others for a common goal is powerful and strengthening in and of itself. Joining with others who are mutually invested in both a sense of personal healing/growth and a dedication toward action allows for the lived experience of interdependence. The following discussions shed light on several historic and contemporary tensions that stop people who are focused either on personal growth or activism from coming together with one other.

Psycho-Spiritual Healing

The U.S. is an individualistic society that places high value on personal autonomy. Yet even spiritual people who lament society's individualism are often influenced by its associated values in ways that deter participation in racial justice efforts. Three connected tensions result from the deeply entrenched value for personal autonomy in the U.S., a self-oriented spirituality born of the modern age, and the way this form of spirituality obscures the value of political action.

Tension

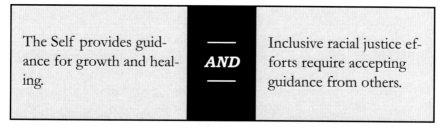

The Self provides guidance for growth and healing.	— **AND** —	Inclusive racial justice efforts require accepting guidance from others.

Many spiritual people today reject individualism. Yet, a close look reveals that even people who believe strongly in humanity's interdependence value personal autonomy, founded in the belief that the truest source of guidance comes from the Self. This has significant effects on people's willingness to take action on behalf of social justice. A brief historical look helps to clarify this issue.

Richard Tarnas writes extensively of the development of the modern worldview in *The Passion of the Western Mind*.[3] The book explores the philosophical shifts that occurred in Europe from the 1500s through the 1800s and charts the movement from the classical and medieval Christian worldview to the modern perspective. There are several important philosophical changes that resulted in modern society being characterized by disconnection and individualism.

According to Tarnas, the history of the modern era involves a splitting between nature and the divine; the body and mind; emotionality and rationality; subjectivity and objectivity; the feminine and masculine. Three psychological shifts played essential roles in the development of these disconnections. First, Descartes' statement "I think, therefore I am" articulated the perspective that the human being is autonomous and "fundamentally distinct and separate from an objective external world that it seeks to understand and master."[4] This is the basis for modern society's contemporary individualism.

Second, the Copernican revelation that the Earth travels around the sun disrupted humankind's sense of significance and connection to a primary deity. No longer inhabiting the center of the cosmos, humans were left to see themselves as existing in an impersonal universe and on a peripheral planet that revolves around one of a billion stars.[5] This led to a sense that humanity and nature may have no inherent meaning and purpose.

Related to this shift, the orientation of the Western mind moved over the course of centuries from the divine being embedded within nature to it being accessible only via priests and, later, toward a secularism that centered more on personal liberty, freedom, rationality, intellectual speculation, and discovery.[6] This shift gave rise to secular humanism and involved the heightening value of rationalism, objectivity, intellectuality, and the "independence of critical judgment."[7] Human beings, for the first time, began to recognize themselves, instead of god or other deities, as holding authority and power. Within this worldview the divine resides within the autonomous human, not within nature or within an external deity.

These shifts collectively prompted the development of a society that is individualistic, values personal autonomy, and views human beings as without inherent divine purpose. Many who hold a spiritual perspective recognize the downside of this orientation, one of which is that people influenced by a modern worldview often develop symptoms of distress. According to Tarnas, whether individuals' coping mechanisms manifest as inflated egocentrism, narcissism, greed, consumption, or addiction, the alienation and disconnection of the era characterized by modernity will eventually lead to the breakdown of society. Tarnas' overall analysis is similar to descriptions of the ef-

fects of collective trauma described by Mary Watkins and Helene
Shulman:

> Individuals begin to feel as if they are completely on their own,
> and a sense of distrust about the world often develops. The in-
> dividualism and isolation felt to be the norm in modern urban
> environments may in fact be the end product of the traumatic
> disruption of communities over time.[8]

The effects of individual autonomy and disconnection negatively impact attempts at addressing a social justice agenda, even for people
working to heal from these symptoms.

Paul Rasor, author of an essay titled, *Reclaiming Our Prophetic
Voice: Liberal Theology and the Challenge of Racism,* notes that racial justice efforts by liberal, religious people are negatively impacted by the
ambivalence of wanting to create inclusive communities while, at the
same time, retaining their individual autonomy. Many people aspire to
be welcoming of diversity, but experience a tension when challenged
by requests to be inclusive that bump up against personal interests
and values. The challenge arises as soon as being "in community" is
juxtaposed with the comfortable or traditional. Rasor attributes the
ambivalence about creating racially inclusive communities to a need
to distance oneself from that which is feared. In other words, when
the idea of being inclusive remains theoretical, it is valued, as it does
not require active (and often uncomfortable) change. But when being
inclusive requires making personal (often significant) changes, follow
through is often radically reduced.[9]

Failing to address this ambivalence head on and locate a
both/and approach allows one to avoid the necessary shifts required
for living within an inclusive community. This undermines not only
one's own growth and healing, but racial justice efforts as well.

❖ To what degree do you value individual autonomy?

❖ How does it affect your decision-making when you are asked
to make a difficult change?

———————

Tension

Knowing your Self can be considered knowing the divine.	— **AND** —	An exclusive focus on Self can undermine responsibility to the collective.

Like many in the United States, I turned away from the religion of my parents and was dissatisfied with individualistic U.S. society. As a result, I have searched for a spiritual practice that offers meaning, a sense of wholeness, and a feeling of being universally connected. This has involved searching for something other than a mainstream religious practice, viewing our contemporary society as "corrupt and disconnected from nature and the sacred,"[10] and attempting to break through the boundaries that separate myself from others and nature.[11] This has led me to the conviction that all of humanity, the Earth's creatures, the Earth itself, and the Divine are interconnected and interdependent.[12]

The search for a different way of being in the world leads many toward a compilation of spiritual ideas and practices falling under the umbrella of "New Age." Although difficult to describe in a way that will satisfy everyone, this blend of influences include "pagan religions, Eastern philosophies, and occult-psychic phenomena," as well as beliefs and practices from Indigenous cultures and what is called the "Timeless Wisdom," including mystical forms of ancient traditions such as Gnosticism, alchemy, Kabbalah, and Theosophy.[13] Although I have never identified with the New Age movement, my spiritual grounding is aligned with many of its associated beliefs. These concepts may influence many people who consider themselves spiritual but who do not identify as adherents of the New Age movement.

Considering the values and beliefs associated with New Age concepts is important because many of these beliefs have become ubiquitous within some contemporary organized religious institutions. Churches influenced by these ideas are more likely to offer a liberal interpretation of the religion's beliefs and mythology. A closer look reveals a rather distressing fact; *there are a number of foundational principles characteristic of modern spirituality that appear strikingly at odds with racial justice efforts.* An exploration of these principles helps to explain why many racial justice advocates lament the self-centeredness they see in contemporary forms of spirituality.

The religious scholar Wouter Hanegraaff suggests that society is witnessing the birth of a new type of religion that is self-created; one that will consist entirely of personal, subjective understandings and experiences.[14] This approach reflects the belief that people should follow their intuition to find a spiritual path that is right for them.[15]

As a result, spiritual experiences are no longer necessarily attached to institutions. This rejection of institutional oversight also involves the ideas that traditional religions depend upon people uncritically accepting dogma and that those who take an individualized approach have broken free from tyrannical religious power structures and are free to discover divinity within themselves.[16] Direct communication with the divine supports the idea that one's ultimate truth and knowledge comes from subjective experience.[17]

Hanegraaff writes that the Self is the "central, unifying symbolism" that best represents this type of individually created spirituality.[18] He explains that "the centrality to western esotericism of gnosis — knowledge of the Self interpreted as knowledge of God — appears to provide a perfect foundation for the individualistic symbolism of the Self in New Age religion."[19] Subsequently, a critical question is posed: If religions have, for centuries, depended upon collective narrative and imagery to make moral arguments and guide behavior according to a "community's code of conduct," what happens when collective symbolism is replaced by private symbolism?[20]

According to Hanegraaff, what is missing from these practices is something that existed within the traditional, esoteric forms of the ancients' religions — a sense of community obligation.[21] With the idea that the unifying center is to be located within each individual and that the Self "undergoes a process of spiritual evolution,"[22] this new religious form suggests that the Self is the vehicle that is able to unlock divine, cosmological mysteries which were previously explained by organized religion. A relationship with, and obligation to, a community is unnecessary for revelation and connection to the Divine.

This individualized orientation, focused on the power of the Self, leads many spiritual seekers to view suffering as existing primarily as a part of people's spiritual education and evolution.[23] This belief aligns with the companion understanding that people are responsible for creating their own reality.[24] These concepts are often linked to the power of one's thoughts, karma, and/or the soul's selection of its physical incarnation. In other words, people's life circumstances are perceived to be chosen by their individual souls as part of the necessary conditions for their evolution of consciousness. Therefore, people's life circumstances are aligned with their divine purpose.

This perspective supports the view that everything happens for a reason. Many spiritual people believe that the hand of the Divine is found resting on all past and present circumstances. In this framework, the divine Self (sometimes conceived of as spirit or soul) is that Divine hand.

In summary, the various beliefs and principles characteristic of this new form of spirituality involve:

- Freedom from religious dogma involves individually constructing one's spiritual path, and eclectic experimentation is acceptable.

- Each individual locates truth within him or herself.

- There is no authority other than the Self.

- Everything that occurs, regardless of how oppressive or discriminatory, can be presumed to be related to people's divinely-directed, self-selected experience.

- Each person is solely responsible for his or her own life situation and only responsible to his or her higher Self.

In this belief system the individual is *not* responsible to take actions intended to relieve the suffering of others. This self-orientation leads to a significant problem for both the spiritual seeker and for racial justice: *Even though many spiritual seekers are attempting to return to a more balanced, harmonious, and interconnected way of life, this approach reinforces the very individualism that is rejected as a problematic part of our contemporary society.*

❖ Do any of the beliefs and approaches sound familiar to you?

❖ To what degree are your beliefs shaped by some of these ideas?

Tension

Positive thinking leads to personal and collective healing.	**AND**	Confronting painful truths is necessary for personal and social transformation.

The personalized approach to spirituality often prioritizes what is perceived to be positive and connecting but which, unwittingly, reinforces disconnection. How and why does this occur? A self-focused spirituality does not generally inspire participation in collective action. Although spiritual and social reform movements in the U.S. during the nineteenth and early twentieth centuries were often aligned, most people currently influenced by the concepts described above are not politically engaged.[25] This is true even though the vast majority of people internalizing these beliefs are politically liberal or progressive. One reason for the lack of political engagement is that spiritual seekers often emphasize that positive thinking is a necessary way to avoid negativity from getting in the way of the healing of self and the planet.[26] Giving attention to societal problems, aligning with political movements, and dealing with messy attempts at political action and collaboration are often interpreted as focusing on negativity.

Resistance to entering the "negativity" found within the political fray is understandable. Engaging with the politics of difference, access, power, and privilege can be unpleasant and may involve interacting with people who are very angry. There are social justice activists who are suspicious of people who focus on personal healing efforts. Many believe that changing the system should be the sole concern and work toward structural change is the surest route to creating healthy communities. For this reason, some activists may not see psycho-spiritual efforts as valuable for either themselves or others. A spiritually oriented person will undoubtedly feel alienated by a group dedicated to a "politics-only" approach. But that does not mean spiritual people should allow this to avert them from engaging in advocacy. In fact, maintaining a positive perspective while engaged in these efforts can be considered powerful spiritual work.

The second way a self-based spirituality can unwittingly engender disconnection involves how it prioritizes actions that *feel* positive over actions in service of the common good. Hanegraaff wonders how the set of beliefs that are a part of a self-oriented spirituality allow for common moral values.[27] Others also question how the freedom to pick and choose what feels comfortable might affect ethical decision-making.[28]

A significant contribution to the tendency to turn toward the Self as the primary guide is that rituals and practices are often conducted in isolation. For example, a study of neopagans found that only 5% said working with other people was centrally important to maintaining either their involvement in, or commitment to, their paganism.[29] The study's authors conclude that, although people feel an immediate sense of belonging to an imagined, large group with common beliefs, the notion of community is "more diffuse and abstract."[30] *This diffused sense of community can significantly reduce one's sense of obligation to another person or group.*

This made me stop and think about my own actions. If I am my own ultimate source of truth and solely committed to feeling good, what will hold me accountable for my behavior? Accountability to one's Self alone may be no accountability at all. It is exceedingly hard to change, take on a new task, or give up something that *feels* right. With my Self as my primary guide, how can I be sure I do not dismiss meaningful, challenging messages too quickly out of attachment, fear, or the individualism that remains embedded within? How can I be sure I am accessing my higher Self when making decisions? The consequences of this current trend of individualism continue to affect many spiritual people in ways that frustrate activists and efforts for justice.

❧ How is your experience similar or different from what is presented here?

❧ How can a personal approach to spirituality work in support of political action?

❧ What helps you determine how and when to take action?

Political Action

It must be acknowledged at the outset that people who focus exclusively on political action contribute meaningfully to racial justice efforts every day. Yet, it is also true that considering the psycho-social dimension as undermining political organizing can lead to a limited diversity of approaches to systemic change, a weakening of their effectiveness, and a turning away of some interested people who simultaneously value spiritual principles.

Tension

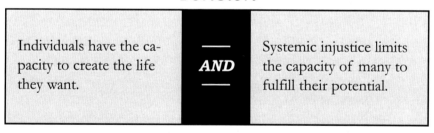

| Individuals have the capacity to create the life they want. | *AND* | Systemic injustice limits the capacity of many to fulfill their potential. |

It is common knowledge that people first need to know about unjust policies before taking the necessary action to rectify them. Therefore, educational workshops on unjust policies are valued. What needs consideration, however, is how data illustrating racial disparities is presented and the meaning made of that data.

It is important to note that most people in the U.S. interpret data using an *individual analysis*. This is due to the fact that U.S. society is based on the belief that individuals are responsible for their circumstances. The focus on personal responsibility underlies the U.S.'s vision of itself as a meritocracy, a society in which all people have an equal chance for success. The consequence of this belief, particularly for white people, is a default perspective that people attain their level of education based on their efforts, live wherever they would like, and enter the criminal justice system when they do bad things. In this individualistic way of perceiving the world, people make personal choices and are exclusively responsible for the results.

An *individual analysis* is very different than a *systemic analysis*. Most social justice advocates learn to use a *systemic analysis* that recognizes how the historical and contemporary policies and procedures of a society (via its institutions) shape people's experiences and life outcomes. A systemic analysis can reveal, for example, how schools offer differential access to advanced placement courses or arts programs, historic lending policies resulted in certain groups living in concentrated areas in the inner cities, and targeted police sweeps and gang injunction policies result in youth being criminalized. The systemic lens reveals how policies and practices of people within institutions make a difference in where people live, find employment, and how likely they are to complete their education or get arrested or incarcerated.

In a society focused on the autonomy and responsibility of the individual, people are not encouraged or educated to perceive how systems affect people. Learning to apply a *systemic* or *structural analysis* is generally a difficult skill to learn, one that contrasts with long-held beliefs and values. For this reason, unless a person is exposed to hard evidence or personal experience verifying the accuracy of a systemic analysis, data presented intended to reveal racial disparities (and demonstrate how systemic practices are injurious and discriminatory) are usually challenged or rejected outright.

Part of the problem is that when activists' workshops identify institutional racism as responsible for society's racial disparities, the data presented does not offer proof that racism is the cause. Unless the data comes from controlled or experimental studies, it is only correlational or descriptive. One group has a rate of X on some measure (like poverty, incarceration, or college attendance rates), while another group has a Y rate on that particular measure. Nothing inherent in the statistics suggests *why* the disparity exists.

This opens the door for interpretations and challenges: Are institutional problems really the root cause of the disparity, and how do we know for sure? For those accustomed to perceiving the world through an individual lens, every potential explanation is brought to bear. "What about...? How do you know it's not because...? Couldn't it be that...?" These questions are predictable because they arise from of a lifetime of having been influenced to see the world with an individual analysis.

For activists who offer a systemic analysis, this can be extremely frustrating. Contributing to the frustration is the fact that in these situations, the data simply cannot answer the question of causation. Activists have generally studied the history of an issue and multiple streams of evidence have convinced them that the current disparities are based on historical and current policies and practices which continue to exacerbate the issue. Theirs is a cry for an urgent response. Getting people accustomed to seeing the world through an individualistic lens to accept the historical and systemic analysis and respond to the call for action often depends on the degree to which activists are able to string together a compelling circumstantial case for their position. This means justice advocates seeking to expand their support base need to formulate a case that offers additional evidence, historical facts, psychological theory, contemporary anecdotes, and compelling personal testimony.

✤ How do you tend to interpret the world - through an individual or a systemic lens – or both?

✤ What do you think will help people view the world through a systemic lens?

———————

Tension

Individuals can control how they react to circumstances.	**AND**	The circumstances of people's lives impact their responses, and these circumstances must be improved through collective action.

Our society's individualism is so pervasive that many people dedicated to social justice believe an unwavering focus on systemic injustice is the only way to create some semblance of balance. This approach, however, may unwittingly discourage people oriented toward psycho-spiritual healing from engaging in political action.

There is no doubt that resistance to a systemic analysis is firmly embedded within U.S. culture. *Hearing that U.S. society is still marked by institutional inequality is not what most liberal, spiritual white people want to believe.*[31] If true, it means there is more work to do, which can feel overwhelming and prompt emotional reactivity. This is one reason why psycho-spiritual healing is so necessary. It can encourage people to investigate and resolve some of the emotional responses that result in denial and inaction.

Exacerbating the situation, however, is that those who offer an unwavering *systemic* analysis can disavow the concept of personal agency — the freedom to make individual choices and work to overcome life circumstances. This often turns off people who value personal growth, balance, and a holistic perspective. Although it is essential to learn how systems operate, it is also important to acknowledge what spiritual people dedicated to social justice know to be true about inherent personal agency. The *both/and* approach is required — systemic factors contribute to people's circumstances and all individuals remain free to react to those circumstances in ways that either support or inhibit their growth. Nowhere in this *both/and* is a suggestion that the playing field is equal, only that people remain in control of their inner experience and outer responses even while being impacted by the social systems surrounding them.

Without this balanced understanding, a number of unhelpful patterns result.

People invested in social justice frequently speak and react to questions regarding personal agency as though there are no individual factors at play. There is often a failure to acknowledge that individuals have some choice in how they navigate systemic challenges. To spiritually oriented people, a singular focus on systems appears to dismiss any attempt or responsibility to provide personal growth and healing opportunities for those who experience injustice.

How does solely concentrating on systemic inequities push away these potential allies? One way is the judgmental response they get from activists when adding the role of individual choice and/or personal responsibility to the conversation. This happens because often their questions and interpretations of the data frequently reinforce racial stereotypes.[32] People new to racial justice issues tend to draw their conclusions based on an individual analysis. The resulting questions or statements can, accurately, strike justice advocates as infused with prejudice.

For example, people might suggest that the reason for the disparity in college attendance rates could be the result of less of an emphasis on education in the home, laziness among students, or any number of other reasons that place responsibility with the individuals affected by racism.[33] As these suggestions are highly offensive to those who know how deeply many parents care about their students' success and how hard many youth in the community have worked to become college ready, compassionate responses are necessary to sustain connection and continue in a way that allows people to feel valued even while they express contrary and often stereotypically racist viewpoints.

Social justice oriented people who want to encourage spiritually oriented people to join their cause can offer a systemic analysis while simultaneously acknowledging personal agency. The role of personal responsibility can be recognized as necessary and desirable while highlighting how individual efforts are regularly undermined by systemic factors. The ability to skillfully honor the questions and concerns raised about personal agency by spiritually oriented people is essential.

People who are new to systemic interpretations should be valued for their interest in learning. Taking the time to support someone in breaking through the limits of an individualistic lens can make a huge difference. Empathy for people going through a process which can be emotionally and psychologically upsetting can go a long way toward encouraging future action. Although exceedingly difficult for those who feel the great urgency in addressing racism, there is no way around the fact that, for many people, this process takes a lot of time and the pathway is often frustrating and messy.

* ❧ How do you relate to issues of personal agency and systemic issues?

* ❧ What strategies do you have for engaging people around issues of social justice?

* ❧ How important is it to you that a group you work with holds a balanced view?

Tension

Expanding consciousness is key to transformative change.	— *AND* —	Action focused on changing systems is key to transformative change.

People invested in social justice unwittingly create tension within their own ranks when making value judgments about different approaches to advocacy efforts. This tension is both sabotaging to the overall effort and off-putting to those newly entering the fold. It begins when consciousness-raising and political action are split off from, or pitted against, each other. Consciousness-raising in the context of this discussion relates to both learning and reflecting on issues of race and racism and developing the skills necessary to navigate situations and relationships in non-reactive ways.

Rarely does the tension between consciousness-raising and political action involve a wholesale rejection of one over the other. It is
commonly understood that consciousness-raising is essential so that
people are inspired to action based on knowledge, have a clear understanding of the psychological and systemic issues at play, and are personally equipped to engage in effective change efforts. It is also
commonly acknowledged that action is essential because personal understanding does not, on its own, result in structural change. Holding
both sides of the work in balance is a goal for those who recognize
that power hierarchies are often reproduced if the psycho-spiritual
dimension is ignored in favor of a purely structural focus.[34] Activist
educators, such as Gloria Anzaldúa and Jacqui Alexander, suggest
that a "spiritual activism" can, in fact, allow people to bring a deep
understanding of themselves to the work in ways that can fundamentally shift power relationships.[35]

However, tension occurs when people concentrate, feel comfortable, and actively participate on one side more than the other. I
am a case in point, leaning toward consciousness-raising activities,
particularly since they draw on my personal strengths and skills. Although I have challenged myself to be part of political action campaigns, it is not where my time and attention is usually directed. For
this reason, I take seriously the activists' caution not to descend into
"navel gazing" in ways that keep one on the sidelines, constantly
seeking more information and dialogue, and never taking action. I remain self-reflective about whether using my voice in the way that I do
is somehow taking the easy way out.

I know many people whose focus is on community organizing,
political action campaigns, and other systemic, institutional change
efforts. While many of these colleagues recognize the value of
doing their own work on personal growth and consciousness-raising, this is not true for all people who are drawn to political action.
Some activists may be shortchanging their capacity for effectiveness
by not devoting more of their time to personal reflection and
growth.

It is possible that the tendency to advocate solely for one approach may involve an element of self-validation. If not attuned to
how psychological needs play a part in all human endeavors, interac-

tions can become unintentionally divisive. An experience that occurred within my racial justice community illustrates this.

For the last decade, AWARE-LA has attempted to structure itself so that it offers opportunities for a well-balanced advocacy practice. The organization values both consciousness-raising (via the Unmasking Whiteness summer institute and Saturday Dialogues) and political action (via the Active Resistance and White People for Racial Justice workgroups). Yet, even as an organization dedicated to the *both/and,* the group sometimes struggles.

A recent tension involved two volunteers who took active roles in the organization's leadership. Both of these racial justice advocates are women in their mid-20s with prior experience participating in social justice efforts. Both understand the need for a balance of political action and consciousness-raising in the work. Both are wholeheartedly dedicated to the organization. And yet, their conflict exposed a long-simmering organizational tension related to each of these women's differing perspectives on what constitutes substantive change. The issue centered around two essential questions: What happens when someone does not participate in more than one workgroup? What does that suggest about that person's advocacy practice? These questions illuminated the underlying differential valuing that existed in our organization between consciousness-raising and systemic change work.

One colleague, who plays a leadership role in both the Active Resistance work group and the summer institute planning group, is clearly dedicating time to both action and consciousness-raising. According to descriptions of the organization's structure, her work is easily perceived as complete and balanced. For her, the conversation about what counts as consciousness-raising or systemic efforts is about honing her analysis and ensuring that there is a clear understanding between group members.

The other colleague, who plays a strong leadership role in developing the Saturday Dialogue workshops, is employed as a K-12 educator. Her advocacy work involves working towards structural change in the school where she is employed. For example, she developed a tutorial program to support struggling students of color to achieve academic success. Further, she is constantly thinking about and working on ways to bring her understanding of racial justice to every aspect of her life. Given her strong valuing of the *both/and* integrative approach, the idea that her efforts are somehow perceived by some other members as not systemic work is hurtful and dismissive. For her, the conversation about what counts as consciousness-raising or systemic efforts is not a purely intellectual question. The judgment she perceives coming from others affects her interest in continuing with the organization.

I began to see the situation more clearly through discussions with both women. Both of their contributions to the organization arise out of their own journeys and how they see themselves as advocates. They both do great work and appreciate each other. The colleague who participates in multiple workgroups has come to realize the wisdom in widening her view of what "systemic" means in order to value the localized efforts of her colleague. Recognizing these efforts as important contributions, she is more apt to offer explicit appreciation. On the other hand, the educator has recognized her need to self-validate instead of looking for validation from others who may not provide it for her.

Demonstrably appreciating everyone's contributions to any aspect of the collective effort is needed. This is important in order to keep individuals returning to groups attempting to work collectively. Recognizing the need for both consciousness-raising and political action and aligning one's behavior to reflect that recognition, is vitally important to the health and effectiveness of social justice organizations. After all, the efforts are interconnected and interdependent. A change occurring in one part of a system (including changes within the individuals who make up that system) results in change in all other parts of the system.

❖ In what ways have you seen explicit or implicit tension between different approaches play out in your organizations and communities?

The Search for Balance

George Tinker draws on addiction studies when he suggests that "it takes people roughly as long to recover from an addiction as they spent being addicted."[36] He suggests that if U.S. society's addiction to individualism and disconnection (and the violence and exploitation it generates) has continued for approximately 500 years, then it will take about that long for the recovery. This means that, although one might consciously reject individualism and seek to create a life involving collective effort, there are layers upon layers to unpeel. This struggle is part of a healing journey that connects spiritual growth and active participation in racial justice efforts.[37]

An essay by Rebecca Parker, in *Soul Work: Anti-racist Theologies in Dialogue,* provides a practical outline of steps people can take to engage racial justice in a way that includes psycho-spiritual development, growth, and healing.[38] Parker writes that social activism is a spiritual practice that allows people to reclaim their humanity and refuse to accept "cultivation into numbness and disengagement."[39] A study of fifty white activists found that a sense of reclaiming humanity and healing from socially conditioned racism propels many of them into racial justice work.[40] The need to recover from the disconnections discussed above are addressed in the work of Michelle Alexander. Focusing on the issue of mass incarceration in the U.S., she provides a powerful example of how the call for social justice action is simultaneously a call for personal healing.

Alexander's work offers a thorough analysis of a number of issues. First, the U.S. War on Drugs has led to an explosion in our prison population that now consists of a huge number of non-violent drug offenders, mostly people of color. Second, laws have been passed that virtually guarantee no redress against claims of racial discrimination. Third, the treatment of, and attitude toward, those swept up into the criminal justice system has created a racial caste system in our country wherein hundreds of thousands of people have had their lives forever altered and their ability to participate meaningfully in society limited.[41]

The disproportionate number of people of color swept up in the War on Drugs is astonishing. By 2000, there were *twenty-six times* more prison admissions for African Americans than there were in 1983. There were *twenty-two times* more prison admissions for Latinos, and *eight times* the number for whites during that same time period.[42] The overall U.S. prison population increased from under 300,000 in 1980 to over 2 million in 2004.[43] How did so many people get so dangerous in such a short period of time? The truth is that people did not get more dangerous. Public officials and voters changed policies and legislation. The danger resides within the political and criminal justice systems.

Unfortunately, many within our society remain willfully ignorant of the personal and social consequences of being caught up in the criminal justice system. People are also generally unaware of what happens to people after they have had their first encounter. One relatively minor infraction (that white kids get away with on a regular basis) or an unintended police error can disrupt a person's life to the degree that they never regain their footing.

To address this injustice, people need to see beyond the individualistic lens that views all those swept up in the War on Drugs as culpable and, therefore, deserving of what happens to them.[44] While the majority of illegal drug users in our nation are white, three-quarters of all those imprisoned for drug offenses are Black and Latino.[45] Why are white people not arrested and convicted at proportionate rates? Alexander's analysis offers answers. The difference is not related to neighborhood crime rates, nor that people of color deal and use drugs out in the open more often. The difference is not that whites are purchasing drugs more often from people of color. None of these common arguments hold up under analysis.

Alexander uses a systemic lens that offers conclusive answers. Studies have demonstrated that, when asked to envision a drug user, 95% of the participants imagined a Black person.[46] Media messages over the last three decades have cemented an image of Black people as more likely to be drug users and both whites and people of color have been influenced by these messages. Alexander notes: "decades of cognitive research demonstrates that both unconscious and conscious biases lead to discriminatory actions, even when an individual does not want to discriminate."[47] This means that discrimination occurs without police, prosecutors, or judges being consciously racist or intending any harm.

Even without intent, the underlying bias toward seeing people of color as criminals leads to a disproportionate allocation of resources and attention in poor communities of color, making it more likely that people of color will be caught up in sweeps. It also results in harsher treatment by the police, courts, and correctional offices. For example, Alexander cites that, among juveniles who are first time offenders and have committed identical crimes, African American youth are *six times* more likely than white youth to be incarcerated.[48] For many youth, this is the start of a lifelong downward spiral.

Alexander concludes that the problem is not simply due to a set of failed policies or the need to change laws. Policy and legislative change is necessary, and the "War on Drugs" must end. But, disconnection and indifference to the experience of low-income people of color is, perhaps, the biggest hurdle.[49] She notes that one of the major challenges is getting people to care about those who have been, and are currently, incarcerated. It is all-too-common for people to believe that those locked up deserved it. Alexander writes that people are in "collective denial" regarding how dire the situation is and how significantly racism influences police and court practices[50] noting, in addition, that it "is this failure to care, really care across color lines, that lies at the core of this system of control and every racial caste system that has existed in the United States or anywhere else in the world."[51] Taking action to end silence and indifference is part of individual and collective psycho-spiritual healing and it requires a *both/and* orientation.

Combining psycho-spiritual healing and growth with racial justice advocacy requires confrontation of the various ways one's psyche has been conditioned to experience fear, separation, and otherness. Alexander notes that, in order to return to the incarceration level the U.S. had in the 1970s, 80% of those currently in prison would have to be released.[52] *Take a moment to imagine. What image arises when you consider every 4 out of 5 prisoners released? What fears and concerns come with that image? Do these questions provoke discomfort? Why?*

I was not conditioned to see the current situation as undermining society. Instead, as a white woman, I was conditioned by media and societal structures to experience feelings ranging from discomfort to terror when considering the prison population. Social conditioning led me to see all incarcerated persons as dangerous, instead of seeing that a vast number of non-violent drug users and their families are deserving of respect and help, not punishment. Providing drug counseling and access to jobs, as well as revising our drug policies, would be a healthier and more effective solution.[53]

It is also essential to consider how this conditioning affects white people's sense of self. It is easy for me to judge people from past decades or centuries for their complicity in racial oppression. I'd like to believe that my moral and spiritual sensibilities would have led me to be an abolitionist if I had lived during the 1800s. Noel Ignatiev recognizes this as a common perspective among white people.[54] He asks white people to consider our current U.S. situation in terms of mass incarceration in order to realistically judge one's level of concern about those living at that time in history. His questions require me, as one who believes that it is wrong to imprison people for non-violent, drug-related offences, to consider what it would take for me to advocate for the release of 80% of those incarcerated today. After reading Alexander's book, I see how the historical work on abolishing slavery is in some ways comparable to contemporary organizing that advocates for prison reduction.

Considering these questions brings me face to face with my fears, disconnection, and conditioned stereotypes. I know people who have spent time in prison. They are dedicated to their families, work hard, and are trustworthy and dependable. Yet, my image of the prison population remains informed by media messages that lead me to believe that *all* those currently locked up are dangerous. I know this is not accurate. My fears regarding personal safety are understandable, but overblown, and I have been influenced by political rhetoric, corporations, and other interests who are making huge amounts of money from the expansion and privatization of prisons.[55] I am challenged to spend even more time with people directly affected by these issues to help my head, heart, and hands become more fully engaged.[56]

Taking up an engaged presence is part of taking responsibility to recover from modern disconnections and the individualism that continues to lie at the very core of mass incarceration. For Parker too, "social action is an incarnational event. It mends the split of mind and body, individual from community, neighbor from neighbor."[57] The capacity to recognize what is going on in society, how one is participating (or not) and why, and then choose to engage differently is a mark of interdependence. This recognition allows one to play a role in disrupting the racism and oppression that continues to perpetuate a racial caste system within the U.S.

❖ What emotions and concerns arise when you think of playing some active role in the racial justice movement?

❖ How deeply have you been affected by the media blitz that falsely implies the majority of drug users are dangerous people of color?

I have heard it said that a movement is built individual by individual. Every person is a potential ally, and there are some issues so dire we need every mind clear, every voice loud, and every body actively engaged. However one chooses to contribute, all are welcome and all are necessary in our collective recovery from individualism.

CHAPTER 4

Common Humanity and Group Differences

In 2006 I first heard Dr. Joy DeGruy, author of *Post-Traumatic Slave Syndrome*,[1] deliver a powerful address to an auditorium full of people. I went home and immediately read her book. A few months later I attended another of her lectures. A week after that, I attended yet another. Her words inspired me because she offers an analysis that argues for a therapeutic approach to one of our nation's deepest wounds.

Her message calls those of us living at this time in history to consider the psychological experiences of those who came before and how unhealed psychic wounds have been passed forward. She speaks of the psychological effects that slavery had on African Americans and the resulting coping mechanisms they generated. She explains how these survival tactics, although no longer helpful, are still in evidence today. She also speaks of the cognitive dissonance that must have existed for white people trying to hold ideas of their goodness while, at the same time, owning slaves. She addresses how the resulting psychological distancing has been passed on through familial and societal conditioning to their descendants. Throughout her exploration of the various eras of U.S. racism DeGruy stops and asks, "And where were the psychologists?" "When was there an opportunity for healing?" There was none. Each era of trauma was followed by another.

After providing the history, DeGruy outlines issues currently challenging the African American community. She explains how they are directly linked to this long history of wounding and the lack of opportunities for healing. The message is clear: At no time in U.S. history has there been a concerted, authentic, and wide-spread effort to provide the therapeutic attention needed to transcend this history and its devastating legacy. And so it is that our nation's racial wounds are trans-generational and festering.

All this being true, many people feel hopeful and filled with possibility during experiences highlighting common bonds across race. Whether part of spiritual community gatherings, sporting events, or other situations where a diverse group comes together in celebration, people engaged in a collective effort can feel a healing moment. The racism and injustice of the past may feel far removed; the future looks bright and focusing on our commonality is celebrated.

Unfortunately, there is a problem if these moments are considered sufficient for collective healing, as these celebratory experiences rarely prompt learning about the particularities of others' experiences. This is especially true when this learning involves hearing about unpleasant situations that continue to provoke deep emotion and upset. The result is an all-too-frequent scenario where people focused exclusively on positivity and future potential remain unaware of how historic and contemporary racism negatively affects people on a daily basis. In these cases, relationships across race often remain superficial and easily disrupted.

More explicit efforts toward healing are needed. Yet, even when there is agreement that large-scale healing is needed, this does not guarantee there will be agreement on what those efforts should entail. Is it better to attend to old wounds, or focus attention toward a collective future? Will healthier relationships be developed by highlighting common similarities among people, or is there value in investigating group differences?

People oriented toward psycho-spiritual healing often respond:

> Focusing on our common humanity and similarities helps people relate to one another. Looking backward to past pains can reopen wounds and block new inspiration. Healing occurs through attention toward the present. We should recognize the inherent freedom to heal ourselves and envision the future we wish to create together.

But, people oriented toward racial justice tend to believe:

> The unhealed past is with us today. Wounds from racism re-
> main open and festering. Paying attention to the histories and
> experiences of our different racial groups reveals that each
> group needs a specific healing process. Moving forward in a
> way that avoids creating new injuries and stops pouring salt in
> already open wounds requires knowledge of history and recog-
> nition of how that history affects our lives today.

Exploring the tensions that arise between these two orientations can
reveal *both/and* possibilities.

A balance between *common similarities* and *racial group differences* can
be navigated by staying open to how racial identity impacts people
differently *and* appreciating that people share experiences that go beyond race. Some use the phrase "unity in diversity" to describe how
to hold this *both/and* ideal.[2] Without this balance, difficulties arise for
both sides.

Common Humanity

Generalizations made about a group (whether positive or negative)
are rarely, if ever, applicable to all people in that group. To assume so
moves that generalization solidly into the realm of a stereotype. If I act
out of a stereotype, the result is often discriminatory and unjust. However, there is value in discussing general tendencies specific to different
racial groups. Without recognizing difference, people fail to appreciate
the lived reality of others, exacerbate unhealed wounds, and overlook
critical group-specific issues that deserve attention.

Tension

Our similarities are numerous and tie us to each other.	— **AND** —	Racial groups experience U.S. society very differently.

It is helpful to begin by recognizing two often-posed questions: Do racial groups experience U.S. society differently? And if yes, are these differences meaningful enough to warrant attention? Exploring how values associated with American culture originated, how those values relate to racial identity, and how the history of American values impacts various racial groups' experiences today can provide a useful context for these pivotal questions.[3]

It is essential to note at the outset that the idea of a "white race" did not exist in law before the 1700s. It was not until 1705, in the Virginia Codes, that the term "white" was used to identify a specific group of people. The various Northern European groups entering and assimilating into the U.S. between the 1600s and 1800s went through a process of racialization that, over time, developed into a white American identity. Supported by cultural writings, cartoons, pseudo-science, economic advantage, and legal decisions, European-Americans were led to believe they exemplified the height of what it meant to be human.[4] *Being white came to mean being autonomous, ambitious, productive, superior, and able to accumulate wealth. All other races, more likely to live by communal values and retain a mystic sensibility, were considered primitive, savage, and inferior.*[5] Not only did these value judgments affect people psychologically, they were used to justify hundreds of years of violence, racism, and unjust laws against groups considered "not white."

From a psycho-social perspective, this history remains significant because these judgments resulted in *white American identity* being associated with what it means to be *Western* and *modern*. As a result, any discussion regarding the "American" experience and all that it is assumed to entail, should be approached with caution. Today, all people in our society, and many worldwide, are influenced by this worldview, with its focus on individualism and personal autonomy. Simultaneously, different racial groups within the U.S. have had, and still have, very different experiences related to these concepts.

For example, although the portrayals of U.S. history generally have offered a positive image of white American culture, the portrayals of people of color have been largely absent or demeaning. In *The Souls of White Folks,* published in 1920, W.E.B DuBois writes:

> This theory of human culture and its aims has worked itself
> through warp and woof of our daily thought with a thor-
> oughness that few realize. Everything great, good, efficient,
> fair, and honorable, is "white"; everything mean, bad, blun-
> dering, cheating, and dishonorable is "yellow"; a bad taste is
> "brown"; and the devil is "black." The changes of this theme
> are continually rung in picture and story, in newspaper head-
> ing and moving-picture, in sermon and school book, until., of
> course, the King can do no wrong, — a White Man is always
> right and a Black Man has no rights which a white man is
> bound to respect.[6]

DuBois refers to "*our* daily thought," acknowledging that the devalua-
tion and negative judgments infected the psyches of all people. Racial
advocates often discuss the infecting nature of these thoughts when
considering the *internalized superiority* and *internalized inferiority* that operates within people in U.S. society — people who continue to be exposed
to, and influenced by, stereotypical messages via media, school, etc.

W.E.B. DuBois' writing provides evidence that, although the il-
lusion of white superiority might consciously or unconsciously influence everyone in U.S. society to some degree, people of color have
always recognized its fallacy. In fact, the argument could be made that
people of color, on the receiving end of the worst of white supremacy's violence, have always been more clear-sighted about the
United States, its cultural values, and the false nature of white supremacy. DuBois states:

> Here is a civilization that has boasted much. Neither Roman
> nor Arab, Greek nor Egyptian, Persian nor Mongol ever took
> himself and his own perfectness with such disconcerting seri-
> ousness as the modern white man. We whose shame, humilia-
> tion, and deep insult his aggrandizement so often involved
> were never deceived. We looked at him clearly, with world-old
> eyes, and saw simply a human thing, weak and pitiable and
> cruel, even as we are and were.[7]

With these words, DuBois calls people to recognize the way white supremacy went hand in hand with the development of the modern
worldview and the creation of a white identity; specifically, a prideful
self-concept of white people as a model for the most evolved way of
being.

White American values — one of which is that success is available to any and all who work smart and hard — were not allowed to be realized throughout our history for most people of color. These differing experiences continue today in many ways, some obvious and some subtle. A survey analyzing perceptions of the prevalence of racism and discrimination in the United States reveals significant group differences. By a large percentage, people of color believe that there is a higher level of racial discrimination in our society than do white people.[8] This difference highlights the wide chasm that still exists between racial groups.

A resulting problem is that a focus on our common humanity generally goes hand in hand with an assumption that people experience the world similarly. This assumption easily translates into offensive behavior toward people impacted by discrimination and racism. If one does not recognize the difference between people's experiences, one's statements which assume a universal reality display ignorance and insensitivity. When asked to reflect on how one's speech or actions might be based on unconscious racism, one is likely to reject the suggestion that racial differences might have anything to do with the offense.

Addressing this tension requires a recognition of the *both/and*. Our common humanity does bind us together. *And* people from different racial groups have varying perspectives based on divergent experiences.

♣ How often do you think about the impact of race on people today, including yourself?

♣ To what degree do you find people interested in and/or willing to discuss racial group differences?

Tension

The physical body is a vessel for the movements of spirit and soul.	—— *AND* ——	The physical body carries historical and ancestral memory.

A factor that stops many people from agreeing that racial differences are real and important is that many spiritual people believe the
physical world is less meaningful than the ethereal. A consequence of
this is that racial group membership, by extension, does not seem important. As a person who learned to value the *both/and* early in my
spiritual journey, this raised an issue that perplexed me for many
years. I struggled to find a way to hold my spiritual evolution as the
most essential purpose of my life while simultaneously holding my
racial identity as a meaningful part of that.

After many years of grappling with this issue, I sought the perspective of a respected spiritual guide, Orland Bishop.[9] In response
to my questioning, Orland said physical bodies are what place us
within *time,* as opposed to a timeless state, and allow us to connect
with the spirit of this historical era. He validated how important the
physical body is as part of an incarnational process. Without my
body, I would not be able to move through the consciousness-en-
hancing experience of human life.

I still wondered how my particular body, including my racial des-
ignation, might be meaningful. He replied that our bodies are not
ours alone, but a psychological and social "group space." My body is
part of the group considered white, and I represent its history simply
by having white skin. I am attached to that history even though I was
not part of its original creation and do not want to be associated with
its historic or ongoing damage.[10] I already understood that my white
skin marks me as associated with old and continuing racial wounds.
What I wanted to know was: How is my association with whiteness
valuable? What does being marked as part of a group to which I do
not feel strongly associated have to do with my conscious evolution?
How might it be purposeful from a spiritual point of view?

As the conversation continued, I realized that Orland was referring to an even deeper relationship — an inheritance that is carried
by one's physicality and connected to one's specific ancestry. He went
on to say that my body is related to more than my individual self and
that I am connected to five generations of ancestral memory through
my body. I, therefore, carry an inheritance of deep memory through
my white, physical body. This was a new and somewhat disconcerting
idea.

I had previously considered my physical form as something that was not fundamentally the "real me." Like many spiritual people, I conceived of my physical body as a temporary structure that housed my inner spirit. It did not carry its own history beyond that of "vehicle" or "receptacle" for spirit and soul. This was less anxiety-producing than the perspective Orland offered me. To see my physical form as coming with a racial inheritance of ancestral memory that requires resolution suggests that I need to deal with pain and grief rooted in my familial history.

This is reminiscent of Eckhart Tolle's, *A New Earth: Awakening to Your Life's Purpose,* wherein he describes how human beings carry the past with them. He says that "negative emotion that is not fully faced and seen for what it is in the moment it arises does not completely dissolve. It leaves behind a remnant of pain."[11] Tolle suggests there is an energy field created from all of that old emotion. He calls this the "pain-body" and states that "the pain-body…is not just individual in nature. It also partakes of the pain suffered by countless humans throughout the history of humanity."[12] This energy field called the "collective pain-body" may be encoded within our DNA.[13] In other words, the energy making up the "pain-body" is not derived from an individual's pain alone. Each person may be carrying pain from those who have come before.

Tolle speaks of how particular groups who have been subject to persecution have very strong pain bodies. He also widens the scope beyond persecuted groups when he writes:

> The suffering inflicted on Native and Black Americans has not
> remained confined to those two races, but has become part of
> the collective American pain-body. It is always the case that
> both victim and perpetrator suffer the consequences of any
> acts of violence, oppression, or brutality. For what you do to
> others, you do to yourself.[14]

If five generations of my ancestors were disconnected from their "feeling life" as part of being bystanders to injustice,[15] as Orland suggests is possible, then something that has been long asleep within me needs to awaken. As the history of white racial identity reveals, I have been conditioned to see myself as representing "the good." My unconscious attempts to navigate a racially discriminatory society have resulted in me closing off from aspects of my perception and distancing myself from negative attributes. By seeing myself and my group as exemplifying only positive traits, I have avoided recognizing how I and my ancestors have been complicit in injustice. Developing a stronger sense of social consciousness is part of regaining my full humanity. This requires me to reconnect and accept all of who I am.

According to Orland, this opening of the heart is a critical part of human beings' soul development. He said that reconnecting to heart-feeling is what can allow people to stop denying what is clearly visible in the world — exploitation, racism, and injury. This awareness will allow people to "stay current with their time body." Orland explained that the "time body makes people responsible for entering the world deeper and deeper, bringing spirit into matter, into this particular given, practical world and spirit potential."[16] The more I open my heart to feel my unresolved pain and grief, the more I will bring my spirit into today's context and respond to the needs of the world.

The suggestions from Orland mirror the reflections of Carol Lee Flinders in her book, *At the Root of this Longing: Reconciling a Spiritual Hunger and a Feminist Thirst*. Flinders' reconciling of spirituality and feminist activism parallels the reconciling of spirituality and race. She speaks of returning to an embodied way of being, reimagining the body and femininity as a sacred, meaningful, and purposeful healing act.[17] Flinders' argument supports the belief that delving deeply into what it means to be living with white skin is also an act of healing that helps challenge participation in an unjust society that thrives on disconnection and individualism.

The more conscious I am of the unhealed pain continuing to swirl around me, the more I will be able to attend to it and work toward resolution. For example, I might support and participate in the creation of healing rituals — either individual or community-based — that recognize racial trauma and seek to soothe ancestral spirits still hungry for acknowledgment and peace. Attending to the pain and taking steps toward resolution does not require me to feel guilt for the original trauma, but it does ask me to take responsibility for the place I occupy within the group I represent and to play a healing role today.

✤ What meaning, if any, do you find in being born into a particular racial group?

✤ Do you feel there are responsibilities that come with your
racial group membership?

Tension

Healing ancestral wounds can be achieved in mul-tiracial community.	**———** **AND** **———**	Some wounds require a group-specific healing ap-proach.

It may be true that healing ancestral wounds can be done
collectively. However, this may not offer a complete picture of
what is needed. There are also personal wounds that occur during
one's current lifetime that may require a particular group-specific
approach.

Over time, I have realized how being raised as a white person
in the U.S. affects me and the way I relate to others. This became
clear the more I attended Saturday Dialogues with AWARE-LA,
my white racial justice community. For the first several years of my
participation, I was continuously surprised to learn I was not the
only one struggling with particular questions, anxieties, and fears.
Slowly I became convinced that most white people in racial justice
circles have wounds in common. However, the Shade Tree community (my multiracial spiritual home) did not validate my growing
belief that white people should work on a healing process with
each other. Some Shade Tree members even saw the activities of
AWARE-LA as exclusionary and misdirected.

I longed for support beyond my experience with AWARE-LA
to justify my focus on race-specific healing. Thankfully, spending
time in other racial justice spaces introduced me to people of
color actively working to address issues that affect their particular

racial groups. A major turning point came when hearing Dr. Joy DeGruy, whose research and work highlights the need for race-specific healing.[18]

DeGruy's perspective did not immediately help me bridge the gap between my appreciation for race-specific healing and the views of my spiritual community, however. Although many members of Shade Tree grappled with issues of racism, classism, and discrimination during annual week-long retreats, most of them did not appear interested in focusing on race outside of that yearly setting. This caused me to question myself, particularly when in racially diverse gatherings dedicated to community well-being. There was so much love, positivity, and mutual appreciation at events devoted to uplifting personal and community healing and growth, that bringing up race felt like I was being the "downer" who could not be satisfied in present moments of joy and togetherness.

I finally expressed my confusion during conversations with Orland. Having already believed for years that a healing process for white people was important, I was curious whether or not Orland would agree with the idea that different racial groups might benefit from group-specific healing processes. So, while asking questions regarding the importance of my current incarnation into my white body, I also asked him what meaning he made of his own racial identity and history. He said,

> The other thing I transitioned into this physical body to do is to be able to represent the cultural age of this group of people considered Black who work on moving through the cultural story to a thought level where a new kind of interpretation can happen. If I did not inherit this body, I could not be a representative for that cultural task. And I needed the American experience to see racism in a certain way, to see social injustice in a certain way. To practice communicating with people in a way that would allow greater understanding about the future. I wouldn't have this task if I stayed in Guyana.[19]

Orland spent his adolescent years in New York, seeing internalized oppression play out among the different groups at his high school. He spoke of choosing to sit with the Haitian kids during their social gatherings, even though he did not speak their lan-

guage, both as a show of support and as a protest act against the
racism the Haitian students experienced from other groups. His
lived experience, therefore, is one in which he stayed open and responsive to the pain that can come from being part of a marginalized group. His spirituality does not shut himself off from
recognizing this pain.

It was at this point in our conversation where our divergent,
yet parallel, pathways regarding healing work became clear. We
spoke of how each of us is attempting to meet the needs of this
time. We were then able to discuss the differential needs of specific groups. Orland recognizes the incapacitating pain that people
of color often experience while incarnated in bodies that carry the
weight of historical and contemporary oppression. This inheritance of the pain body is profound. A focus for him, therefore, is
providing the insight and inspiration necessary to recover a sense
of freedom. Although he does not focus exclusively on the African
American community or people of color in general, his experience
in his own skin, with its particular inheritance and experience, allows his voice to emerge in a way that mine could not.

For my part, I recognize the fear of the incapacitating grief
and shame that arises when white people consciously accept ancestral and contemporary ties to white supremacy and all of its consequences. The emotional impact of coming to awareness of this
racial trauma can be profound. The depth of racism's residency
within white bodies is profound as well. This is something I know
intimately. I recall feeling so disgusted by all that I learned about
historic and contemporary racism and my unconscious complicity
with it, that at one point I felt revulsion about my own skin and
everything associated with it. This resulted in me pushing away
from my white family, friends, and community for some time.

I also asked Orland about the work he does with white people
who seek him out because of his spiritual orientation. I wondered
if he has generated any specific insight from working with so many
white people. He said the primary conversation involves him asking white people to consider: *To whom, and for what, do you feel responsible?* He recognizes that connecting with the body can be
emotionally overwhelming because the physical body takes on a

kind of stress when it encounters the anger, fear, and doubt of past and present racial pain. He suggests that white people have to be ready to engage in psychological and emotional healing work, because the modern world has not yet created rituals that call for the kind of giving that stretches a person beyond his or her self-interest. As Orland challenges people to give to others out of a sense of freedom, he recognizes they are often disoriented and unprepared, having spent generations being influenced to withhold, accrue wealth, and see others as less worthy.[20]

This conversation with Orland helped me see a new layer of the group-specific healing work that is needed, a layer that others perceive as well. While telling a story about a white man who was unconscious of his privileges and fully invested in the trappings of modern capitalist life, Noel Ignatiev lamented, "This is not what human beings are supposed to be like. This is not the purpose of existence. To me, the most damaging effect of whiteness is that it constricts the mind. It dissolves, it restricts the imagination."[21] It is, in part, this restriction of imagination that has stopped many white people from resolving the ancestral inheritance that comes with being born with white skin.

❧ Do you believe your racial group could benefit from group-specific healing?

❧ What might that healing process need to involve?

Racial Group Differences

An exclusive focus on racial group differences can result in unintended negative consequences. They include people becoming exhausted by storytelling, being treated as a stereotype because of an assumption they have gone through particular experiences, and feeling so defeated that the potential for healing actions is disrupted.

Tension

Retelling painful stories can open wounds and leave people exhausted.	**— AND —**	Sharing stories across racial difference provides important insight.

Can retelling stories of racial pain be more damaging than healing? This is an essential question because there are many people who create multiracial dialogues intended to inspire learning across race which do not serve everyone equally well. Investigating why this occurs may help people interested in playing a role in advocacy employ less harmful approaches.

I am a prime example of a well-meaning white person who spent years attempting to support growth-enhancing processes without understanding that all efforts are not equally beneficial. In the years following my awakening to race, I led a number of efforts to bring multiracial groups of women together in dialogue. My purpose was to create a healing space where women could gather to discuss racial issues. What I failed to realize was that this simple effort involved complex dynamics and that the dialogues would have benefited from additional knowledge and facilitation experience on my part. Although I felt energized by the conversations and I did not experience them as harmful, I cannot say the same for the women of color who participated. Although I am unaware of any specific trauma or distress they experienced, I now realize how easily that may have occurred with my limited awareness.

Like many white people who answer the call to learn about race, I was interested in hearing stories from people of color whose lives were different from my own. It made sense that this should be done via multiracial dialogues. If part of healing is opening my heart-space and getting to know more about other people and their lives, then meeting together multiracially seemed the obvious way forward. What happened, however, is that attendance at the dialogues diminished over time to the point where only white people attended.

Several women of color shared that people of color often do not find value in merely talking for the sake of increasing consciousness and building interracial relationships. Some action steps needed to result from the dialogues in order for the time spent to be worthwhile. An evening sitting in discussion with a group of other women does not fundamentally change people's challenging circumstances. From what I have gathered from others, what happened within our group is common.

All too often, white people are the ones who benefit from these types of multiracial dialogues. People of color tell their sad or anger-provoking stories of discrimination, while white people sit and listen, hopefully learn, are sometimes deeply impacted, and often respond in ways that are filled with guilt and/or other self-focused reactions. Often enough, white people also respond with intellectualized comments that seem to ignore the emotion just laid bare. The result is that people of color experience their trauma all over again with no positive effect for themselves.

White people who have spent their lives seeing themselves primarily as colorblind individuals enter multiracial dialogues without an ability to speak about themselves as racialized beings. They are unable to share stories about what it has meant for them to be white and how it has affected their lives. Without this ability, white people tend to value stories from people of color exclusively and are not able to appreciate that white people who have spent time learning about race have a lot to offer other white people about what it means to become racially aware.

Reflecting on my experiences, in setting up the dialogues as venues for sharing basic knowledge about racial differences, the people of color were positioned as the teachers for a bunch of neophytes. Although well-intentioned, most of the white attendees were not sufficiently far enough along in their learning process to provide much of value to the discussion.

This is not meant to suggest that working multiracially is unimportant. It is both worthwhile and necessary. However, there are numerous stereotypic and prejudicial conceptions that white people need to examine and disentangle. Exploration of them is the only way to counteract them. But doing this in the presence of people of color, or with the unconscious expectation that people of color will provide the content for white people's learning, is neither appropriate nor helpful.

The idea of getting a group of white people together to gain basic knowledge about issues of race *prior* to engaging in multiracial dialogues never occurred to me. Why would it? Most people believe that would be a form of segregation. As I had never experienced race-specific dialogue groups (also called *affinity groups*), I did not know how helpful it can be for white people dedicated to social justice to have a space where these issues can be grappled with among one another.

It is easier for white people to sit and listen to people of color tell their stories of discrimination. However, white people must seek out initial learning experiences that do not depend so heavily on people of color's deeply emotional sharing, which can leave them exhausted and often times frustrated. There are so many videos, films, and texts available as learning tools that there is no need to have one's co-workers and neighbors of color re-traumatized. Others have already put themselves forward through published resources that offer insights. The content of this published information may be more general than hearing from a neighbor or colleague, but it supports a critical and necessary foundation for multiracial discussions that are productive and focused on topics that benefit everyone.

Attending to this concern is vital for people who are relatively new to race dialogues. All the best intentions in the world will not protect against re-traumatization unless there is experienced and educated facilitation navigating the process and ensuring that participants come to these dialogues ready to face what will inevitably emerge. Even then, there are always risks involved.

The concern here is not only about re-traumatization. When people come together for these difficult dialogues and they result in injury, it reinforces the idea that meeting to talk about race is dangerous and futile, thus discouraging further participation.

❖ Have you experienced multiracial dialogues that seemed to go awry or cause more harm than benefit? What happened? What harm ensued? Who was affected?

❖ How might you play a role in supporting future dialogues to proceed that are productive, given this discussion?

Tension

| Each person's life journey is unique and leads to different understandings and capacities. | **AND** | Differences exist between racial groups in how they experience and perceive systemic racism. |

There are a couple of ways that an exclusive focus on racial group differences can negatively impact racial justice efforts. The first is when people assume members of a particular racial group have had similar experiences. One downside to believing that all people of color are subject to the same experiences with ongoing racism and in a better position than white people to comment about the effects of racism is that these assumptions often lead to people of color being asked to be representatives of their entire race. This reinforces racism by experiencing people as only members of a monolithic racial group, not as unique human beings. Although this problem is readily understood by many, it still occurs quite frequently.

In subtle ways, a version of this pattern plays out especially when there is a single member of a racial group in a dialogue and that person's experienced is heard and received as though it represents the entire group's perspective. This results in catering to the opinions of one individual with a strong voice, even though any subsequent actions taken are perceived to be honoring the needs of an entire racial category. Avoiding this situation requires an approach that invites many voices to contribute, employs a cycle of questioning, reflection, and feedback, and involves the underlying understanding that each person speaks as an individual, not as a representative of his or her race.

A second challenge occurs when there is a suggestion that all members of a particular group are in need of the same type of growth and healing. A few stories weaved throughout this book describe moments when I was convinced that *all* white people are significantly damaged in particular ways and I felt so strongly about my perspective that it became a bias. During that time, I was assuming all white people were equally troubled. I engaged in an all-out effort to teach people solely out of my own experience, and there were times when this approach took on a rigidity that did not allow for individual differences. This resulted in people feeling unfairly judged and, therefore, less interested in further participation with equity efforts.

I am still involved in efforts to teach through the medium of personal testimony. But my primary motivation is not to suggest that all white people need to go through the same process. Hopefully, the use of words and phrases such as "may" and "might be useful" allow readers to feel invited to consider the ideas, but not feel that a definitive statement is being made about them personally.

A related issue is that many people do not *feel* the trauma or injury of societal racism. This is certainly true for a lot of white people, as the psychological effects are usually buried in the unconscious. Among people of color, however, there are also those who feel fully empowered and not victims of institutional racism. Although to some it may seem fruitless (and perhaps damaging) to try and convince people that there are institutional forces negatively affecting them, this is precisely what many advocates attempt to do when they are invested in getting people on board with political change efforts.

Regardless of whether or not there are underlying issues to reveal, ultimately, people hoping to influence others to become active in social change efforts can avoid suggesting that *all* people of color feel victimized by U.S. society. Recalling that each person arrives at his or her racial identity and life perspective via myriad of factors helps. Race is only one of many social identities we have, and each unique individual has varying experiences in how significant a role race plays in his or her life.

❧ In what ways have you experienced yourself or others being treated as representatives of their race?

❧ What do you see as the value and/or danger in attempting to raise people's awareness about societal racism and its psychological impacts?

———————————

Tension

Reimagining one's personal story can initiate a powerful healing process.	— **AND** —	Retelling stories of personal trauma can help others understand the need for racial justice.

Attention to the past is needed, personal stories about past pain can be revealing, and there is a lot more individual and systemic change work to do. Advocates *do* need to give voice to the open, festering wounds of the past in a society that is engaged in a full-throttle effort to distance itself from its history of racial violence and trauma. *And,* in order to achieve a measure of balance, a view that accounts for personal freedom, allows for new interpretations of personal stories,[22] and honors the significant societal changes that have occurred are important as well.

At the root of the challenge is that people of any background can get stuck in the past through attachment to stories of personal trauma. This can disrupt the ability to resolve inner turmoil, work effectively with others, and inspire participation in advocacy efforts. People invested in racial justice can improve their practice by doing their own emotional and consciousness-raising work.

These words may be read as a personal challenge to those who value significant anger and emotional upset as part of the drive to remain engaged in activist-oriented efforts. Even so, those who suggest the need for balance see consciousness-raising as a fundamental ingredient if long-term transformation is to take place.[23]

Holding the *both/and* orientation can be challenging to practice, particularly when conversations lean heavily to one side or the other of the continuum. One anxiety-provoking experience occurred for me while listening to Orland address an audience at one of Shade Tree's public *indaba* events.[24] Orland spoke passionately to the group, composed primarily of people of color, about the freedom and potential inherent in human beings. He suggested that no circumstance could take this freedom from anyone, no one has any more advantage than anyone else, and all people have the freedom to transcend their histories. The focus was on one's inner experience and its relationship to living out one's potential. The audience responded with great enthusiasm.

The energy in the room was palpable, as was the hope born from the call to dream and expand beyond perceived constraints. The message was that people are not defined by their background, and that past experiences can be reimagined in order to envision a different future. Orland encouraged people to tell their stories differently, both to themselves and to the world. He said that people are free, even when challenged by physical barriers, even a jail cell.

I heard the truth in his words. This message of freedom is essential for continued striving, particularly among people facing significant external challenges. Over the years, I have been witness to people achieving life-altering gains from circumstances that looked bleak or hopeless. This is what Orland meant when he spoke of his sense of purpose in being born into his racial group. He is a radical visionary of human potential. All of us can benefit from reimagining personal narratives that tether us to pain and affect our present sense of self.

In the midst of this enlivening talk, Orland also said, "privilege doesn't exist." Although he said it in the context that everyone has abundance and opportunity available to them, I struggled with the fact that this message was received by white, spiritually oriented attendees already inclined to reject the idea that racial differences affect people's experiences. I was immediately cognizant of my wish to amend Orland's message to include my version of a balancing *both/and.*

My wish to always name the *both/and,* even in situations such as those, is a tension I continue to navigate. It is a challenge that faces others who are dedicated, above all things, to raising awareness about the impact of racism. Highlighting the negative impacts of race at every turn sometimes hinders the ability to validate other important messages, such as those about personal agency, healing possibilities, progress achieved, and our commonalities.

❖ What are the stories you have told most often about difficult experiences in your life?

❖ How might your self-image and potential change if you told a new story?

The Search for Balance

An essay by Rebecca Parker provides steps for how to engage racial justice efforts in a way that attends to some of the tensions between our common humanity and our group differences.[25] Parker recognizes that although every person is an individual, for white people, there are some common soul tasks that come with racial inheritance. To attend to them, she suggests that people deconstruct cultural images and search out additional education about race and how racial differences impact people. She also invites white people to engage in a process of deep, internal inquiry as part of a recovery from the distancing that sits at the heart of the racial identity development process. This can help us learn about what it means to live in a white body at this time in history and support us becoming increasingly responsive to what contemporary life requires.

Part of recognizing the influences that have shaped one's racial inheritance involves investigating the ways the stories and imagery embedded in cultural and/or spiritual traditions continue to have psychological effects. For example, although a person may not self-identify as a Christian, Christian stories may still influence a person's thinking and behavior, as each of us is part of the *collective consciousness* of the U.S.[26]

One example I often discuss with teachers-in-training is how U.S. society is deeply influenced by the myth of the savior/hero. In comparison, examples of collective achievement are rarely recognized or celebrated. When my classes watch films involving portrayals of teachers, students notice how many of them show the one good teacher amid the other failures. In class discussions we note that almost all of the good teachers in the films are white. We question the implications and explore how the portrayals could impact expectations of ourselves and others. We wonder how this hero/savior myth translates into a culture wherein teachers too often fail to seek out support from others or engage with colleagues to solve problems. In general, people in the U. S. are socialized to expect either rescue (salvation) from a white savior, or to go at it alone. This pattern gets in the way of people working together to solve social and political problems.

Parker also proposes that Christianity offers a wide-reaching and problematic interpretation of the Garden of Eden story.[27] She suggests that the way the story is commonly told and understood sanctions a lack of awareness. It teaches people that having abundance provided for them is good and not to be questioned. Further, the serpent who entices Eve with knowledge of good and evil is devalued. Parker's analysis concludes that "when religion sanctions ignorance, it cultivates alienation from life. It blesses segregation and encourages people who are comfortably provided for to remain compliant with the created order."[28] Even though Parker rejects this interpretation of the Eden story, its cultural influence still can trigger her defensiveness and shame when she is challenged. She recognizes the importance of resisting her attachment to being "innocent, guilt-free, good."[29] She proposes that our culture needs a new theology that supports inner healing to mend the fragmented self and encourage engagement with the realities of society.[30]

These are but two examples of how inherited cultural and spiritual influences can be unconsciously linked to concrete, personal reactions to life's circumstances — including racism — and function to keep people oblivious to the need for healing.

✤ What are the stories and images that influence you most?

✤ How have the stories and myths of your cultural and/or spiritual upbringing taught you to see the world?

✤ How might these influences impact the way you interact with people and react to stuations?

———————

Another way for white people to accept their racial inheritance is to become better educated about historic and contemporary racism. It was not until taking doctoral level courses in my late twenties that a class forced me to look seriously at the effects of racial injustice. Even then, the content only scratched the surface of racism in United States history and its continuing legacy. Years of teaching in public schools and reflecting on how the history of racism is handled has helped me understand why our nation remains largely ignorant. Educational standards, curricula, and assessments do not prioritize teaching about the painful and controversial aspects of U.S.

history. While major events such as slavery, Westward expansion, and Jim Crow laws are introduced, their superficial treatment leaves the depth and scope of racial trauma unrecognized.

Educators argue over how much of the story to tell. There is significant tension between those who wish to present information that intends to bind society together to promote patriotism, national pride, and a sense of collectivity and those who want to inspire critical thinking by exposing the systemic violence that allowed the U.S. to become a superpower. The result is that there are multiple generations of teachers — predominantly white — who have neither the educational background nor the understanding via personal experience to effectively deal with race in the classroom. As Gary Howard suggests, "You can't teach what you don't know."[31] Too many teachers do not know race well enough to navigate the subject successfully.[32]

Parker suggests that white people need a process of remedial education. She lists the authors that expanded her understanding, citing Howard Zinn's *The People's History of the United States* and Ronald Takaki's *A Different Mirror* as primary resources. She also refers to the many authors of color who have created an expanded version of how society has developed. It is only by taking the time to explore the history of race and racism that a relatively informed view is built. Parker also notes that knowledge develops through groups of people inquiring together. Participating in experiences where shared learning occurs allows for continued growth and may be part of a valuable healing process.

❖ How effective was your education in informing you about U.S. history regarding racial injustice?

❖ How do you know if your knowledge of history is complete?

❖ What resources will you choose to support you in learning more?

❖ Which individuals and/or groups support you in integrating what you learn so you can share it?

———————————

The themes discussed here are also highlighted by many others who call for an opening of mind and heart to imagine, to dream, to create community, and to participate in the co-creation of our future.[33] They call for a perception of the world that is accurate enough for injustice to be named and recognized and a course set toward healing.[34] These voices hold the *both/and.* They recognize that racism has injured us differently and with unequal severity *and* we all have collectively been hurt. Each group has its own ancestral inheritance *and* we all carry pain. Each group has its own healing work to do and that work includes recognizing and caring for our common humanity. The past needs attention *and* the future is not yet determined. Awakening to the work of the soul requires recognition of one's birthright of freedom *and* the obligation to confront experiences of privilege and disadvantage.

CHAPTER 5

Belonging and Appropriation

Belonging is a universal need[1] that helps people feel connected, grounded in their lives and practices, and reinvigorated in their daily efforts. In addition to meaning acceptance or membership, the word belonging also refers to the concept of ownership. To what, or to whom, does something belong? What are the implications when discussing belonging in a spiritual context?

Many people today practice spiritual traditions that do not come from their cultures of origin. This is called *appropriation,* and for people invested in racial justice it is a serious concern. Inner conflict can arise in the face of competing spiritual and racial justice principles. People searching outside their culture of origin for a spiritual path that is meaningful and feels relevant to their lives often express:

> Spiritual truth is universal, spiritual paths are open to everyone, and spirit cannot be the sole property of any one person or group. The spiritual practice I follow feels right for me even though it isn't from the culture I was raised in. I love the sense of belonging and close connection my path gives me. I've finally found my true home.

The underlying tenet is "When it comes to spiritual practices, it doesn't matter who you are or where you come from."

In contrast, people focused on racial justice cite the profound damage caused by colonization and often state:

> It is a problem when white people take on spiritual traditions that are not from their own culture. Too often this comes with exploitation of the original culture and inappropriate use of sacred beliefs, objects, and practices. It ignores the destruction that has been, and continues to be, done to the people in that original cultural group. White people should return to their own roots to find spiritual grounding.

The tenet here is "It is problematic to participate in a spiritual practice that is not of your own culture — especially if you are white."

Understanding appropriation, and how it relates to the consequences of colonialization and a lack of ancestral grounding, will provide an important foundation. We can then explore tensions related to how a history of oppression complicates the contemporary appropriation of spiritual practices across cultures.

An Introduction to Appropriation

Religious scholars and anthropologists describe how cultures and religious traditions have historically influenced one another through interactions over time and evolve in ways that incorporate new and different forms of expression and practice.[2] Cultures and religions are, therefore, not considered "fixed."[3] However, when groups have an historical relationship wherein one group has been oppressed by the other, this significantly affects how cross-cultural interactions and cultural changes are perceived and experienced. Because of this, there is disagreement about whether and/or how the process should take place.[4]

According to Sybille De La Rosa, appropriation occurs when a person or group intentionally takes a term, idea, symbol, image, or practice out of its original context, alters its meaning, and then uses it without including the original group in the new form.[5] This pattern of modification and unsanctioned use is particularly common when there is a history of unequal power between groups, such as between white and Native Americans. The history of violent oppression and attempted genocide of Native Americans and their practices is so severe that use of the terms "adopting" or "borrowing" undermines acknowledgment of this devastating history and overlooks the harmful impact of appropriation. Intentional or not, this serves to validate those doing the appropriating. Given this, Native American writers generally refer to appropriation as "taking" or "stealing."

There are many reasons why people appropriate other groups' cultural symbols or practices. Oftentimes, it is not done with conscious intent to injure. During a time period when I traveled to a number of countries, including Guatemala, Costa Rica, and Indonesia, I returned home with objects that would remind me of the journeys, countries, and cultures I had experienced. They were purchased at tourist outlets and were intended to be placed on my walls, shelves, beds, and floors. I thought they would add color and richness to my life. Never having heard of the term appropriation, I considered adorning my home with objects from "far-off lands" a demonstration of my appreciation.

At the same time, if you had asked me about my own culture, I would have stumbled. Like many white people of mixed European descent, connections to my ancestral cultures were traded in by my family for the privileges of assimilating into whiteness. No German, Russian, or Italian was spoken in our home. Only isolated remnants of traditions remained. I was one of the many white people who would have said: "I have no culture," "I'm just normal," or "I'm just American." By my mid-twenties, my perception of American culture was that it was mostly about consumerism, individualism, competition, and getting ahead at the expense of others. It was not meaningful or positive.[6] Confronted with feelings of guilt and ambivalence over my country's history — a history to which I increasingly did not want to be associated — the feeling of being without meaningful roots compounded my sense of ancestral and cultural disconnection. This sense of disconnection can be described as "cultural loss," and it provides the basis for many white people's search for inclusion in other group's cultural practices.[7]

My lack of connection to my ancestors prompted me to participate in appropriation in a way that went beyond simple acquisition. I was searching for meaningful connections and a different way of being in the world. Yet, I gave no thought to how different objects or symbols purchased were distortions of those cultures' traditions. And I had no understanding of how many Indigenous groups' cultural and spiritual expressions are intrinsically intertwined.[8] Because of this, many objects once displayed in my home reinforced the commercialization of various group's treasured religious identities. My home became a visible testament to my desire for a stronger sense of belonging in the world. Having grown up in a culture that views cultural traditions as commodities that can be customized at will, I was oblivious to how my actions were part of a widespread lessening of the value of a culture's sacred objects and practices. I was also unaware that they were an unconscious attempt to escape from the pain bred from my unresolved issues with my whiteness.

During this time I became an elementary school teacher who was earnestly striving for spiritual grounding and racial understanding. Given my lack of healthful connection to a culture I appreciated, my growing awareness of racism did nothing to diminish my appropriating. I continued to purchase objects that made me feel connected to cultures I perceived as having qualities I longed to have myself. I also adopted styles of dress patterned after African people. Although part of the intent was to connect with my African American students and demonstrate the value of their ancestry, my approach was misguided. My students did not need me to *act* like I was African in order to highlight the value of African contributions to U.S. society. My fifth graders knew I was white and was trying to act like I was not.

Part of my change in dress was a direct response to being challenged about how my daily behavior mirrored distressing stereotypes of white culture. I did not want to be white, and therefore, this exterior change was a reaction to my inner discomfort about my racial identity. Around this time I also became part of a multiracial community that participates in ceremonies with origins in Indigenous African and Native American cultures. Participating in these rituals and ceremonies satisfied my desire to experience a spiritual belonging my white community left unfulfilled.

❖ To what degree have you felt adrift and without a meaningful cultural grounding?

❖ Have you ever wished to escape from the stereotypes associated with your racial group?

❖ In what ways do the appropriating behaviors described sound familiar?

Belonging

What happens when seekers focus on their need for belonging and are unaware of, or insensitive to, the negative consequences of appropriation? What follows is an exploration of what happens when non-Native people appropriate Native American imagery, symbolism, rituals, and practices. I highlight this particular example because it is the one with which I am most familiar. Readers are invited to consider how the following tensions also relate to the appropriation of other oppressed cultures and traditions.

Tension

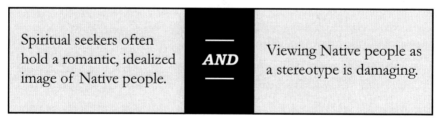

| Spiritual seekers often hold a romantic, idealized image of Native people. | ——— *AND* ——— | Viewing Native people as a stereotype is damaging. |

Many spiritual seekers hold a romanticized image of Indigenous people. I fell into this pattern myself during my early phase of recognizing the disconnections in modern life and moving toward spirituality as a healing response. The idealized image of Native Americans as communal, in tune with nature, and purveyors of wisdom served as a stark contrast to modernity. I saw Native people as inherently spiritual naturalists.[9] This image also symbolized my wish to become more connected to the earth and to a culture characterized by harmony and balance. Even though Native Americans were not my own ancestry, to my mind they represented a group of people who knew how to stay in touch.

What could be the problem with Native Americans being held up as models of a better way to live? For quite some time I thought my idealized image was respectful. It took me a long time to learn that there is a downside. Seeing an entire group of people through the lens of a stereotype is a problem.[10] In this case, idealized images, even if seemingly positive, do not respect and honor the complexity of Native American people's lives. Instead, they encourage treating living, breathing individuals as mere symbols.

Holding a stereotype of Native peoples leads some people to believe they know what it means to be a "true" or "real" Native American. In *A Native American Theology*, Clara Sue Kidwell, Homer Noley, and George Tinker explain:

> Native Americans remain the one racial/ethnic minority that non-Natives, even those who would be sympathetic to Native causes and issues, will not let move into the twentieth — let alone the twenty-first — century. In their mind's eye, they still imagine "real" Indians living in teepees and hunting buffalo from dappled ponies. Anything or anyone who does not fit this romantic stereotype is labeled as inauthentic....It fails to take into account the incredible diversity among Native nations and the change over time that occurs in any living culture.[11]

Shelly Johnson Khadem, in her dissertation on spiritualists and representations of Native Americans, describes how this can lead to white people contradicting Native voices and telling white audiences what someone who is truly acting like a Native would do or say. Khadem offers an illustrative example from a white interviewee:

> White man has stolen their land and their dignity and their lives and now their ceremonies, and so of course, a lot of people are going to have a chip on their shoulder and say, "You're not even native, how can you do our ceremonies?" And yet the true native shares.[12]

Beyond addressing the arrogance that allows a white person to make this statement, it is essential to note that when a significant number of white people hold an idealized (stereotyped) image of what a Native American would do or say, it encourages other white people to see actual Native Americans as inauthentic if they do not fit into that image. This can lead to the disparagement of Native people who speak up in protest against white people appropriating their cultural and spiritual practices, as is evident in the example offered.

Additionally, when Native Americans are revered simply as representations, as opposed to diverse communities of people, it decreases motivation to address the socio-political realities Native peoples' face. The romantic image of the Indigenous of our nation serves as a feel-good cover that allows white spiritual seekers to avoid facing our complicity in Native peoples' oppression. It shields us from attending to how they are even now striving to maintain their cultural identities[13] and, in many cases, their very survival.[14]

Another problem to highlight is that creating a sense of self that is other than modern by idealizing Native Americans and their practices is perceived by many white spiritual seekers as reviving the old traditions. It is not only considered part of a conscious effort to transform oneself, it is considered a way to transform the world.[15] Beyond being an expression of self-importance, this belief among white spiritual seekers generally does nothing to inspire political action to support the survival of Native peoples and their cultures. It is, therefore, both hollow and disrespectful to the Native people who are battling the U.S. government for the right to practice their traditions in their own way on the land of their ancestors.

Overall, the issues related to the idealized image allow non-Native people to feel a strengthened relationship with nature while simultaneously reinforcing a disassociation from living Native Americans and the socio-political issues that affect them.

❖ How does this pattern relate to how other marginalized groups and their practices are treated?

Tension

Creatively modifying ancient spiritual practices provides a sense of continuity and connection for spiritual seekers.	**AND**	Modified ancient spiritual practices are destructive when perceived as representing the original.

While investigating how appropriation of spiritual practices misrepresents Native American cultures, I learned about many important issues. In Susanne Owen's comprehensive analysis, *The Appropriation of Native American Spirituality,* she observes that at the heart of all of the critiques is the way in which spiritual seekers frequently take ancient traditions, modify them, and practice these newly created forms in ways that are significantly different from the original. The results are distortions that can no longer be called Native American.[16] The way these new forms and practices are publicly perceived to be representing Native American spiritual traditions is damaging.[17]

Take the Lakota sweat lodge as an example. Imagine the leader has made significant changes to the construction and/or process of the lodge which were never validated by a recognized authority within Native society. In this case, a Lakota person attending may not recognize the lodge as upholding either the protocols or specific intent of the ceremony. Imagine that attendees have invited hundreds of non-Native seekers into that lodge over a span of years. Add to this that the lodge has been described as a Lakota sweat lodge at each event. All those people walked away with a false understanding of what is practiced among Native groups. Multiply this scenario by many thousands.

According to James Young and Conrad Brunk, in *The Ethics of Cultural Appropriation,* if enough people talk about aspects of Native culture or practices based on experiences such as the distorted version of a lodge in this example, it can begin to change "the widespread understanding in the dominant culture" and this would do "harm to the people and to that original culture."[18] I understand how the pattern described above could distort the understanding of a culture. This is problematic in and of itself. I wondered, though, how could it damage Native people if non-Natives have a misunderstanding of their cultural practices?

To consider this question, take as an example an organizer of a seminar who is not part of the Hopi clan. This person publicizes a workshop to teach about the Hopi people and performs Hopi rituals at a hotel. The audience includes people who have no relationship with Hopi people and have no plans to create any such relationship. According to David Howes, in *Cultural Appropriation and Resistance in the American Southwest,* this kind of public display "pollutes the sanctity of the rituals" and "violates the constitution of Hopi society."[19]

Depending on how widespread its use, this kind of misrepresentation can affect not only the understanding of those from the dominant culture, but also Native Americans who are subject to these messages.[20] Cynthia Kasee highlights problems related to this misrepresentation. When Native traditions are rendered mundane and removed from their sacred context, they end up being "parodied" by non-Native people in ways that results in a loss of "dignity in the eyes of the rest of the world."[21] Spiritual seekers may have good intentions, but this does not stop Native American practices from being trivialized. Native American practices are then vulnerable to ridicule in the dominant culture. This can have tragic consequences.

Kasee describes how some recovery programs in prisons throughout the country help Native men and women to gain "a sense of pride in themselves and their people through a return to tradition."[22] This healing is undercut when the tradition is misrepresented in U.S. society. From her work with Native women who are recovering from substance abuse she has recognized that Native traditions can be "a lifeline," helping women regain a sense of identity and self-esteem by recognizing their ancestral roles on this continent.[23] However, misrepresentations and parodies lead to a distorted understanding of the "commitment, reform, and diminution of ego" that the Native tradition requires.[24] These are considered by Kasee to be necessary to a successful recovery effort, and the lessening of the power of the Native traditional message undermines the women's ability to find strength in their own traditions. In other words, the very qualities of Native American cultures which are so highly prized by many non-Native spiritual seekers end up being negatively portrayed through misrepresentation. This is destructive to Native people trying to recover from challenges that stem from the destruction of their traditional way of life.

Additionally, misrepresentation has an impact on the political struggles faced by Native Americans today who still fight for their rights to practice certain ceremonies on the land of their ancestors. Kasee challenges readers to take this injustice seriously:

> It is very difficult these days to convince the average American that Native people do not have a constitutional guarantee of religious freedom. Firstly, they do not realize that anyone is excluded under the Constitution. Secondly, they know a place locally where you can go to a retreat house for a weekend and they'll set you up on a vision quest, for a modest sum, of course. "How can you people say your religions are endangered when there are plenty of listings in the Yellow Pages for shamans?" (You can hear the patronizing tone in that delivery, can't you?) The parodying of Native religion diminishes it, creates a plethora of misinformation, and takes the heat off legislators considering yet again whether to grant Indians constitutional guarantee of free practice.[25]

The spiritual is inextricably connected to the socio-political. Ignorance about the ways appropriation distorts ceremonial practices allows it to continue unabated and undermines Native peoples' healing efforts, equal protection under the law, and practice of their spiritual traditions.

❖ To what extent have you seen misrepresentations of Native American traditions?

❖ How does this pattern relate to how other groups and their practices are discussed and treated?

Tension

Some people believe reso-nance with another group's cultural or spiri-tual practices is attributed to past life experiences.	**AND**	Non-natives identifying as "Native in spirit" harm Native people.

The pattern of white people taking on Native identities is long-standing and can manifest in many forms. A profound example is when the Camp Fire Girls and Boy Scouts of America turned to Native American culture when developing their programs. Each group encouraged their youth to "play Indian" by selecting Native names, participating in dress up, and infusing Native influences into various other activities.

The Camp Fire Girls are still in the process of "weeding out" activities which entail copying Native American styles or activities.[26] Reflecting on what that experience was like as a young participant in the 1960s, Pauline Turner Strong writes:

> My Camp Fire friends and I fashioned ourselves as Indian princesses: We chose or invented "Indian names," designed a symbolgram to visually express that name, sewed our own fringed ceremonial gowns, made beaded headdresses on a handmade loom, and decorated our gowns with strings of colored beads representing our achievements.[27]

Many young people, primarily white, had this early experience. There was a concerted effort within these organizations to have participants adopt the identity of a Native American. This is offensive and racist, even if it does not fit into what non-Natives generally understand to be racism.[28]

Some go a step further. A book chapter, titled *The Indian Way Is What's Inside,* written by Karlyn Crowley, details how gender and race issues intersect in such a way that many white feminists, out of a purported move toward gender empowerment, adopt the idea that they can be Native. There are many women who believe they are taking up this position as a healing vision and feel themselves to be Native "at their core" or "in spirit," suggesting they are, deep down, Native themselves.[29] Crowley explains that this has led to a very problematic and destructive pattern wherein white women have put themselves forward as representatives of Native cultures when their relationship to those cultures is either absent or tenuous.

Another manifestation is when white spiritual seekers claim legitimacy for the appropriating of a Native identity — and its cultural/spiritual practices — by referring to past lives.[30] Andrea Smith, who wrote *For All Those Who Were Indian in a Former Life,*[31] directly, albeit sarcastically, criticizes this pattern:

> Nowadays anyone can be Indian if they want to, all that is required is that one be Indian in a former life, or take part in a sweat lodge, or be mentored by a medicine woman, or read a how-to book.[32]

Native people are harmed by the pattern of white people claiming to be Native. Smith likens this type of appropriation to a form of sexualized violence.[33] She notes that sexual violence is ultimately about power and ties the sense of intimacy required to truly "know" someone — biblically recognized as a reference to sexual intimacy — to the breaking down of barriers between people. Spiritual seekers who act like they know all about what it means to be Native via the claim of being Native in spirit transgress those barriers unilaterally. She points out how taking on the "knowing" of someone, and thereby their knowledge, is a way that white people continue colonizing oppression and abuse of Native people. Smith continues:

> This practice of taking without asking, the assumption that the needs of the taker are paramount whereas the needs of the one being taken from are irrelevant, mirrors the rape culture of the dominant society. Thus, it is particularly ironic that this colonial practice, structured by sexual violence, is often perpetuated by white feminists in their efforts to heal from the wounds of patriarchal violence. Sadly, they do not consider how such practices may hinder Native women from healing as well. Native counselors generally agree that a strong cultural identity is essential if Native people are to heal from abuse because a Native woman's healing entails not only healing from any personal abuse she has suffered but also from the patterned history of

abuse against her family, her nation, and her environment. When white women appropriate Indian spirituality for their own benefit, for whatever reason, they continue this pattern of abuse against Indian peoples' cultures. This exploitation has a specific negative impact on Native peoples' ability to heal from abuse.[34]

Although white people may seek healing from disconnection and imbalance through the forms of appropriation described here, this cannot justify the resulting misrepresentations and subsequent negative consequences for Native peoples.

❖ In what ways have you witnessed people identifying with another cultural group?

❖ What were the results of this identification? In what ways have these efforts appeared harmful or unhealthy?

Tension

The dissemination of spiritual traditions by outsiders makes life-sustaining practices available to all.	**AND**—	The adoption, modification, or commodification of sacred knowledge and objects is immoral and dangerous.

The taking of sacred objects, knowledge, and spiritual practices out of context, modifying them, and turning them into products that are bought and sold in the marketplace is offensive and destructive to Native people. The ways people participate in those ventures and the claims made regarding authenticity are included in this critique. At issue is not simply monetary gain. Spiritual practitioners may not necessarily make a profit from their activities.[35] A primary issue is the manner in which traditional knowledge and practices are treated and transferred to others. Offensive or objectionable pursuits include each of the categories described below.[36]

Blending traditions with other practices or world-views

The individualistic approach wherein rituals are selected, manipulated, and altered in the name of creative freedom is antithetical to Native American spirituality and traditions, the beliefs regarding proper authority, and the attempts to maintain Native cultures.

Selling sacred objects, symbols, or experiences as a commercial venture to anyone who can pay

According to Khadem, this involves "spiritual practices, sacred objects, [and] cultural knowledge" being turned into a transferable resource to be marketed, bought, and sold.[37] This is one of the most widespread offenses.[38] It includes offering workshops and ceremonies that are part of an economic exchange. Traditional ceremonies do not require payment for participation and sacred pipes are not for sale. When brought into a commercial context, these ceremonies and objects are desacralized.

Writing misleading books

A number of regularly referenced authors, such as Lynn Andrews and Carlos Castaneda are denounced for offering information that misrepresents Native American beliefs, cultures, and practices.[39] They are also criticized for profiting from their commodification of Native American traditions while Native American communities themselves are still working to recover from colonialization economically, socially, and culturally.[40] These authors' activities are considered immoral.[41]

Becoming an "expert" after one course or workshop

Particularly offensive are non-Natives who claim to be "shamans" or "medicine teachers" of Native American traditions without having ever participated in the sustained and dedicated training process undergone by traditional people within a tribal context and under the tutelage of an elder.[42] According to Brunk and Young, it is all too common for spiritually inclined white people with cursory experience to set themselves up as "experts" and claim the authority to "correct Indigenous people about the nature of their beliefs."[43] Khadem also notes that the "trainings" may require such minimal investment as paying a registration fee and participating in a half-day workshop.[44] A book chapter by Ward Churchill entitled *Spiritual Hucksterism: The Rise of the Plastic Medicine Men* offers a strong critique of this phenomenon.[45]

Ignoring protocols

Along with the myriad misrepresentations of Native American traditions available to experience via purchase, there are countless ceremonies conducted which claim to be Native American but which do not follow traditional protocols. It is probable that some non-Natives who have been granted "permission" to run these ceremonies do not even know the correct protocols.[46] Many others simply do not stop to consider that self-selected modifications essentially change the ceremony. This is not to suggest that changes never occur among Native American practitioners. They do, but as George Tinker explains:

> ...this occurs as a natural process inherent in their organic composition and purpose, and as result of the adaptations made by the spiritual teachers of the communities in accordance with the changing times and situations brought on by virtue of the Fourth World existence of American Indian peoples.[47]

These objections make clear that, for the most part, those who appropriate are criticized for *how* they approach the spiritual traditions as opposed to *who they are* as racial beings.[48] The fundamental truth is that white spiritual seekers desacralize Native American objects, traditions, and beliefs when they participate in commercial endeavors, are not grounded in the kind of knowledge, cultural competency, and experience required of Native people, and conduct modified or distorted forms of traditional ceremonies by failing to follow proper protocols. Native critiques are not ambiguous or gentle, and my language and descriptions are perhaps too mild given the writing put forward by others (see Vine Deloria, George Tinker, Wendy Rose, etc).[49]

The critique is strong because the consequences are significant. Tinker suggests a number of ways the commodification of Native American traditions have destructive influences on Native American populations.[50] First, young Native Americans are exposed to individualism in ways that disrupts their ability to view their own culture through eyes undistorted by self-centeredness. Second, Native Americans become tempted to cater to white spiritual seekers in order to focus on careers and economic gain. Finally, and more subtly, in order to accommodate white participants, Native Americans shift their own thinking so that their beliefs are more easily understood. None of this is considered a worthwhile cultural exchange. This situation also highlights the irony that a common reason white seekers want to adopt Native American traditions in the first place is to move away from the individualism of modern U.S. society.

♣ Have you purchased objects or participated in activities that have their origin in another group's spiritual practice?

♣ What thoughts and feelings arise as you consider how a large group of white spiritual people adopting Indigenous practices influence people to become more individualistic?

♣ How might these concerns be reflective of experiences of other Indigenous groups who have many white people adopting their traditions?

Appropriation

Despite knowing the harm done by widespread, consumerist appropriation, seekers may still experience significant internal tension when deciding whether or not to participate in traditional ceremonies and cultural practices. For this reason, a discussion highlighting a set of interrelated differences of position and perspective is necessary. First, there exists a fundamental difference in the formation of religious/spiritual identities of Native and non-Native people. Second, there is the ongoing significance of the difference between Native and non-Native peoples' participation in the popularization of Lakota practices during the 1960s. Third, there remains disagreement among Native practitioners regarding including non-Natives in ceremonies. Finally, questions prompting white seekers to evaluate their participation re-center individual-oriented reflection and decision-making.

Tension

Spiritual seekers believe people of any background may participate in any spiritual practice.	***AND***	Native people do not select which tribe with which to affiliate.

A fundamental tension comes into focus when recognizing that traditional Native and non-Native people experience religious identity in starkly different ways. Whereas Native people's identity is "tribal," non-Natives have approached religious affiliation primarily as a voluntary choice, at least since the 18th century.[51] *In Spirit and Resistance: Political Theology and American Indian Liberation,* Tinker explains:

> [I]n America — as in Europe — religious membership and participation are free choices of the participants, and making a change from one denomination to another is as simple as taking a short membership instruction course or filling out the appropriate membership forms. To the contrary, being Indian is a matter of birth. Changing one's tribe of birth is not possible; even a person's clan membership (within the tribe) is a given that cannot be changed at will.[52]

The difference in how Native and non-Native people experience religious identity is also illustrative of the collective versus individualistic mind frames that distinguish Indigenous from white culture.

This is an important element in understanding why Native and non-Native people often view "ownership" of spiritual traditions so differently. Tinker highlights this difference when he writes:

Typical of the view of New Age adherents of Native spirituality is that of Gary Snyder, a non-Native poet and self-pro-
claimed "shaman"' Snyder states that religion cannot be
"owned," contending, "In this sense, it seems to me that I
have as much right to pursue and articulate the belief systems
developed by Native Americans as they do, and arguments to
the contrary strike me as absurd in the extreme." By contrast,
Native Americans often see the issue as exactly one of ownership. They see appropriation as an attempt by Amer-Europeans, whose ancestors conquered this continent, to "own"
the heritage of Natives as thoroughly as they claim to own
the land and its resources.[53]

This difference in perspective has significant consequences.

The belief held by many white seekers today that "all elements
of any spiritual tradition are available to anyone" is widespread.
Many individuals, seeking to construct or augment their own private
spiritual practices, take on ancient forms of worship. Non-denomina-
tional spiritual centers often draw on an eclectic set of traditions to
offer a generalized spiritual experience. Some contemporary, progressive churches even include yoga, meditation, or African drumming in
their offerings. A common set of beliefs encourages this behavior:

- All societies are part of a "global village."

- Spiritual traditions are not the private property of any particular tradition.

- Spirit is universally available.

- People are free and encouraged to practice and/or spread their
  understanding of spirituality in ways that will benefit the
  whole.

These beliefs are often used to justify *anyone* making use of
any part of *any* spiritual tradition in *any* way desired.[54] They also
support the conviction that any person has the right and authority
to modify cultural and spiritual objects, symbols, and practices for
use in a new context for the sake of personal and communal transformation.[55]

According to Michael York, in his article *New Age Commodification and Appropriation of Spirituality,* this reinforces the view which re-

jects that "one can be told what to believe" and, consequently, "also denies that one can be told, at least spiritually, what not to take."[56] Khadem suggests "this perspective is arguably one of the most significant reasons for the seeming callousness of New Agers with regard to Native American objections to their appropriations."[57]

The fact that the majority of people who venture beyond their cultural borders are white is significant to this discussion.[58] Again, Tinker provides insight when he writes:

> Many of these spiritual seekers are genuinely well intentioned and seriously searching for something more substantial than the spiritual experiences of the church into which they were born and raised, or they seek a more life-affirming and meaningful experience than is available in their secular society. Typically, they see themselves as sharing a worldview with Indian people, including concern for environmental issues, openness to the universe as some expression of pervasive divinity, a sense of the interrelationship of all things, especially all people, and a sense of the immanence and accessibility of spiritual power. All these may be thought of as laudable, yet however laudable these beliefs, they are still White, euro-american thoughts rather than Indian thoughts.[59]

Good intentions aside, this individualistic mindset all too often involves seekers hoping to gain personal power through participation in the ceremonies.[60] This mindset lies in stark contrast to the intentions of Native people. From reading Tinker's full argument it is clear that non-Native people's individualism (and privilege) is seen as disrupting (infecting) the practices of Native people and their ability to keep their cultural values, ceremonies, and communities intact.[61] It is also considered a continuation of colonialization.[62]

None of this is to suggest that Native people are silent on the question of how non-Natives can work toward healing. Tinker suggests that the core values of Native peoples are essential for all when he writes, "Perhaps the most precious gift that American Indians have to share with other peoples is our perspective on the interrelatedness of all of creation and our deep sense of relationship to the land in particular."[63] It is clear that the objection is not about non-Natives valuing Native perspectives. In fact, incorporating them into our way of life is viewed as a step toward healing.

Tinker provides a set of nine suggestions for how we all, both Native and non-Native, can move toward collective healing in service of restoring balance in the world (see notes for a fuller description). This list includes white people needing to take responsibility for our past and learning the importance of respecting all our relatives in the created world. All of us, both Native and non-Native, must also identify and work to dismantle structural oppression, recognize the personal risk we each face in doing so, become serious about reducing consumption, learn to respectfully relate across cultural boundaries, know ourselves and our communities sufficiently to avoid misappropriation of others' cultures, replace individualism with broader ideas of community, and create a new vision for the world where domination and privilege are seen as unnatural.[64]

Exploring this tension with authentic concern leaves non-Native spiritual seekers with an important set of tasks for participating in mutual healing. It also raises the difficult question of what kinds of community-oriented spiritual practices are viable in the interim, when one's original religious upbringing may not value the principles and steps suggested that would help us live together in harmony and balance.

❧ What practices from spiritual traditions outside of your cultures of origin have you participated in that could be considered acts of appropriation (yoga, meditation, sweat lodge, smudging with sage, African drumming or dance, etc.)?

❧ How have you felt about your participation before reading this? How do you feel now?

Tension

Many non-Native spiritual seekers, with no ties to a Native community, joined in Lakota ceremonial practices in the 1960s.	*AND*	Participation in traditional Native ceremonies generated pride and became connected with Indian political resistance during the 1960s.

A second issue contributing to the tension felt by seekers is the dramatic difference between Native and non-Native peoples' participation in the popularization of Lakota practices during the 1960s. It is essential to note that Native ceremonies were banned in the U.S. until 1934.[65] It was in the 1960s that white New Agers began attending commodifying, tourist-attracting events that brought Lakota spiritual practices into increased public consciousness.[66] Most of these spiritual seekers were not creating long-lasting relationships with a Native community, nor were they taking up the political interests of Native people. Instead, the majority approached the predominantly Lakota-style ceremonies in a way that resulted in the ceremonies being seen as a new, exotic way to commune with nature.[67]

For Native peoples, on the other hand, participating in traditional ceremonies became a matter of cultural pride. This occurred around the same time period as the formation of the American Indian Movement (AIM) in 1968, "a group that generated renewed pride in being Indian and helped many to affirm Indian cultures, values, and religious traditions."[68] According to George Tinker:

> What had been hidden or practiced by only a few in remote locations for so long, suddenly began to claim a place in the public consciousness of Indian communities in one nation after another...What had been revived as a tourist attraction at Pine Ridge in the cities was brought back into the open as legitimate ceremony. No longer produced as mere voyeuristic spectacle, and with stricter and more traditional observance, Sun Dances in the seventies took place at Porcupine and Kyle on the Pine Ridge reservation, and at Ironwood Hilltop and Crow Dog's paradise on the Rosebud. With this spiritual renaissance, Indian identity was rekindled with a new pride, which became more and more intimately connected with the Indian political resistance of the day.[69]

This resulted in Native ceremonial practices becoming a "symbol of resistance, making it more attractive to young Native Americans."[70] An important part of this movement was AIM's focus on "aspects of Native American cultures that had their roots in pre-colonial times."[71] It spoke to Native peoples need to "reclaim the religious traditions and ceremonies" that the missionary system and federal laws banned for so long.[72] The fact that so many Native people today are leaving Christianity and returning to their ancient ceremonies highlights the importance of these traditional ways in the ongoing process of liberation from the effects of colonization.[73]

This dramatic difference in approach continues and affects how non-Natives who appropriate Native traditions are perceived. Many non-Native seekers may be sincerely searching for a pathway away from Christianity's value of human dominance, individualism, and Western mindset. However, we are largely perceived by Native activists as tourists who approach their traditions as "something to dabble in" or "an exotic expression of the return to nature."[74] As there is scant evidence that white spiritual seekers have taken up the political struggles of Native Americans over time, it is hard to justify arguing that, as a group, we should be seen any differently.

❧ How might non-Natives be responsive to the critique that their investment in Native traditions is individualistic and devoid of Native peoples' political concerns?

Tension

Many Native practitioners have continued to invite non-Natives into ceremonies.	**AND**	Many Native practitioners who spread Native knowledge to outsiders have alienated themselves from their tribal communities.

There is much disagreement regarding the value of sharing traditional Native ceremonial practices with white people. Oren Lyons, Faithkeeper of the Turtle Clan, and member of the Onondaga and Seneca nations, speaks of a conversation among Native elders in 1969 wherein they discussed white people showing up at their doorsteps and a prophecy that foretold this phenomenon. The elders

agreed that if this prophecy was true they could try to help by passing on knowledge.[75] Tinker notes that, "many, especially a number of
Lakota practitioners, have welcomed non-Indian participation and
have come increasingly to consider their spirituality as a human universal."[76] Bron Taylor, in *Earthen Spirituality or Cultural Genocide?*, notes
that there are some Indians who say that "Native American religious
practices are crucial if the world is to be preserved" and that non-
Natives "need to adopt the beliefs of Indigenous people 'if humans
are to re-harmonize life on earth'."[77] Oren Lyons appears to concur
with this belief when he calls for us all to have the same ceremonies
for our survival.[78] However, this inclusionary approach shared by
many practitioners is not the majority view.

The majority of activists hold an opposing stance — and this
opposition to white people participating in Native ceremonies has
intensified over time. A primary concern expressed by Tinker is that
many of the Lakota practitioners who shared knowledge became
"spiritual salespersons…[who] made the teaching of native spirituality a for-profit industry."[79] In response to this pattern, in 1980 a Resolution on the 5th Annual Meeting of the Traditional Elders Circle
was passed which outlined concerns regarding "people who use spiritual ceremonies with non-Indian people for profit."[80] It warned
non-Native people to be wary of Native Americans passing themselves off as medicine men who have not actually been given the
permission and training they claim. In 1984, a more stringent document was released by AIM. As with the earlier Resolution, it focused
on commercialization, but in addition, it encouraged the disruption
of ceremonies held by those continuing to falsely claim they are
medicine men.[81]

By the 1990s, there was no reduction in the sale of Native American practices. If anything, there was an increase.[82] In 1993, a document
called the "Declaration of War against Exploiters of Lakota Spirituality" was issued. It had been "passed by 'five hundred representatives'
from 40 different tribes belonging to the Lakota, Dakota, and Nakota
Nations."[83] The Declaration indicated their concern that:

> [F]or too long we have suffered the unspeakable indignity of
> having our most precious Lakota ceremonies and spiritual prac-
> tices desecrated, mocked, and abused by non-Indian "wannabes,"

hucksters, cultists, commercial profiteers and self-styled "New Age shamans" and their followers…"[84]

This declaration called for immediate action to protect Native American's spiritual traditions, including "whatever tactics are necessary and sufficient — for example demonstrations, boycotts, press conferences, and acts of direct intervention."[85]

Another Proclamation was issued as a result of a Protections of Ceremonies meeting held on March 13, 2003 calling for Native people to prohibit non-Natives from participating in Lakota ceremonies.[86] Debate continues on the issue of white peoples' participation in ceremonies, in part, because "among the Lakota, there is no centralized single authority."[87] Also, some people, like Vine Deloria Jr. appear to have taken a more "case by case" approach, recognizing that there are instances of respectful participation in some ceremonies. He makes a distinction, however, between participating in a sweat and some of the other ceremonies that have "deeper significance."[88]

These divergent views help explain some of white seekers' confusion, as "non-Natives are accused of 'appropriating' what they believed was given to them."[89] White people then must determine whether or not to continue participating in ceremonies. This is often conflict-laden because the advice of a trusted elder, regardless of Native heritage, may be considered suspect.

In the face of these challenges, Tinker suggests that a different question becomes important: "Who are the appropriate spokespersons for giving an authoritative answer to [the question of who can participate]?"[90] Three core considerations ultimately concern how non-Native participation affects the community. The first is how non-Natives often take advantage of the hospitality of Native people even when Native persons would like to say no. Second, the Native person may not have the right to extend the invitation since the ceremony is a community event. In other words, non-Native participation affects more than only the issuer of the invitation. Third, non-Natives have a responsibility to question their own motives before seeking or accepting an invitation.[91]

These cautions provide important guidance for white spiritual seekers who find themselves interested in, or invited to, participate in ceremonies alongside Native people. There is another challenge to discuss, however, and this is how non-Natives navigate questions regarding whether or not participating in ceremonies occurring in urban environments led by non-Native people can ever be considered valuable and a contribution to community healing.

♣ How should a non-Native determine what action to take when facing differing messages from Native people?

♣ Is there a way that non-Natives can respond that respects both sides?

Tension

Some Lakota-style ceremonies held off Native-controlled lands, led by non-Native leaders, are attempts to support collective healing for a multiracial community.	——— *AND* ———	Ceremonies held off Native-controlled lands, led by non-Native leaders, are not authentic representations of Lakota traditions.

The final tension is one that continues to challenge me. I have attended a sweat lodge ceremony on a regular basis for approximately 20 years. Throughout the majority of those years, I did not seek out activists' writings and was unaware of the widespread damage caused by white people appropriating Native American practices. Embarrassed, I see myself reflected in many of the critiques named in previous sections, particularly related to white seekers' frame of mind. My participation began during a time when I was personally searching for meaning, my idealization of Native peoples was evident, I paid little attention to Native peoples' political, cultural, and economic concerns, my religious identity was seen as an individual choice, and my privilege allowed me to enter the lodge without considering its larger context or impacts.

For many years, I quietly questioned the contradictory messages I received about my participation in lodge. On one hand, the lodge community was comprised of a multiracial group of individuals dedicated to mentoring young people, convinced that our participation was part of a beneficial, healing process. On the other, I attended anti-racist community events where appropriation was soundly criticized as we spoke of privilege, racial identity development, and systems of oppression. I understood that wanton appropriation for the sake of personal gain or economic benefit was wrong. Yet, I also figured that there were both good and bad ways to go about cultural boundary crossing. In the face of the conflicting messages, I wondered if I was a problematic appropriator. A number of issues influenced my thinking and kept me participating in lodge.

First, I witnessed the sweat lodge save people's lives. For years, the sweat lodge has been a sanctuary space for many Black and Latino youth of color in Los Angeles. These young people need a pathway that is different from the dominant culture, a culture which holds no spiritual meaning for them. My participation allowed me to bring young people to lodge who otherwise would not have gone. One who found sanctuary within this ceremony was a young Latino student of mine in a dangerously disconnected state and clearly longing for the type of connection to the Earth the lodge provides. I imagine my experience is not dissimilar to others who have been part of youth programs that include the sweat lodge as part of their programming. With some exceptions, these types of programs have been seen as conducting the ceremonies responsibly by at least some Native people.[92]

Second, my multiracial community has benefited from mutual participation in ceremonies for many years and would not see it as a step forward to have some of its members stop attending the purification ceremony based on their racial background. My Latino and African American friends looked at me with concern when I talked in ways that led them to think I might stop participating in lodge because I am white. I never considered challenging them about their participation, assuming that being part of a traditionally marginalized and oppressed group made them exempt from concerns over appropriation.[93] Reflecting now, it is possible that the use of the distinction "Native" versus "non-Native" implicates them similarly, as they have also been raised in an individualistic culture that has been separated from Indigenous ways of being. Thus, their participation might be seen as infecting the Native ceremonies in a similar way as my own.[94]

Third, questions about intentionality took center stage in my thinking, and there were moments where clear distinctions between my actions and those I saw as 'gross appropriators' arose. For example, in October 2009 people died in a commercialized and de-contextualized sweat lodge held as part of a "spiritual warrior" retreat. I wrote a blog to highlight my concerns. A portion of it read:

> That lodge was not the safest place on Earth, as my elder calls it. Instead, it was rendered deadly. The ego and hubris of a non-Native man turned a sacred Native American ceremony into a money-making venture. A purification ceremony within mother's womb was turned into a trial to be overcome. A sanctuary space for prayer was turned into a prison from which people begged for release.
>
> … Cultural appropriation often distorts the beauty of the original form. Worse, blind appropriation and defensive egos shield people from recognizing the harm they perpetuate. Within weeks of the deaths, the white man was busy offering workshops and lectures, telling audiences that he prays for the families of those who died. At no time does he publicly recognize the role he played, his lack of humility and use of privilege to take and modify what he had no right to desecrate.[95]

My stance during this phase was that the lodge I attend is wholly unlike those criticized by activists and scholars. By this time, I saw myself as a person who attends lodge in order to support community healing, since the messages conveyed by the lodge community were of communal responsibility and the need to heal our ancestral inheritance.

To illustrate this, the founder of Street Poets has allowed me to share a spoken word poem he performs. What struck me is how he interweaves the struggles faced by so many of the young people he works with in Los Angeles with the recognition that he and his white ancestors are partly responsible for the young people's current pain. It highlights the personal responsibility white people have to work for social justice.

From the Fire

My ancestors came to me
Between the seams of Sweatlodge dreams
With a request for healing
Hearts muffled & torn by dead silence born
From horrors too big to face
Seeking grace on sacred ground
Paved with false promises

My ancestors came to me
To claim responsibility
For the rape and enslavement of millions
Of one, your son
Who was once elder, chief, healer
Of a tribe that knew nature and beauty
Like the river knows tears
My ancestors' fears fed flames
That consumed original names & songs
Turned ancient healing rites to wrongs
Harnessed hell for profits that today
Build prisons to contain the same shame
Under different names:
Bloods, Crips, Sureños, Norteños
Hatred fueled by wounds
That live in unmarked tombs
Watery graves between home and here
There are days when we are all slaves to fear
Smoking, drinking, buying
To forget the dead and dying
Flying bombs far beyond backyards
Where bullets trace scars in night skies
Ripped wide by cries for help

How can one explain a baby
Sold like crack cocaine
As blood rains from her mother's womb?

My ancestors came to me
With that blood on their hands
And the blood of every man-child
Murdered in drive-bys by living lies
Too high to heal
Running the streets between destiny & deceit
Every village burned
Every girl turned out by broken boys
Once token toys tossed aside
By uncles drunk on Night Train
Still staggering into children's bedrooms
Mimicking slave masters orchestrating disasters
For future generations to deny

My ancestors came to me
With tears in their eyes
And taught me a song
That belongs to you & you & you
And maybe someday
Me too.

Chris Henrikson
Street Poets Inc.[96]

This poem speaks to the understanding that a spiritual practice ties me to others, acknowledging a sense of belonging in the world such that you matter to me and, hopefully, I matter to you. Native Americans' experiences matter. So do the experiences of people from other cultures who witness the appropriation of their sacred rites. This is what has kept the question alive for me: Is this understanding, along with commitment and mindfulness, sufficient to warrant continued participation?

After almost 15 years participating in lodge, I began to investigate this question seriously. It was then that I encountered the myriad critiques by activists and scholars that make up the majority of this exploration. Based on much of that information, I thought determining authenticity might be possible by evaluating the degree to which a ceremonial leader followed traditional protocols and avoided commodification. However, verifying that a group or leader follows correct protocols is not as straightforward as I hoped.

The story of the lodge I attend is illustrative. I was first invited to participate in lodge in 1996, at which time I met Miguel, the elder who runs the lodge. Miguel is a half-white, half-Guatemalan man trained in the Lakota tradition. I never presumed to question his authority or his ethnic relationship to the practice. For many years, I actually assumed he was Native. I now know that one of his teachers was Wallace Black Elk, a Native American man who is said to have believed at least at one point in his life that "the power of the Sacred Pipe is for everyone."[97]

From all I have read and experienced, it seems that Miguel's approach attempts to adhere to tradition and he follows the protocols taught to him. At the same time, Miguel often refers to his primary teacher, Marcellus, when he states that we should "learn this ceremony really well this time, because it will all be different the next." He always says this with a hearty chuckle and says that he was trained not to be a "methodist," focused on the methodology, but to recognize the intention of the ceremony. I was, therefore, heart-sick upon reading the name of Wallace Black Elk as among those who have been criticized as supporting appropriation and commercialization.[98]

A strong sense of dread arose within me that the lodge I attend is characteristic of those critiqued by advocates and activists. I was hoping that was not true, however. I considered the fact that even though Miguel jokes about not being a "methodist," the same protocols that were in evidence during my first sweat are still in place today. Our manner of entry, our movements, the way the stones are treated, who can say what when, the blessings, the way the water is poured, the fact that I must stay home during my moon time (menstruation), refrain from alcohol, etc. remain unchanged. Additionally, when I was invited to participate in a lodge run by a Native elder living in a city just north of Los Angeles, that elder followed the same protocols. For this reason, I recognize in Miguel's approach both the understanding that this is a sacred tradition that cannot be changed out of personal preference and that our intention and sincerity are critically important to supporting the process. The statement about it "all being different the next time" seems to have more to do with our personal experience of the ceremony, rather than the ceremony itself.

In all my years of attendance, no money exchanged hands in order to participate, beyond offering donations for the purchase of fuel for the fire. There was no publicizing of the ceremony. There were no flyers, no associated workshops, no purchasing of objects or any other economic exchange for knowledge. There was never any indication that we could be quickly trained to lead a lodge ourselves. There was, however, always the invitation for us to arrive early to help and to learn. Only through dedicated practice over years could one earn the right to conduct a lodge and then, only through a long mentorship process.

Miguel echoes his teacher, Marcellus, when he says that those of us who are white come to lodge because our ancestors did not. So much devastation would have been avoided if white people had understood and respected Native ways upon arrival to this land. Therefore, I have come to see my participation as part of my responsibility to ensure better tracks are laid for those who come after me.

Although I was convinced that the lodge I attend attempts to be respectful, the reading I encountered troubled me. So I talked with Miguel regarding his experience and perspective. We discussed his life journey and how he had come to know Wallace Black Elk and the teachers he has had in subsequent years. I asked whether he ever experienced negative reactions and charges of disrespectful appropriation. It was then that Miguel told me of an experience he had once when an unknown group arrived unannounced at a Sun Dance ceremony decades prior. A group he participated with was preparing for the ceremony. A number of people they did not know arrived at the location. The group suspected they were AIM members that had come to disrupt the ceremony. After observing for a while, and recognizing the group's sincerity in following protocols and fulfilling traditional obligations, that group joined in to support the process.

After hearing Miguel's story and considering all the readings, I determined to remain open to hearing further critique. But, I also felt somewhat satisfied that my participation in lodge was not a problematic form of appropriation, given the adherence to protocols, the lack of commodification, and the fact that Miguel remains connected to his spiritual teacher.

Quite some time later, however, reading more of George Tinker's work provoked additional concerns.[99] Much of what Tinker writes corresponds with what other activists and scholars offer. This includes the critiques about white spiritual seekers' commodified versions of ceremonies and their damaging effects. Tinker also criticizes how non-Natives approach ceremonies in ways that retain Christianity's influence. Whether the topic was the role of reciprocity, the understanding of the meaning of *mitakuye oyasin,* the circle, interrelationship, humanity's place in the web of life, spatiality, or the role of vicarious sacrifice, what I read fit with my understanding.[100] Again, I felt relieved to know that the lodge I attend conveys these understandings.

The fact that I carry these understandings within me deepened my hope that the lodge I attend is not one of those that extends colonization and undermines Native cultures. My investment is strong because participating in lodge has helped me deepen my responsiveness and attention to my white community's healing and well-being.[101] My intention is for us to become better able to respectfully relate across cultures, as Tinker refers to in a set of suggestions for our collective healing.[102]

On the other hand, the reality is that regardless of my understanding and intention, I cannot escape the charge that I am complicit in the following:

> For euro-americans and Europeans, the addiction to power and dominance is enhanced as they take the illusive surface structure of Indian ceremonies and colonize them into just another religious resource for themselves, a resource clothed with the appearance of righteousness, much as statutory rape can be clothed with the claim of prior mutual consent.[103]

While I may not want to believe that this applies to me and my lodge community, the fact remains that by virtue of the lodge occurring away from its original context with a primarily non-Native group, white thinking surely influences and affects the ceremony.[104]

I may believe wholeheartedly that I am acting with full respect and have been appropriately invited in to this ceremony. Yet, I also must account for the fact that the lodge community has changed over time and regularly includes white people who do not recognize issues of white privilege and their complicity with structural injustice, and are therefore, less likely to engage in political struggles. For this reason, I cannot argue against Tinker's critique:

> White involvement in Indian ceremonies is actually harmful to our White relatives because it reinforces the inbred sense of White privilege that is the birth heritage of every White person in North America, just as male privilege is the inescapable birth heritage of every male....we hurt our White relatives and friends when we naively invite them into our private, community ceremonial life. We are only encouraging the final act of colonization and conquest. ...This becomes a primary reason for arguing that the inclusion of White folks in the community intimacy of our ceremonies is not healthy for those White relatives, especially if they really do want to make a difference in the world and find creative ways to do things differently."[105]

What strikes me most deeply about this is that Tinker's perspective forces me to confront how my own analysis has to some degree been filtered through an individual lens. What is right, given who I am? What is right, given my elders' relationships and approach? What has been much more difficult is attending to the question, what is right, given how my *entire white community* handles these issues? Individualism remains alive and active within me.

I am left with the question of how to proceed. A clear pathway forward includes continuing to work to encourage my white community to confront privilege and structural inequity as part of our own healing process. I wonder about how best to do that. Would discontinuing my participation with my lodge community support that overall effort? Or, might it be of value to continue my participation, consistently bringing this complicating perspective and analysis to the group? In other words, is remaining a participant, while engaging them in critical conversations about appropriation and privilege during our social moments, a messy, but useful approach?

Either way, I am not the only one wrestling with these questions. Anyone hoping to avoid damaging forms of appropriation while also participating in yoga, meditation, or another Indigenous ceremonial practice must confront similar questions.

❖ Do you struggle with the tension between a wish to do no harm to others via appropriation and the perceived value of participating in traditions from another culture?

❖ How is the example of my lodge participation similar or different from concerns raised by other groups who find their traditions widely used by spiritual seekers from outside their tradition?

The Search for Balance

Avoiding harmful appropriation and working for justice while staying true to one's spiritual principles requires continual reflection and sustained effort. While I am not entirely certain how to best move forward, there are some considerations that are essential. These include building authentic relationships with Native people, reconsidering our relationship with the land, and recognizing the priceless nature of the sacred. My intention in offering these ideas is to invite others to share in community what has been thus far, for me, a largely private dialogue. My hope is that this will prompt integration of this knowledge among fellow spiritual seekers so that we can develop a responsible approach to living in this tension.

Building Authentic Relationships

It is important to consider what is required for people to give up an idealized, romantic image of Native Americans. There are three related struggles that must be faced. The first involves grappling with the possibility that much of the damaging spiritual appropriation occurring today may be connected to a "white women's culture" that involves a "fantasy multiracial sisterhood."[106] Karlyn Crowley makes this connection:

> Just when women of color challenged feminism and women's and gender studies for its racist foundations in the 1980s and 1990s, many white women turned toward New Age spiritual practices that "allowed" them to live out fantasy unions with

women of color that were disrupted in the public, feminist-po-
litical sphere.[107]

Even though I was not engaged with political/academic issues during the '80s or '90s, I have been left wondering about the degree to
which my spiritual practice has allowed me to *feel* a sense of connection to *all* women without needing to develop real relationships
with them.

A second struggle concerns how hard it may be to accept the
implications of this fantasy because of a deep investment in being
"racially innocent."[108] Again, Karlyn Crowley offers perspective:

> For any possible authentic multiracial feminist community, we
> must attend not just to the spiritual realm but to the material
> one as well: as Jean Wyatt points out, "antiracism based on the
> all-too-real lack of social justice could provide a more solid
> grounding for crossrace feminist solidarity than the imaginary
> yearning for identification." The spiritual is, almost by defini-
> tion, a space for "imaginary yearning," but it must be coupled
> with a greater self-consciousness about white women's suspect
> desire for a "racially innocent feminism."[109]

Her proposition goes far beyond issues of feminism. This critique
challenges one to accept that growing up in our society involves being
steeped in racism, whether overt or subtle, and that privilege may
shape one's entire approach to life, including spirituality. The inference
is that any step toward authentic relationship requires an exploration
of personal culpability and an investment in actions for justice.

The third struggle concerns how to engage in the material realm
in a way that is connected to spiritual growth and practice. Thankfully,
there are numerous models for this *both/and* approach. The writings of
women of color are resources for this "spiritual activism," particularly
those, such as Gloria Anzaldúa, who incorporate spiritual beliefs in a
way that embraces the realities of the social-political world.[110] Their orientation to spirituality involves three interlocking dimensions — political awareness, spiritual consciousness, and enhanced creativity.[111]

Ultimately, this move into political awareness is essential because, as the neopagan and feminist author Starhawk writes:

> Any real spiritual power we gain from any tradition carries with
> it a responsibility. If we learn from African drum rhythms or

the Lakota sweat lodge, we have incurred an obligation not to romanticize but to participate in the very real struggles being waged for liberation, land and cultural survival.[112]

Becoming allies in the struggle to change systems that perpetuate oppression is a path that can lead to authentic relationships.

❖ To what degree do you recognize the challenges described here?

❖ How does your spiritual understanding support you to confront the challenges described?

Considering the Land: Confession, Repentance, and Relationship

Attempting to live out spiritual principles derived from Indigenous peoples and remaining accountable to racial justice involves acting in solidarity with those from whom the principles originate. Specifically, it includes reconsidering how we are related to the land.

A first essential step is recognizing ancestral inheritance. This is particularly true for white people. One way of thinking about this inheritance from a metaphysical standpoint comes from my mentor, Orland Bishop[113] who describes two companion concepts: *soul stream* and *time body*.[114] Orland describes the soul stream as the thousands-years stream of memory that tells where one's soul has traveled throughout various incarnations. This concept can explain how a person might have memories of previous incarnational events. Unfortunately, this has all-too-often been used to justify many white spiritual seekers who claim memories of having been Native in a previous life. As previously noted, there are many reasons to reject most of these purported memories as wish-fulfilling fantasy, serving to allow white people to escape the need to confront their own racial identity. Therefore, the *soul stream* concept is unlikely to encourage people toward actions for justice.

What can provide encouragement, however, is the related concept of the time body. According to Orland, the *time body* provides the raw material for this incarnation's soul work and refers specifically to one's blood ancestry. The memory tied to the time body includes the five preceding familial generations and one's genetic inheritance. From this perspective, I have personally inherited the history of my white ancestors, the consequences of their choices, and the need to heal what has been passed down to me and injured others. It is because of my time body that I take responsibility for contributing to humanity's healing process.[115] It is the sense of being tied to my group, to my time body, that allows me to see my relationship to European people who became white and were unable to reach across difference and refrain from land theft.

The recognition of my ancestral and personal complicity in the wrongs perpetuated against Native peoples is what allows me to offer the *confession* (using a Christian frame) that is asked for as a first step toward healing.[116] The personal sense of complicity (which includes the emotion of guilt) for the historic and continuing injury, whether intentional, active, or inherited, provides an impetus to take the second step required, *repentance*. To be clear, this is not a call for white people to get mired in guilt and remorse. It is, instead, a call to fully admit our relationship to grave injustices in order to pave the way toward a proactive set of action steps that lead toward justice.[117]

This brings the issue of *belonging* front and center. Of primary concern to Native peoples is the return of stolen land. This is a straightforward request. Yet, it likely pushes non-Native spiritual seekers into new considerations of what it means to fully live out spiritual principles. What I have come to realize is that the only way to actually live out the principle of interrelatedness and move away from individualism and modernism is to recognize my role as an occupier of stolen lands and, therefore, support actions that will result in the return of land.

Tinker writes of what would occur if a process was initiated whereby Native people regained control over land currently held by the U.S. He writes,

> The relatively simple act of recognizing the sovereignty of the Sioux Nation and returning to them all state-held lands in the Black Hills (for example, national forest, national park, and South Dakota state park lands) would generate immediate inter-

national interest in the rights of indigenous, tribal peoples in all state territories. In the United States alone, it is estimated that Indian nations still have legitimate (moral and legal) claim to some two-thirds of the U.S. land mass.[118]

Reading this prompts an important set of considerations regarding how efforts for racial justice may deepen spiritual life.

What would it mean to return *all* U.S. public lands? For me it might mean that visiting land I find regenerative would no longer be permissible. If Native people determined that a time of healing and regrouping would necessitate the exclusion of non-Natives from those lands, this would provide me with an opportunity to think, act, and relate differently than those who came before me. It would be an opportunity to understand and accept that there are boundaries I must respect for the sake of collective well-being and justice.

Reflecting on my likely response, this would first prompt me to want to work toward building a relationship that might eventually allow me to be invited in to those lands. I would then have to recognize the likelihood that, given how individualism and modernism characterize my ways of living, Native people might not feel it to be healthy for them to build a relationship with me or allow my re-entry. Accepting this could be a prompt to deepen my spiritual healing. It would be a call to strive for a life characterized by the kind of non-hierarchical communalism dedicated to harmony and balance that originally attracted me to Native practices in the first place. My acceptance of the need to stay away would reflect not only a dedication to supporting another groups' healing process but also an appropriate detachment from personal desire.

In addition to Tinker's call for the return of land as a necessary part of healing and justice, he provides a radical vision for all of us that includes a movement toward smaller, autonomous communities that would require an end to our reliance on private property, borders, and hierarchical government structures.[119] The arguments that support this vision of a life-sustaining return to a state of harmony and balance are compelling. And they lead to questions regarding how non-Natives can navigate their longing for spiritual belonging while knowing that the fundamental issues of land ownership remain unresolved. Starhawk speaks to this when she says:

> People of European heritage, out of hunger for what their cul-
> ture lacks, may unwittingly become spiritual stripminers, dam-
> aging other cultures in superficial attempts to uncover their
> mystical treasures. Understanding the suppression and ground-
> ing ourselves in the surviving knowledge of the European tra-
> ditions can help people with European ancestors avoid flocking
> to the sad tribe of Wannabes, — want to be Indians, want to be
> Africans, want to be anything but what we are…[120]

Because ancient European traditions have, in many respects, been
lost, this can prove challenging. In cases where there are threads of
the past to follow, the surviving fabric can be too thin for a viable tradition. This situation underlies the felt need among many white seekers to adopt an approach that allows for the personal freedom to
craft one's own spiritual path as well as recreate one's ancestral traditions using inspiration from existing ones.[121]

Some spiritual seekers in Britain are using Native American ceremonies as models to revitalize what may have existed on European
soil during the Bronze Age. Archeological evidence supports that
something like a sweat lodge existed, but there is nothing to suggest
the format, protocols, etc.[122] Practitioners, inspired by the Native
American sweat lodge, connect the lodge to their land and traditions
by substituting plants indigenous to Britain instead of using sage or
tobacco.[123] While recognizing that they draw inspiration from Native
American practices, these British Druids dissociate their rituals from
Native American ones by calling their ceremonies "Native European
spirituality."[124] They appear to be sincerely grappling with the moral
and ethical dilemma that, "The more [a] ritual is represented as the
practice of another culture, the more problematic it is likely to be.
And the more it will be appropriately characterized as 'theft'."[125]

I do not know whether or not this is what Native Americans
have in mind when they suggest that white people return to their
roots. Yet, it is a reflection of the considerable challenge facing descendants of Europe. Since European earth-based spiritual practices
were largely lost, reviving them requires inspiration from somewhere.
The hope of these European practitioners is that the use of distinguishing titles, such as Native European, will avoid the misrepresentations that have led to harmful distortions of Native American beliefs
and practices.[126]

In considering these efforts, I reflect on the fact that my ancestors were not British or Celtic and I have no blood ties to that land. Nor do I live on European land now. Given my mixed European roots (German, Italian, and Russian), claiming a Druid or Celtic tradition would be a different form of appropriation.[127] My ties to the earth were compromised by a long line of ancestors who did not practice earth-based spirituality. Yet, investing in non-descript forms of pagan, goddess, or Wiccan spirituality is also problematic. The first reason is that its feminist forms — those most prevalent around me — include an essentialist approach to women that has felt incongruous with my expanding understanding of issues related to gender and sexuality.[128] Also, goddess worship tends to be a predominantly white movement.[129] My initiation into spirituality involved a multiracial community, and this is something I value.

A continuing challenge for me is that in discussions with my mentors, Orland and Miguel, they have suggested that I can reconnect directly with the land where I reside. They advise that I can allow the land to lead me, that the land itself holds answers and will reclaim me, and that I belong to it no matter where I go or what I do. Their suggestion invites me to spend time in a forest or on a mountain and get my hands in the earth. Gardening is a reconnecting effort. It is generative and often leads to association with others, creepy crawlies included. The exchange of zucchini or tomatoes enhances relationships with neighbors. The sharing that abundance inspires allows connections to deepen and lowers barriers between self and other.

The practice is, essentially, about listening to the natural world. The full moon invites reflective time spent in a place where the tides offer evidence of our planetary and stellar connections. These sorts of individually-performed, nature-based rituals are not necessarily tied to any particular tradition. They simply reinforce that one is related to all the elements of nature and that there is a purpose for one's life which includes others. These pursuits address some aspects of the cultural loss I once felt.

The complication is that my mentors' approach involves a broad understanding of what the term "Indigenous" means. In this way of thinking, we are all Indigenous. We are all people of the land. This is a radically different way of considering what it means to be "of the land." It is completely depoliticized, does not depend on me being Native, and does not require me to address the fact that I live on stolen lands and have an obligation to address this issue.[130] For this reason, I attempt to hold these perspectives with an attitude of *both/and.* I live on stolen lands to which I cannot lay claim, such that I am required to support its return to Native control. *And,* I am related to the earth and all of its creatures, and therefore, belong to it, regardless of where I am situated.

♣ What questions does this raise related to your life and spiritual practice?

Recognizing the Priceless Nature of the Sacred

A final consideration is that we must avoid that which has been easily gained and commodified via appropriation. Cynthia Kasee offers a set of reflective questions that are useful in identifying the potential for harm:

> Ask what elements of the New Age pseudo-Indian hodge-podge ring false with the most cursory of examinations. Are they charging me for this knowledge? If the answer is "yes," walk the other way....Are they telling me to avoid "real" Indians (i.e., Traditionalists, reservation dwellers, activists, etc.)? Do they say these people don't want me to learn this because I'm not Indian? Do they say they are fulfilling a prophecy supposedly made in the 1960s to teach Indian faiths to non-Indians despite protests by other Indians? If they tell you to avoid "real" Indians, they are doing it to protect their profits (not their prophets!).... Yes, it is possible to learn these ways without being a Native, and non-Indians have done so for five centuries. However, it takes a lifetime of commitment shown in very mundane ways, and knowledge is not given simply because it is desired...Finally...you must ask yourself if you have been told that men and women should participate in all rituals together, regardless of the time of month or year. When you found out that traditional rites were often segregated and women were not active participants in some rituals in the case of menstruation, pre- or post-parturition, or seasonal cycle,

were you told that the inclusiveness of New Age rituals strikes down the inherently sexist nature of the Old Ways?...A further admonition is to be wary of amalgamations. If you truly seek to follow a Native path, there are ways to do so. They will no doubt involve years of study with one or another holy person, probably in site-specific ceremonies. This will probably be initiated only after you have sufficiently proven your diligence...If, after many years of this, you can accept with equanimity the fact that you may be told to "Get lost! No Indian wisdom for you here!," then you have walked the path to Traditionalism many of us have walked.[131]

This is not a comprehensive list. But it is a start. Devotion and humility play a monumental part. Receiving spiritual wisdom easily is a surefire sign that something is amiss. The feeling that one has the right to make demands or argue that the requirements set forth are unfair indicates that ego is playing too large a role.

Ancient spiritual knowledge that is easy to access and acquire has, almost by definition, been cheapened. Spiritual wisdom is a priceless gift given by holy people and, therefore, a price tag attached to it is a sign of it having been commercialized. Becoming a sage, shaman, or teacher of timeless wisdom is not easily achieved, nor does it come with a certificate. It is a labor that takes time, attention, devotion, and sacrifice.

There are many white spiritual seekers working to become increasingly responsible. A white woman named Michelle Kleisath, along with her partner Chilan Ta, presented a workshop entitled *Healing Orientalism* at the White Privilege Conference in 2013. Kleisath shared about her years living in India learning about Buddhism by witnessing the practices of a local family and she offered some thoughts that invite important consideration. Part of the presentation was a thorough — and thoroughly disconcerting — history of how white privilege and institutional racism played a role in Buddhist meditation practices becoming popularized in the United States. Kleisath spoke of the politics on both sides that prompted white seekers to go toward the East and Eastern practitioners from Tibet to come to the West. She revealed governmental funding sources that set up centers and programs aimed at influencing U.S. citizens against communism.

Kleisath also spoke of alterations made to Buddhism that made it palatable for white Westerners. Her research aligns with academic literature that describes how white U.S. poets during the 1960s were instrumental in bringing practices associated with Tibetan Buddhism to the United States.[132] Most importantly, this white woman's story included her understanding of meditation as primarily practiced by monks *after* they had gone through a process of giving away their worldly possessions and *after* many years of dedicated study. She described how meditation is not a common practice in the homes of practicing Buddhists in India. Her Asian American partner, Chilan Ta, verified, from her experience, that the U.S. conception of meditation as an easily accessed way to learn Buddhism is decontextualized to the degree that it is problematic. Western people may practice a form of meditation diligently, but the kind of devotional practice that involves study and the giving away of one's possessions as a way to reduce ego is, most often, absent.

The conclusion offered by these two women was not, as I had anticipated, that white people in the U.S. should refrain from learning the practice. Instead, what caught my attention was Kleisath's recognition that there is great healing to be found in learning how to sit quietly. Our frenzied modern world moves too quickly. Learning how to stop, sit, and breathe is healing. The suggestion she made was that spiritual seekers should not mistake this centering, anxiety-reducing practice as traditional Buddhist meditation and that, perhaps, it should not even be called meditation at all. She went on to say how she sees group stretching as very healing, particularly when involving bending the body in shapes that imitate animals. This tongue-in-cheek statement contested the practice of this kind of group stretching done across the U.S. being called yoga.

Both meditation and yoga have their origins within religious and/or spiritual practices that require years of devotion and dedicated study. The two presenters invited people not to be fooled into imagining that the types of commercialized training programs available in the United States are reflective of the original practices, nor are the health-related forms that have been born out of these commercialized versions. The commodification and desacralizing of these practices have turned them into exercises, leaving the public with a radical misunderstanding of the original forms and how they fit into their cultures of origin.

A court case in San Diego, California illustrates the point.[133] A set of elementary schools began teaching yoga to students as part of the health curriculum. The program is funded by a grant from a yoga studio linked to a foundation supported by followers of Krishna Pattabhi Jois. The school district's Superintendent said he hopes the program will "decrease instances of fighting and bullying" and that the district is "not instructing anyone in religious dogma…yoga is very mainstream." The school district was sued with the claim that the program violates the "state law prohibiting the teaching of religion in public schools." The plaintiff suggested that "yoga poses are integrally linked to religious and spiritual beliefs." The judge upheld the program, explaining that the district "has taken out any references to Hinduism and its liturgical language, Sanskrit. Yoga, the judge said, is similar to other exercise programs like dodgeball."

It concerns me that the U.S. process of commercialization, commodification, and decontextualizing is able to take yoga, derived from a religious/spiritual tradition, and turn it into a practice likened to dodgeball. Maybe Kleisath is right. Maybe group stretching is good. But I wonder what distorted understanding about Hinduism results when the world believes that current forms of yoga practiced in the U.S. are the same as traditional yoga.

❖ To what degree have you adopted an exercise, breathing, or relaxing technique that has its origin in a devotional, spiritual practice?

❖ In what ways have some practices been so commercialized that they have lost their sacredness within the forms you encounter?

Developing the awareness of how approaches to spiritual practices today often involve damaging forms of appropriation is an important step toward creating a more authentic sense of belonging. This awareness alone, however, is not enough. Fundamental differences in spiritual principles complicate decision-making, and we are challenged to modify our beliefs and actions when we learn that our valued practices might injure others. We must consider how one may both maintain loyalty to a sense of inner truth and remain accountable to racial justice principles at the same time.

CHAPTER 6

Inner Truth and Accountability

Be strong then, and enter into your own body;
there you have a solid place for your feet.
Think about it carefully!
Don't go off somewhere else!
... just throw away all thoughts of
imaginary things,
and stand firm in that which you are.

Kabir

Sometimes the hardest thing to do is stand firm. This has been a challenge for me recently. I have been learning how to listen to my heart instead of simply my head, learning how to accept and honor my own needs without feeling obligated to explain or justify them to anyone else, learning to say "no" to stepping off center because of "shoulds" or guilt, and to stand firm in my own sense of integrity.[1]

In the month prior to writing this piece, I received an email that began with the poem and message above. The poem invited me to be embodied, grounded, and fully incarnate in my present self. The message which followed emphasizes the need for self-trust. This email reminded me that guilt is paralyzing and living with integrity takes strength. Standing firm requires me to value and follow my inner voice on a daily basis.

Many spiritual people attempt to access their "inner voice" as part of a healing process. Yet, there is often a need to evaluate the degree to which an "inner guide" and sense of integrity come from one's most conscious Self and not simply an unconscious desire for comfort.[2] The search for the truth of one's inner voice can be deep spiritual work.

Becoming involved with racial justice involves uncovering unconscious motives and habits. Standing too firmly in one position can inhibit growth and learning, cross-race relationship building, and effective collaborations for justice. Therefore, there must be an attempt to stay true to an *inner truth* while also engaging across race in a way that is *accountable* to others and to racial justice. This is not a clear and easy path.

This tension is faced by many who try to navigate between a spiritual practice and a racial justice one. These are, too often, contradictory perspectives.

People following a spiritual path often state:

> Locating the truth that lies within allows for an authentic voice. Being liberated from confining social structures means listening to what emerges from my deepest core, my divine Self. Trusting my inner voice is part of living out of my freedom. I also do not judge another's truth. We all need to find that deep, guiding voice within.

The guiding principle is *"I turn to and trust my inner voice to locate my truth."*

In contrast, white colleagues focused on racial justice often express:

> Being white makes it impossible for me to have total clarity about how I carry lingering racism and internalized superiority. I must listen to people of color to understand myself better, even if their analysis is counter to what resonates for me. Relationships of accountability wherein I take a step back, listen, and learn, reveal my false assumptions and harmful behaviors. It is painful to hear that I am wrong, but it's all part of undoing racism.

The guiding principle is that *"Racism has warped my perspective and I need others to help me see clearly."*

The *both/and* is clear. Spiritual growth requires humility and openness, and being willing to learn from others allows for reflection on how to best serve and lead. At the same time, having the grounding and conviction that comes from a sense of inner truth is also important, because good advocacy requires an unwavering voice. Therefore, individuals invested in both spirituality *and* racial justice must figure out how to balance them both simultaneously.[3]

This chapter offers an overview of the concept of accountability as it relates to racial justice work. The focus is on areas where navigating the tension between *inner truth* and *accountable obligations* is often unclear and anxiety-provoking. A concluding section offers some ideas to support doing a self-check on one's perspective when in vexing situations.

An Introduction to Accountability

My first direct experience with accountability occurred through the Alliance of White Anti-Racists Everywhere - Los Angeles (AWARE-LA) and our participation at the White Privilege Conference (WPC) in 2006. The theme of the conference prompted members of the group to reflect on how our organization was accountable to people of color. At that time, each of the members of the leadership team had close relationships with people of color and multiracial organizations. We felt secure in the value of the organization's work because so many colleagues of color were strongly supportive of it, and our informal, personal accountability relationships seemed solid. We were taking up the call to do our personal work with other white people —— an oft-heard request from people of color.

The messages delivered at the conference, however, prompted us to work on creating a more formal accountability structure for our organization. The story of that effort was published in a book about white accountability in a chapter entitled, *Powerful Partnerships: Transformative Alliance Building.*[4] It chronicles the research, attempts, and misfires we encountered while trying to set up an accountability board.

Underlying the entire experience was a tension between our understanding that people of color's perspective and collaboration are essential and our need to trust our insights regarding working with white people.

As we engaged our friends of color in conversations about how we could develop an accountability structure that would oversee the organization's work, they asked us to strive to find a form that did not solely depend upon people of color to evaluate and validate our efforts. They stated that AWARE-LA members knew more about the workings of the white psyche than they did. This sparked disturbing realizations amongst our leadership team. We came face to face with how several of us had been initiated into a form of accountability wherein relationships had been unidirectional, with white people locked into a subordinate position. These unequal relationships resulted in poor communication between white people and people of color and less effective advocacy efforts. These experiences also left some of us believing there was little room for us to place trust in our own perspective if it ran counter to the views of people of color. These insights did not become clear right away; it took time to determine how to move forward differently. Along the way, we discovered a different approach to accountability, one that held expectations for everyone involved.

As a human being, to whom am I responsible, and for what? This is a fundamental question my spiritual mentor asks white people. For many whose spirituality derives from a religious tradition, the answer might be that one is accountable only to God. Accountability in this form may be considered transcendent, and is accompanied by the belief that there is no secular or material entity that holds any authority over a person's actions.[5] To others, the answer is that one is accountable first and foremost to one's own soul — what Michael Meade refers to as "the first agreement" in life.[6] Neither of these perspectives necessarily support the idea that one must be accountable to other human beings as well.

Gillian Burlingham, a white anti-racist activist, offers an approach adopted by a group of Quakers which is described within their *Faith and Practice* guide:

> Friends testimony on equality is rooted in the holy expectation
> that there is that of God in everyone, including adversaries and

> people from widely different stations, life experiences, and religious persuasions. All must therefore be treated with integrity and respect…Friends recognize that unjust inequities persist throughout society, and that difficult work remains to rid ourselves and the Religious Society of Friends from prejudice and inequitable treatment based upon gender, class, race, age, sexual orientation, physical attributes, or other categorizations. Both in the public realm — where Friends may "speak truth to power" — and in intimate familial contexts, Friends' principles require witness against injustice and inequality wherever it exists.[7]

This approach holds authority as immanent within human beings, and requires members to act to ensure that all people are recognized as inhabited by a divine spark and treated accordingly, thereby bridging spiritual and material realms.

Accountability as it applies to racial justice usually takes a purely secular approach. People are accountable to people. Within racial justice circles, accountability primarily involves upholding a set of intentions and practices within the context of a relationship or organization. One is obligated to act in a certain way or do certain things. This kind of obligation manifests in various ways, and within different racial justice communities it can have different meanings. Some definitions include individuals being dependable, reliable, practicing ethically, building relationships with whites or people of color that are characterized by trust and authenticity, and being loyal to an organization or group wherein trust is built over time. For groups, it means holding themselves accountable to the "movement" and the values and norms that go along with the analysis, practices, and vision of their community.[8]

There are both formal and informal kinds of accountability.[9] In the case of AWARE-LA, we were only able to move forward once we worked through our past experiences and came together formally to create a mutually accountable Racial Justice Alliance (RJA) — a multiracial group that supported one another but did not oversee the organization's activities directly. Simultaneously, relationships among friends and colleagues continued to serve as informal accountability. We discuss race regularly and offer each other feedback. We call on each other for check-ins when we are confused or struggling.

A spiritual definition suggests accountability starts with a heart connection, then moves to the head. In this view, a loving connection precedes the philosophy underpinning accountability. Accountability begins with the desire for those we love to have their basic needs fulfilled and to enjoy success, resources, support, and self-determination. There is no room for patronization, a sense of superiority, or a savior complex. It is about equalizing power and ensuring that resources are shared equitably.[10]

What does being accountable involve? Those who are at the forefront of movements for racial justice are clear that accountability needs to function in ways that are psychologically and socially healthy for everyone. These leaders and their organizations strive for relationships of shared power where the guidance of all is honored, as opposed to relationships where people strive for power over others.[11] These leaders hold the *both/and,* acknowledging that white people must support leadership of people of color in solidarity actions *and* that white voices are essential for the overall movement's success. White people are called to be both humble *and* vocal, expected to be open to advice, criticism, and direction, *and* invited to bring their best thinking to the table when making decisions about how to proceed.[12]

The white anti-racist group, European Dissent, offers their Accountability Statement in three parts: (1) accountability of whites to the organization, (2) accountability of whites to other whites, and (3) accountability of whites to people of color.[13] Included in their Statement are general agreements to be honest, respect one another, and create spaces where people can share their ideas. Notable are the sections that mention the use of one's truth and sense of wholeness. In regard to commitments made by white people to white people, they "commit to the appreciation of the whole of each other's personhood" and to "question without a sense of one-upmanship."[14] The white membership recognizes the need to both accept the leadership of people of color and to avoid uncritically following their leadership.

It should be noted that equally present in the Statement is the recognition that accountability requires that manifestations of racism or privilege be challenged. Honoring a person's full humanity does not in any way imply that a person's viewpoint or action will go unchecked. Compassionate challenge is necessary because white people advocating for racial justice can inadvertently undermine the work in a myriad of ways. For example, a white colleague may take action with a sense of urgency and passion that is tainted by individualistic arrogance and, in this way, the collective effort necessary for success can be subverted.[15] A feeling of overconfidence in one's knowledge of racism and privilege might prompt the insertion of oneself in situations involving colleagues of color without taking the time to find out what those colleagues of color want.[16] Internalized superiority and habits of privilege find their way into well-meaning actions regularly and, therefore, staying open to constant review is essential.

How can one meet expectations of accountability? Accountability statements are important. They are also limited. They describe what to expect from oneself and others, but they do not describe what it looks like to fulfill those expectations. They are only guides. Reading them does not protect against pernicious habits of privilege sneaking their way into one's behaviors. Reading these statements also does not guarantee that people will interpret each other's actions in the same way. Individuals may disagree about what it means to act with respect, for example.

Out of the desire to be an effective advocate and avoid making mistakes, most white people newly engaging in racial justice ask for something like a "Top 10" list to guide their behavior. There are some general things that can be said. For example, step back and listen, leave your guilt at the door, avoid appeals for affirmation, admit you do not know, stay in the conversation, ensure you are not taking over by talking too much or trying to lead without being asked, accept leadership from people of color, don't be defensive, accept feedback, and interrupt racism and privilege when you see it.

In addition, a comprehensive study that interviewed fifty white activists resulted in a series of suggestions regarding how to build trusting relationships with people of color.[17] These include: be prepared to prove yourself over time in order to earn trust, make a long-term commitment to a place (like a particular organization or town) where you can nurture authentic relationships, accept that you will make mistakes, recognize when you are exercising your privilege, check yourself, but don't be inauthentic and false, question colorblind approaches, be in a constant mode of self-reflection, ensure those most affected by an issue lead the action against it, construct balanced leadership, and develop "right relationships."

These statements are helpful, yet exactly how to live them out remains unclear. A major complication is that no two people are the same, and what it looks like to be accountably following any particular guideline is subjective. Accountability occurs within the context of relationship, as does one's personal growth. Activist, organizer, and educator Raúl Quiñones-Rosado states,

> Growth occurs in and because of relationships, particularly if these relationships are with others who are also engaged in consciousness-in-action, and are with people who can hold each other accountable to the values and principles inherent in liberation, transformation and integral well-being.[18]

The surest pathway appears to be getting to know people well by building trusting relationships, and allowing those relationships to reveal the way forward.

Navigating Dilemmas

What follows are a series of situations that are perplexing even within relationships with agreed upon accountability guidelines. The tension underlying each situation involves how people can use their authentic voice and honor their inner truth while also acting accountably. These situations are important for individuals and groups to discuss so that people are more likely to meet each other's expectations regarding racial justice advocacy, respect each person's full personhood, and engage in more effective efforts.

Tension

People should not be judged based on their skin color.	**AND**	White people need to demonstrate knowledge about racism in order to earn trust from people of color.

Imagine yourself in a multiracial circle of people attending a community dialogue. The facilitator opens the conversation by presenting a set of communication guidelines for the group to agree to as norms and expectations. One of the statements reads: *Assume positive intent.* A woman of color states her past experience will not allow her to offer trust so easily to a group that includes white people.[19]

Difficult feelings may immediately arise for people who have been led to see themselves as inherently trustworthy, innocent, and good until proven otherwise, and it can be a challenge to accept that trust can take a very, very long time to develop. This can result in statements like: "Unless I have failed you personally, I should be experienced as an individual, not lumped in with those who have trespassed upon you in the past." Exploring why there is discomfort when being told one is not immediately trustworthy is important for two reasons. First, this perspective among white people is generally considered a product of social conditioning and privilege. Second, sufficient understanding is necessary so that individuals who do not trust easily are not perceived as flawed.

The statement from the woman of color offers an important opportunity to double check one's ego investment. Part of being an accountable white partner in this context is recognizing and accepting that different life experiences mean that one needs to demonstrate awareness, authenticity, and dedication first (and for an extended period of time) *before* trust is established. Only then is it possible that partners of color who do not offer trust quickly may choose to risk engaging more fully.

Successful trust building across race occurs when people are engaging with one another meaningfully in places where people are living, working, and learning together.[20] A major challenge is that, at the beginning of the process of uncovering privilege, white people are generally unaware of how privilege is infused in one's thoughts, speech, and actions. Arriving at a dialogue with the belief that "I should be accepted because I am a fellow human being" often comes with other patterns that betray privilege. Two examples include when one conflates being *uncomfortable* with being *unsafe* and when one says that "I understand what you (a person of color) experience with racism because I (a woman) have dealt with sexism." White people will generally not be trusted to do no harm until demonstrating an understanding of their privilege and a commitment to keeping it in check. The more time spent crossing racial boundaries, the more that is learned and the more one's authentic voice bears the mark of that learning. The implication of this is that accountability requires humility and self-understanding. Demanding that someone who has been negatively impacted by racism should offer trust at the outset is unrealistic and unfair.

❖ How easily to do you offer trust?

❖ What may allow you to trust someone who says he or she cannot trust you?

Tension

The intention to do no harm is a core, spiritual tenet.	**AND**	The impacts of one's words and actions are more important than the intent.

Accountability involves knowing how words and actions affect others and making choices that avoid replicating historic, dominating, and injurious patterns. From a racial justice perspective, the *impact* of words and actions are essential considerations. Spiritual people, however, frequently believe that one's *intent* should be of primary importance, and how people are impacted is within their own control. This tension leads to questions worth considering. One is whether or not there are situations in which being white means one shouldn't say certain things.

There are circumstances when being a white person means I am not the best messenger for certain ideas or that extra attention to how I will impact the situation is required. Although this idea may be challenging for many to accept, when framed in light of how one's behavior could either support or detract from the goals of racial justice, the benefits become clear.

For example, I believe that the history of race in the U.S. is replete with trauma which affects everyone to some degree, consciously or unconsciously. I have also experienced a sense of liberation when orienting toward my transcendent self. Recognizing that each racial group requires its own healing process to work through the consequences of past and present racism and white supremacy (some call this a "decolonizing" of the mind),[21] conversations with cross-race colleagues have allowed me to imagine what a healing process might involve for other racial groups.

None of this means that these thoughts should be shared everywhere, with everyone, and at any time. There are some situations in which my voice is not helpful. My whiteness makes a difference and affects the *impact* of my words, regardless of my *intention*. Since my racial appearance carries meaning, I may not be the best messenger for certain ideas in certain situations.

A spiritualized racial justice practice allows for the consideration of all aspects of a situation to determine the strategic moments to use one's authentic voice. This need not be felt as a constraint on one's inner truth. For if one believes that upholding spiritual truth means sharing one's perspective all the time, the approach may be fueled by ego more than an attempt to play the most useful role possible. Recognizing when one's ideas are valuable in any given moment requires an evaluation of the context, including one's racial group membership.

A moment early in my work with racial justice education offers a prime example of this dynamic. I had learned a lot from my first year and a half with AWARE-LA, and was beginning to recognize how pervasive white supremacy was within the highly diverse educational system in Los Angeles. At the time, I was a middle school teacher in a community south-west of downtown Los Angeles. The Principal was Black and the Vice Principal was Latino. Both implemented harsh disciplinary policies that I feared set many students on a path toward dropping out of school, joining gangs, and entering the criminal justice system. Having already spent nine years in Los Angeles area public schools, I recognized how both whites and people of color involved in the system were complicit in maintaining institutional racism.

This was at the forefront of my mind while participating in a workshop in which the facilitator explained to a room of educators why it was essential that schools have administrators and teachers of color. Some of the rationale had to do with people of color adding different sensibilities particularly with regards to racial/ethnic considerations as well as the need for students of color to experience people from their backgrounds in leadership positions and as powerful role models. I raised my hand and suggested that simply having people of color in positions of power is not enough. People of color can also buy into and act out white supremacist culture.

My intention was to add a layer of complexity to the analysis. However, the timing and tone of my comment added fuel for those in the room who were already resistant to the facilitator's ideas, revealed my lack of consideration that people of color in leadership positions experience constraints that make it more difficult for them to push up against institutional racism, raised the issue of internalized oppression in a way that was likely to derail the focus of the workshop, and showed myself to be an ineffective advocate by trying to make myself look and feel good while, at the same time, criticizing leaders of color. All these points were true, and I was not conscious of any of them at the time.

The facilitator responded with a comment about the need for white people to stay focused on supporting people of color in leadership positions. I felt shut down and misunderstood. For years, I consoled myself with the belief that the primary issue was one of regional differences. I rationalized that Los Angeles was already diversified and dealing with "next generation" concerns, concerns that arise *after* people of color attain leadership positions and institutional racism remains. It was not until years later that my analysis of that situation shifted and I realized the ways in which my comments were not helpful.

A little bit of knowledge can be very dangerous. My contribution to that workshop did not advance the conversation. It unfortunately reflected a mixture of relative ignorance and ego. What I learned from this situation is that acting as an ally often means sufficiently analyzing a topic before contributing, understanding the objectives of a particular meeting or dialogue to ensure that a contribution is supportive and useful, and reflecting on one's motives for speaking up or taking action.

- ❖ How comfortable are you with the idea that your racial position can make your voice more or less easily heard?

- ❖ How might privilege play a role in your contributions to a conversation?

- ❖ Have you ever experienced a time when you felt your opinion was not accepted, only to find out later that your timing, tone, or accuracy was in error?

Tension

Respect for one's humanity and a belief in fundamental equality involves everyone being held to the same standard.	— **AND** —	Working with groups requiring one-sided accountability can support justice and healing efforts.

The poem that opens this chapter supports the idea that staying grounded and impervious to the "shoulds" of the world helps one stay true to one's inner voice. Many interpret this as having "healthy boundaries." This is at the heart of a struggle spiritual people may face if they engage with a group who expects white people to be unilaterally accountable to people of color.

Those who expect one-sided accountability usually hold that traumatic U.S. history makes this a requirement and any expectation white people place on people of color is inappropriate. For spiritually oriented white people seeking to be part of organizations where this is a guiding principle, some soul searching may be necessary. Those who can view these situations as moments for the ego's outer layers to be shed and as opportunities to delve deeply within for strength may be able to transcend what feels unhealthy and continue to participate.

For example, one AWARE-LA Saturday Dialogue included a white female college student who expressed concern over a situation while volunteering for a multiracial community organization. A group of white volunteers had participated in the organization's meetings only sporadically because emails alerting them to the scheduled meeting times were not sent reliably. The organization had been planning a trip for members and volunteers that required the purchase of air tickets, and the white student volunteers had never confirmed their intentions to go because they had not received the emails with the information. As a result of not hearing from this group, the organization delayed purchasing the tickets. When the women did express their desire to participate, the organization had to spend additional funds due to a rise in the costs. The white volunteer was present for a subsequent meeting called by the leader of the organization to address this issue.

During this interracial conversation, the Latina leader of the organization informed the white volunteers that the organization considered them responsible for the extra expenditure of funds. The woman who told this story described the conversation as "messy" and "confusing." The group of white students left with varying feelings. Some never returned to the organization, feeling upset and unfairly blamed. The student at the Saturday Dialogue was trying to figure out how to repair the damage. She felt she was asked to be obligated to the organization in a way that did not feel fully justified because there was no acknowledgment of the poor communication on the part of the organization.

Participants of the Saturday Dialogue asked the white student to consider the following:

- Do you believe in the work of the organization?

- Did the miscommunication result in the organization having financial constraints that impact their overall work?

- Regardless of blame, is there something you can do to recuperate the organization's funding?

- Can you release your feelings around blame in order to do whatever is necessary to allow for the organization to be financially sound?

As it turned out, despite the lingering sense of unfairness, the white student volunteers were already planning a fund-raiser to cover the additional funds spent.

The important insight gained through this Dialogue was that there are times when the need to be "right," should be set aside for the benefit of a common goal. Being conscious through these moments allows one to stay engaged without holding resentment. It is, ultimately, in each person's power to stay or to walk away. Too many have walked away. Healing results from finding a way to remain engaged and acquire what new insights are available.

- ♣ To what degree are you able to offer understanding to another while feeling personally mistreated?

- ♣ How willing are you to remain within challenging circumstances for the sake of the greater good?

Tension

Any person should feel free to challenge someone mistreating another.	— AND —	Skin color carries historic and contemporary meaning and affects conversations and relationships across race.

Imagine being a white person who is part of a meeting where a multiracial group is gathered to discuss immigrant rights. You are a relatively new member. As the group is preparing to start the meeting, you hear one of the leaders, a Latino, talking casually to other members using negative stereotypes of African Americans. There are no African American members in the group. In addition, he is mildly verbally aggressive during the meeting with some female members. Glancing around the room, no one else appears troubled by this person's behavior. How would you respond?

If racial justice advocacy is part of one's spiritual practice, then all efforts should support a sense of being interconnected and responsive to others' needs. When troubled by a person's behavior toward another, one should be able to approach that person, regardless of that person's racial/ethnic background. A spiritual sensibility may require people's accountability to reflect their full humanity and allegiance to justice for all.

The commitment to accountability raises significant issues for activists and educators. Exploring the following questions may help white people clarify some ambiguities inherent in this critical aspect of their racial justice practice:

- When is it appropriate for a white person to question people of color who use language that disparage other people of color?

- How well do white people need to know people of color before expressing concerns about their dominating behavior?

- If the people of color involved have different experiences of privilege based on their multiple social identities (such as class, gender, education, or sexual orientation), is it appropriate to question how that privilege might be impacting the situation?

- Is it only appropriate to raise questions about a person's exercise of privilege if one is a member of a marginalized group (i.e. a white *woman* challenging a *man* of color about sexist behaviors)?

- Is it only appropriate for someone from one group to challenge another from the same group (i.e. a *white* person challenging another *white* person)?

- Is someone from a privileged group ever the right messenger to suggest how internalized oppression might be playing out for someone in a subjugated group?

These questions are important to discuss within groups that strive to be accountable to one another. Some people have clear answers to these questions. The contexts, however, vary considerably — and for many the phrase, "It depends on...." would begin almost every response.

A great realization came during a conversation I had with one of my fellow AWARE-LA members and two of our colleagues of color while preparing to give a presentation together.[22] The colleagues of color were two seasoned activists, an African American woman and an East Asian man. I had previously interviewed each of them regarding their views on accountability as part of our efforts to create an organizational accountability structure.

The meeting to prepare for this presentation occurred a year after conducting the interviews. Our organization had collectively concluded that we should develop relationships of mutual accountability, where everyone was expected to develop non-violent communication skills and do self-reflective, consciousness-raising work. As we sat together to finalize our PowerPoint presentation, the two colleagues of color noted that our slide on what white people could expect from people of color was blank, and they asked us what we wanted it to say.

My white colleague and I looked at each other. We were speechless. Eventually we answered that, as white people, we did not think we were allowed to ask for what we needed from people of color. We thought they were the ones who would say what they were willing to offer. The AWARE-LA leadership had talked at great length about our needs, so we knew what we wished would be on that slide, but neither my colleague nor I expected to make the request. We were grateful for our collaborator's capacity to hold us as full human beings, but we thought our positions as white people meant we should not expect any particular kind of support or care.

We were asked once again to say what we needed. We looked at each other a second time and finally said we wanted to be recognized as human beings who, although bound to make mistakes, could be held as people worth their investment of time and trust. With the recognition that it was our job to participate in ways that would develop that investment in time and trust, we wanted some agreement that any particular mistake, once rectified, would not result in us being given up on and cast out. We also wanted to be free to express concerns and know that all of us, including people of color, were expected to communicate non-violently and do the self-reflective work necessary for healing.

Our colleagues of color accepted our expectations and we included them on our slide. Given what we had heard from many other white activists, this felt radical. To follow our colleagues' direction, we

had to hold in balance two ideas: we are positioned differently because past and present racism has resulted in our unequal access to
power and addressing this inequity requires white people and people
of color to come together in ways that are mutually accountable in
order to build a foundation of equality.

According to Raúl Quiñones-Rosado's framework for using consciousness-in-action for liberation and transformation:

> The demanding work of integral change requires a heart-felt
> sense of connection, of relationship based on reciprocity, soli-
> darity, and camaraderie, and motivated by friendship, respect,
> love, and/or the realization of oneness. It is the context of re-
> lationship that accountability among community members and
> commitments to struggle can be sustained.[23]

✤ In what ways have you been held accountable in relationships?

✤ How have you held others accountable?

✤ How does historical inequity complicate white people and
people of color coming together as mutually accountable?

Tension

One must trust oneself and not relinquish control over one's life's path to another.	**AND**	People of color offer essential insights to white people invested in racial justice.

Vance Aniebo, an African American man, was my first mentor
regarding race. He pushed me to see my racial position as a white person as meaningful. Years later, I met a Latino who engaged me in extended conversations about my work on what it meant to be white. I
recognized this man as one who could contribute significantly to my

next phase of development. During one conversation, he mentioned that all white people needed a mentor of color to support them in knowing what their next step should be in developing their racial justice practice. Somewhat facetiously, I asked him, "Who has the approved list of mentors for white people?" I explained that, over the years, I had perceived what felt like a contradiction within racial justice circles. What I had heard regularly from both white people and people of color was that white people could never fully trust themselves with regards to race, but I was also advised by many colleagues of color to remain a critical thinker when following people of color's leadership.

I asked this new friend and potential mentor to clarify a fundamental question: Who makes the final decision regarding what a white person is supposed to do in any given circumstance? I was troubled by two primary questions:

- What if two people of color who figured prominently in one's life held different perspectives and offered conflicting advice? Having heard people of color speak critically of other people of color who were less attentive to social justice issues, it became clear that simply being a person of color did not make one a qualified mentor. A valuable mentor needs to have analyzed racism and have sufficient experience in combating it. How is a white person supposed to judge that? Can a white person ever judge that?

- How can white activists decide which of two mentors of color to listen to, assuming both *are* highly conscious of race issues? How can they discern whether their choices are a reflection of their ego or that which their soul, and the movement for social justice, needs for growth?

This new friend was not inclined to trust white people's insight about race. His concern is common and understandable. Being new to racial justice work, I did not fully trust myself. I was facing an existential conundrum. On one hand, it was not possible for me to relinquish control over my life's path to another. I had to trust myself. On the other hand, evaluating a statement or suggestion from a person of color felt like a slippery slope ending with a lack of accountability if relying solely on my inner voice for guidance.

Trust in one's inner guide to navigate this dilemma takes time to develop. This means staying as open as possible to all input, seeking out as much support as needed to clarify understandings, and only then making the best choice possible. Everyone, regardless of background, must ultimately follow their deepest core, even when this means evaluating advice from people of color.

❖ How do you make decisions when you feel pulled in two different directions?

❖ How do you know that you are making the best decision as opposed to the easiest one?

❖ Are there people who help you stay accountable for your decisions?

Tension

A lack of personal well-being and balance is unsustainable.	***AND***	Personal capacity limits should not be used as an excuse to avoid discomfort.

The underlying premise in Raúl Quiñones-Rosado's work is that each *individual's* well-being affects *society's* well-being, and vice versa. He writes:

> …the greater the level of well-being of individuals within a society, then: (1) the greater the level of well-being of the collective in the present; (2) the greater the potential for future development of the collective; and (3) the greater the ability of the collective to be self-determining on an on-going basis.[24]

This view is held by many spiritual people of all races within racial justice circles.

Personal well-being is essential. If our mental, physical, emotional, social, and spiritual aspects are not in balance and we are not living in harmony with ourselves, then whatever we attempt will be less effective and/or unsustainable.[25] Even with an expanded consciousness, imbalance compromises the *will* and the ability to mobilize our various functions (mental, physical, emotional, social, and spiritual).[26] Focusing too much on any one particular area of life — even activism — leads to the neglect of other aspects of life and can negatively impact the effectiveness of our racial justice work.

Writing about their experience facilitating their Challenging White Supremacy workshop, a group of veteran social justice organizers recognized that today's activists approach things differently than those of past decades. These veteran organizers describe the various questions they faced while trying to figure out how their curriculum and approach could respond to the needs of today. One of their considerations includes the recognition that:

> "Back in the Day," white activists and activists of color believed that the revolution was around the corner so our pace of activity was frantic. Many of us felt we weren't serious revolutionaries if we worried about "taking care of ourselves." Today, many white activists prioritize taking care of themselves as revolutionary work, a way to stay in for the long haul. They prioritize having a more balanced life, with time for friends and relaxation, as well as paid work and political activities. How do we develop a rigorous, tough curriculum which also respects the desire for a balanced life?[27]

This need for a balanced life accurately reflects the perspective of most people I know who are invested in social justice work. However, the veteran organizers' concern about the need for a challenging curriculum is also important. It ensures that a focus on creating a balanced life does not result in people feeling self-satisfied with offering minimal or no effort to social justice action. The challenge lies with how one honestly determines capacity in a way that does not, inadvertently, allow one to avoid hard work.

A parallel to this particular challenge may be found in social activist Robert Jensen's analysis of environmental issues. He is deeply despondent over our planet's current health status, which he believes if left unabated will result in the eventual demise of humanity. He notes the following about participation in environmental change efforts:

> We do not live under conditions of our own individual making, and if we want to participate in the culture in a way that allows us to be politically effective, then we will never be able to claim a position of purity. The question we should ask is not, "Have you met <u>the</u> standard?" set down by some arbitrary authority, but instead, "Are you willing to confront the problem and make a good-faith attempt to move in the right direction?"[28]

This statement from a dedicated activist acknowledges that there will always be ways that we are complicit with our collective problems, and each individual ultimately determines what it means to be *at capacity*. There will always be more that can and should be done. At some point, we may become saturated and exhausted. The inner voice is the only source that can confirm when we have done enough on any given day.

This is true up to the point where we find that listening to our inner voice results in a failure to satisfy obligations made to our partners in justice efforts. If this occurs, it is an indication that there is a need to become more conscious of our capacity before agreeing to future tasks.

* Given all that you already do in the world, where is there room to do something that supports racial justice?

* What is one additional thing you can commit to that would still allow you to maintain balance?

* What concerns does this discussion of capacity raise for you?

Tension

It is unethical and spiritually problematic for people — particularly whites — to benefit financially from the existence of racism.	**AND**	People who are skilled in racial justice work should receive adequate financial compensation.

A final tension involves the issue of people earning money from racial justice work. This is a critical component of any thorough discussion about accountability. Two key topics frequently arise in the conversation: Does earning money from racial justice efforts prompt an unconscious desire for racism to continue to exist? In what ways can people accountably handle funds generated from their advocacy efforts?

The first issue relates to a spiritual concern regarding benefiting from something that one is actively working to end. Some people believe that workshop leaders who benefit economically from anti-racism efforts energetically, albeit unconsciously, do not truly want racism to end. However, given that racism is so entrenched in our individual and collective psyches and our institutions, most advocates I have encountered understand that it will take generations of effort by many more people to experience an equitable society. There is, therefore, no need for concern around ending racism too rapidly and ending a source of economic support. All people who develop essential skills related to activism and educating for racial justice should use those skills as much as possible. Since we all need money to take care of our basic needs, some financial compensation is not only appropriate, but essential, and does not detract from the overall effort.

The second issue relates to the questions of what is fair compensation and what does one do with the earnings? There is a wide monetary range in what people earn from advocacy activities. Some people's entire income derives from this work, while for others it supplements unrelated employment. What if the money is used to support and perpetuate unjust systems, like sending a child to an elite private school or purchasing a home in a gated community? Does it make a difference if an activist's racial justice work has resulted in repeated death threats that prompt the move into a more secure environment? How is the complexity of any individual situation to be understood and measured?

A related question revolves around who benefits from racial justice work. Do white people get hired to teach about race more readily than people of color, with white privilege continuing to replicate itself? Often enough, the answer is yes. Do educators who do consciousness-raising work make more money than activists who concentrate on community organizing? Again, often enough, the answer is yes. What does it mean to be accountable in this context?

Some white advocates believe they should always partner with a person of color, thereby sharing resources. Some call for those who earn money from advocacy efforts to donate 25% of all earnings to community organizations which work on political action campaigns. This is a systemic approach. Others choose to share their funds individually and privately, for example, by subsidizing housing or tuition for people of color in need, contributing to specific non-profits doing work to address the consequences of generations of racism and white supremacy, or ensuring an equal balance of pro bono, volunteer work. The individual approach seeks to address the harm experienced by people of color due to racism, but it does not challenge the systems that perpetuate it.

Everyone faces the question of how to give freely within a culture that values hoarding. It may be a deeply personal struggle, but being open to conversations wherein varying approaches are discussed is one way to receive the kind of critical feedback necessary to stay accountable.

❖ What concerns do you have about people making money from racial justice efforts?

❖ How would you suggest people handle these issues?

———————————

Overall, the tensions explored deal with significant questions many face. Key to facing them is the recognition that feeling uncomfortable, questioned, and challenged is not detrimental. On the contrary, being uncomfortable, questioned, or challenged is often what leads to significant spiritual growth. Those who challenge one another on the dilemmas described above often express care through their willingness to stay engaged, even if it is exhausting. Through their commitment to accountability, they respond to the needs of their colleagues for the sake of a common vision of racial justice.

The Search for Balance

Becoming active in racial justice efforts is a major step for most white people. Often, the first steps are small. It is particularly difficult to be watched, evaluated, and expected to quickly gain a measure of competency far beyond one's current capacities. Staying engaged, especially when it challenges one's spiritual sensibilities, is exceedingly hard. Three connecting ideas described below support growth, expanded perspective, and authentic relationships across difference.

The first strategy is to distinguish the higher Self from the ego. Cultivating the ability to notice and hear one's inner voice is not easy. There are many situations, some more obvious than others, where the ego wraps itself in rationalizations that one wants to believe come from the higher Self. The question is how to know the difference. In attempting to find a way, I asked Orland Bishop how he knows when he is responding to his higher Self and not ego. He said he knows it because of the way he reflects on his motivations. If his words and actions are about caring for others, a kind of future arises out of those interactions that is in service of more than him alone. Instead of seeing himself as simply creating his own world, he sees the process as all of us co-creating our collective world together. Therefore, he does not make decisions only with himself in mind. His decision-making is, in fact, primarily informed by the needs of those around him. The effect his actions have on others provides the validation of his approach.

Most people are a long way from primarily acting out of concern for others, even if there is an underlying hope that it is a driving motivation. Taking the time to actively question ego investment and deciding to take steps to challenge what is normally considered one's "authentic voice" is the only way to get closer to this goal. Some questions that can help discern if a principle or action is inspired more by ego than the higher Self are: Are you the only one benefitting from your action? Whose needs are not being met? What response on your part will do the least harm to people you encounter?

A second strategy is to engage in reconciliation efforts. It is hard to stay in situations where one does not feel comfortable, worthy, and validated even when actively working on shrinking the ego for the sake of something greater.[29] Inspiration can come from reconciliation processes wherein people are forgiving the unforgivable.[30] They are a way to check perspective and recognize how minor one's concerns may be in comparison to what many others are facing. The challenges experienced by white people navigating the tensions discussed in this chapter are lightweight in comparison to the gravity of abuses ad- dressed in reconciliation efforts occurring throughout the world. These global efforts offer great insights.

One such insight calls for transparent vulnerability.[31] This in- volves being authentically interested in finding out how one might be responsible for causing pain, contributing to animosity, and sustaining disconnection from others. As explained by Watkins and Shulman, this requires conveying personal questions, anxieties, and hopes while also cultivating deep listening skills that help strengthen relationships and emotional sharing.[32] Mary Watkins and Helene Shulman hope that, someday in the future, these skills will be sufficiently honed so that those of us in this country will be able to approach accountabil- ity in a way that promotes healing. They write: "To honor together the divinity in…people would help the healing for which we thirst."[33] As more people stay engaged and resist the desire to flee from dis- comfort, society moves one step closer to this possibility.

A third and final strategy involves increasing the ability to re- spond to situations instead of simply reacting. Raúl Quiñones- Rosado sheds light on how to move from a state of *reacting* (unconscious and out of our control) to a state of *responding* (con- scious and self-determined).[34] To control internal, emotional reac- tions in order to develop *response-ability* is considered resistance to a culture of imposition and the dynamics of oppression. This *ability* to *respond* helps one to select ways of interacting that reinforce and sup- port balance and harmony.[35] Although it might not be possible to stop from having particular feelings, one can acquire the ability to "transcend — to embrace yet move beyond — [one's] reactions."[36]

How does one do this in the midst of a challenging situation? Par- ticularly useful is Quiñones-Rosado's analysis of ways to shift *perceptual positions*. Each level in the shift offers an expanded ability to respond.[37] According to Quiñones-Rosado, the first position is the personal "I" perspective that people normally use. The second is imagining how the "other" person perceives the situation. When *reacting* one may only be able to project one's own ideas onto the other person. The ability to get to the second perceptual position already requires an ability to *respond*. The third position calls for perception as from an outside, detached observer. A question that helps one arrive to this place is, "What would my mentor say?" The fourth position is a system-wide perspective — the point of view taken by the organization or community to which one is accountable. From this position, historic patterns influence perception. The fifth position expands to include large-scale considerations of societal development, evolution of humanity as a whole, and/or the influence of spiritual beings. A question that characterizes this position is, "How will this be viewed 10, 50, or 100 years from now?"

Using this perceptual position analysis as a frame of reference when trying to navigate questions of accountability may be useful. For example, the white student volunteers at the Saturday Dialogue who felt conflicted about the request to raise funds for their community organization were asked questions that invited them to consider a position four perspective. A level of clarity emerged when the white students were able to assess their own position, imagine the viewpoint of the other, recognize that there were other possible interpretations, and then consider what the organization needed from them without letting their egos impede their responses. Ego needs and uncomfortable feelings were able to be held in perspective.[38]

♣ How do you distinguish between *reacting* and *responding?*

♣ What support do you have in helping you increase the ability to *respond* instead of *react?*

♣ How can the framework offered of shifting perceptual positions support your ability to stay present within uncomfortable dialogues?

———————

Coming together to bridge racial differences and construct a just society which embraces the full scope of our common human family is still a long way off. Accountability within communities makes it possible to stay connected, explicit about goals, and clear about how each person wants to interact with one another.

Reflecting on her experience within the Quaker community, Gillian Burlingham uses the metaphor of a lever to describe how leverage is an important part of organizing work. She writes:

> As Archimedes said, 'Give me a place to stand and with a lever I will move the whole world.' Leverage is the potential to make change; the lever is the tool used to instigate change; a leverage point is a connecting point, a soft spot, a sweet spot, at which the lever can be inserted to exert pressure for a movement.[39]

It is necessary to be centered and stand firm on solid ground in order to engage leverage for change. It is also important to be sure that one is not standing upon unconscious assumptions and habits born of privilege. When challenged about internalized superiority or racism, it is important to stay engaged and responsive, allowing one's soul to expand. The result is a nimble and flexible balancing upon a sturdy foundation of justice.

Chapter Notes

Introduction

1. john a. powell, "Does Living a Spiritually Engaged Life Mandate Us to Be Actively Engaged in Issues of Social Justice?" *University of St. Thomas Law Review* 1, no. 1 (2003): 30–38.
2. Shelly Tochluk, *Witnessing Whiteness: The Need to Talk About Race and How to Do It* (Lanham, MD: Rowman & Littlefield-Education, 2010).
3. See the Living in the Tension page at ShellyTochluk.com.
4. Carol Lee Flinders, *At the Root of this Longing: Reconciling a Spiritual Hunger and a Feminist Thirst* (San Francisco: Harper Collins, 1998).
5. Flinders, *At the Root of this Longing,* 135.
6. Leela Fernandes, *Transforming Feminist Practice: Non-Violence, Social Justice and the Possibilities of a Spiritualized Feminism* (San Francisco: Aunt Lute Books, 2003), 11.
7. Fernandes, *Transforming Feminist Practice,* 12.
8. Fernandes, *Transforming Feminist Practice,* 17; AnaLouise Keating, "'I'm a Citizen'," 53–69 also offers important insights. She writes, "Anzaldúa's theory of spiritual activism is designed to meet twenty-first-century needs; it offers valuable lessons for feminists and other social justice activists. Her politics of spirit demonstrates that holistic, spirit-inflected perspectives — when applied to racism, sexism, homophobia, and other contemporary issues — can sustain and assist us as we work to transform social injustice" (p. 56). Further, "spiritual activism begins within the individual but moves outward as these individuals (or what Anzaldúa calls 'spiritual activists') expose, challenge, and work to transform unjust social structures" (p. 57). She also states that, "For Anzaldúa and other spiritual activists, self-change and social transformation are mutually interdependent" (p. 59).

9. Fernandes, *Transforming Feminist Practice,* 13.

10. Raúl Quiñones-Rosado, *Consciousness-in-Action: Toward an Integral Psychology of Liberation and Transformation* (Caguas, Puerto Rico: ile Publications, 2007).

11. Quiñones-Rosado, *Consciousness-in-Action,* 148.

12. Quiñones-Rosado, *Consciousness-in-Action,* xviii.

13. Quiñones-Rosado, *Consciousness-in-Action,* xix.

14. Paulo Freire, *Pedagogy of the Oppressed* (New York: Continuum, 1970).

15. Quiñones-Rosado, *Consciousness-in-Action,* 100.

16. Barry Johnson, *Polarity Management: Identifying and Managing Unsolvable Problems* (Middleville, MI: Polarity Management Associates, 1996), 24.

17. Johnson, *Polarity Management,* 44.

18. Johnson, *Polarity Management,* 45.

19. Johnson, *Polarity Management,* 65.

20. Corinne McLaughlin and Gordon Davidson, *Spiritual Politics: Changing the World from the Inside Out* (New York: Ballantine Books, 1994), 153.

21. McLaughlin and Davidson, *Spiritual Politics,* 88; Also see AnaLouise Keating, "'I'm a Citizen of the Universe': Gloria Anzaldúa's Spiritual Activism as Catalyst for Social Change," *Feminist Studies* 34, nos. 1/2 (2008): 53–69 for a discussion of how this is described in spiritual activism.

22. McLaughlin and Davidson, *Spiritual Politics,* 88–89.

23. Zeus Leonardo, "The Souls of White Folk: Critical Pedagogy, Whiteness Studies, and Globalization Discourse," *Race, Ethnicity, and Education* 5, no. 1 (2002): 29–50. This article references the idea that there is a "third space" needed wherein neo-liberal whites who struggle against whiteness are considered neither ally nor enemy, a space in which white people can do the continuing work of liberating themselves from whiteness.

24. Quiñones-Rosado, *Consciousness-in-Action,* 126.

25. McLaughlin and Davidson, *Spiritual Politics,* 14.

26. Fernandes, *Transforming Feminist Practice,* 10.

27. Depth psychology focuses on the relationship between the conscious and the unconscious. Carl G. Jung is the depth psychologist that most influences the material in this book. Essential understandings include the ideas that 1) the layers of the unconscious have their own autonomous power, 2) that which is unconscious becomes Shadow material that emerges in symbolic ways through-

out a person's life, and 3) becoming a true individual in the world requires one to see through the collective consciousness (the taken-for-granted values and expectations of one's culture or group). Liberation psychology, founded by Ignacio Martín-Baró, focuses on supporting oppressed people to understand the socio-political structures that affect them. As opposed to the individual approach taken by traditional forms of psychology, liberation psychology holds that becoming conscious of the social structures underlying one's life circumstances generates a more accurate self-concept and an ability to resist dehumanizing messages such that action for justice is possible.

28. I appreciate the care john a. powell takes to note that a definition of social justice is not easily agreed upon. When I use the term social justice advocacy, I am referring to any effort taken to equalize the playing field by ending discriminatory policies, actions, attitudes, or speech. I say this understanding that actions always take place within a local context, in a particular time, within a specific community. Therefore, broad statements generally lack the ability to capture what the reality of a socially just outcome would look like. That said, a statement written by Vernon Wall titled, "10 Myths of Social Justice" provides another understanding of this term. Although the definition provided focuses on social justice education, it also frames my thinking. Wall refers to Bell, Adams, and Griffin who define social justice as a process and a goal as they write, "The goal of social justice education is full and equal participation of all groups in a society that is mutually shaped to meet their needs. Social justice includes a vision of society that is equitable and all members are physically and psychologically safe and secure." Social justice is the broad goal. When speaking about racial justice particularly, I appreciate Race Forward's definition, which is "the systematic fair treatment of people of all races, resulting in equitable opportunities and outcomes for all." References: john a. powell, "Does Living a Spiritually Engaged Life," 30–38; Vernon Wall, "10 Myths of Social Justice," accessed August 22, 2015 uncw.edu/sustain ability/documents/10MythsSocialJustice.doc; Maurianne Adams, Lee Anne Bell, and Pat Griffin, *Teaching for Diversity and Social Justice* (New York: Routledge, 2007) 1; "Race Forward," accessed August 22, 2015, https://www.raceforward.org/about.

29. Kimberlé W. Crenshaw, "Mapping the Margins: Intersectionality, Identity Politics, and Violence against Women of Color," *Stanford Law Review* 43, no. 6 (1991): 1241–99.

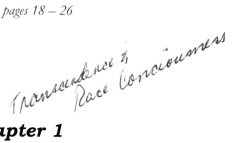

Chapter 1

1. "Lead Facilitator," *The Indaba,* accessed August 16, 2015, http://www.theindaba.com/leadfacilitator.html.

2. "Lead Facilitator," *The Indaba,* accessed August 16, 2015 http://www.theindaba.com/leadfacilitator.html.

3. Orland Bishop describes a "seeing" that is deeper than the sense of vision. From this standpoint the eyes are metaphoric, not literal, and the blind can see just as well as anyone.

4. "Sawubona," *Global Oneness Project,* accessed August 15, 2015, http://www.globalonenessproject.org/library/interviews/sawubona.

5. William Cohen and Janet Langhart Cohen, *Race and Reconciliation in America* (Lanham, MD: Lexington Books, 2009).

6. Ruth Frankenberg, *White Women, Race Matters: The Social Construction of Whiteness* (Minneapolis: University of Minnesota Press, 1993).

7. Eckhart Tolle, *A New Earth: Awakening to Your Life's Purpose* (New York: Penguin Group, 2005).

8. Tolle, *A New Earth,* 57.

9. Tolle, *A New Earth,* 58.

10. Tolle, *A New Earth,* 65.

11. Tolle, *A New Earth,* 87.

12. Tolle, *A New Earth,* 173.

13. James Cone, in *A Black Theology of Liberation* (Maryknoll, NY: Orbis Books, 1986), 51 is clear that there is no room for white people to judge Black people. Using the language of sin, he writes, "Black theology rejects categorically white comments about the sins of blacks, suggesting that we are partly responsible for our plight…Only blacks can speak about sin in a black perspective and apply it to black and white persons. The white vision of reality is too distorted and renders whites incapable of talking to the oppressed about their shortcomings."

14. Tolle, *A New Earth,* 102.

15. This is a very serious problem, as it harkens back to times when Christianity suggested to Blacks that heaven awaited those who endured their suffering as a tool of suppression. Cone, in *A Black Theology of Liberation,* writes of, "the tendency of classic Christianity to appeal to divine providence." He states, " To suggest that black suffering is con-

sistent with the knowledge and will of God and that in the end everything will happen for the good of those who love God is unacceptable to blacks. The eschatological promise of a distant, future heaven is insufficient to account for the earthly pain of black suffering... Black theology also rejects those who counsel blacks to accept the limits which this society places on them, for this is tantamount to suicide": 16–17

16. Dick Anthony, Bruce Ecker, and Ken Wilber, *Spiritual Choices: The Problems of Recognizing Authentic Paths to Inner Transformation* (New York: Paragon House, 1987), 50.

17. Tolle, *A New Earth,* 159.

18. An important caveat to note within this discussion is that the ego is an essential part of our psyche. If we reduced our ego to nothing, we would have no impetus to stand and open a door. The ego itself is not necessarily bad, although so much spiritual literature focuses on its reduction that many in the U.S. are led to believe so.

19. According to Derald Wing, Christina Capodilupo, Gina Torino, Jennifer Bucceri, Aisha Holder, Kevin Nadal, and Marta Esquilin. "Racial Microaggressions in Everyday Life: Implications for Clinical Practice." *American Psychologist* 62, no. 4 (2007): 271–86, microaggressions are, "brief and commonplace daily verbal, behavioral, or environmental indignities, whether intentional or unintentional, that communicate hostile, derogatory, or negative racial slights and insults toward people of color."

20. Tolle, *A New Earth,* 160.

21. Tolle, *A New Earth,* 100.

22. George Yancy, *Look, a White!: Philosophical Essays on Whiteness* (Philadelphia: Temple University Press, 2012), 167.

23. Yancy, *Look, a White!,* 168.

24. McIntosh, Peggy, Unpacking the Invisible Knapsack, " excerpted from Peggy McIntosh, "White Privilege and Male Privilege: A Personal Account of Coming to see Correspondences through Work in Women's Studies," (Working Paper 189, Wellesley, MA: Wellesley College Center for Research on Women, 1988).

25. "White Privilege Conference Recommended Resource List," http://www.whiteprivilegeconference.com/resources/WPC-Resource-List-July2012.pdf

26. The comparison to a right-handed person not recognizing that the world is made for them is particularly apt. It was not until completing college and beginning to study issues of racial justice that I was alerted to how college classrooms generally had only a few "left-

handed desks" (which felt wrong when I accidentally sat in them when a room was full. I never even took note as to why the desk was created as it was. And it was not until I was a substitute teaching in a kindergarten class that I learned that there were left-handed scissors when a child came up to me complaining of difficulty. Only by trying to use the scissors myself did I learn that items privileging right handed people simply do not work for left handed people. My ability to be ignorant to this simple fact for so long is a privilege right handers experience.

27. Yancy, *Look, a White!*, 166.

28. Some authors to note include Thandeka, bell hooks, and Michelle Alexander. Collectively, they describe the psychological, social, and systemic impacts of racism and white privilege.

29. Yancy, *Look, a White!*, 161.

30. Yancy, *Look, a White!*, 166.

31. See the National Bureau of Economic Research for a pair of postings related to a study of labor market discrimination detailing differential callback rates for applications where the only difference was an applicant's fictitious name. These include: "Are Emily and Greg More Employable than Lakisha and Jamal? A Field Experiment on Labor Market Discrimination," by Marianne Bertrand and Sendhil Mullainathan, and "Employers' Replies to Racial Names," by David Francis. The articles discuss evidence suggesting that having a stereotypically African-American name results in fewer callbacks. The two articles can be found at: http://www.nber.org/papers/w9873 and http://www.nber.org/digest/sep03/w9873.html, accessed August 16, 2015. Also see *The Geography of Opportunity: Race and Housing Choice in Metropolitan America,* edited by Xavier N. De Souza Briggs (James A. Johnson Metro Series, Brookings Institution Press, 2005) and Benjamin Howell, "Exploiting Race and Space: Concentrated Subprime Lending as Housing Discrimination," *California Law Review* 94, no. 1 (2006): 101–47, for information about housing discrimination.

32. Yancy, *Look, a White!*, 164.

33. Mary Watkins and Helene Shulman. Toward Psychologies of Liberation (New York: Palgrave Macmillan, 2008), 56.

34. "Steven Aizenstat," accessed August 16, 2015, http://www.dreamtending.com/about.html.

35. Mark Warren, *Fire in the Heart: How White Activists Embrace Racial Justice* (New York: Oxford University Press, 2010), 117–18.

36. Jacob Needleman, *The American Soul: Rediscovering the Wisdom of the Founders* (New York: Putnam, 2003).

37. Needleman, *The American Soul,* 25.

38. This transcript of an interview of Oren Lyons by Bill Moyers titled, "The Faithkeeper, Interview with Bill Moyers, 3 July 1991 Public Affairs Television" includes Oren Lyons discussing the influence of Native forms of governance on Benjamin Franklin's thinking. Subsequent notes validate statements made by Oren Lyons. "By his own account, Franklin said: "It would be a strange thing . . . if Six Nations of Ignorant savages should be capable of forming such an union and be able to execute it in such a manner that it has subsisted for ages and appears indissoluble, and yet that a like union should be impractical for ten or a dozen English colonies, to whom it is more necessary and must be more advantageous, and who cannot be supposed to want an equal understanding of their interest." The quote is cited as coming from Albert H. Smyth, editor, *The Writings of Benjamin Franklin.* New York: Macmillan, 1905–1907, III, p. 42. Accessed August 15, 2015 at: http://www.ratical.org/many_worlds/6Nations/OL070391.html. Readers are also encouraged to refer to *Exemplar of Liberty, Native America and the Evolution of Democracy,* by Donald A. Grinde, Jr. and Bruce E. Johansen (Los Angeles: UCLA American Indian Studies Center, 1991) 96–98 and *Forgotten Founders, Benjamin Franklin, the Iroquois and the Rationale for the American Revolution,* by Bruce E. Johansen, (Ipswich, Mass: Gambit Inc., 1982), 65–66 for more information.

39. Needleman, *The American Soul,* 235.

40. Marjorie Bowens-Wheatley and Nancy Palmer Jones, eds. *Soul Work: Anti-racist Theologies in Dialogue* (Boston: Skinner House, 2003), 96.

41. Needleman, *The American Soul,* 343.

42. Watkins and Shulman, *Toward Psychologies of Liberation,* 177.

43. In a somewhat related way, when AnaLouise Keating writes about the problems inherent to either/or thinking found within identity politics she addresses the issue of how it leads to attitudes and speech that do not serve social justice movements. She says, "When we structure our teaching, our politics, or, more generally, our lives according to this dualistic sameness/difference framework, we assume that there is only one right way to think, act, theorize, or self-define. These oppositional energies become poisonous when we direct them toward each other, as we too often do. In such instances, we engage in what Timothy Powell describes as 'corrosive exchanges' and embark on '[a] downward spiral of ever more hostile counteraccusations.'" Keating, AnaLouise, "'I'm a Citizen of the Universe': Gloria Anzaldúa's Spiritual Activism as Catalyst for Social Change," *Feminist Studies* 34, nos. 1/2 (2008): 53–69.

44. Corinne McLaughlin and Gordon Davidson, *Spiritual Politics: Changing the World from the Inside Out* (New York: Ballantine Books, 1994), 204.

45. Michael Meade, *Fate and Destiny: The Two Agreements of the Soul* (Seattle: Greenfire Press, 2012), 118–20.

46. Meade, *Fate and Destiny,* 172.

47. Yancy, *Look, a White!,* 158.

48. Tolle, *A New Earth,* 275.

49. Tolle, *A New Earth,* 294.

50. Tolle, *A New Earth,* 294.

51. Watkins and Shulman, *Toward Psychologies of Liberation,* 37.

52. Watkins and Shulman, *Toward Psychologies of Liberation,* 37.

53. Watkins and Shulman, *Toward Psychologies of Liberation,* 38.

54. Watkins and Shulman, *Toward Psychologies of Liberation,* 165.

55. "AWARE-LA," Accessed August 16, 2015, http://awarela.wordpress.com/models/.

56. Warren, *Fire in the Heart,* 87.

57. Watkins and Shulman, *Toward Psychologies of Liberation,* 47.

58. William Cohen and Janet Langhart Cohen, *Race and Reconciliation in America.* (Lanham, MD: Lexington Books, 2009), 158–59.

Chapter 2

Self-Acceptance & Self-Improvement [handwritten annotation]

1. Kathy Obear, "Facilitating Workshops with Whites to Dismantle Racism." Unpublished handouts (2013), 18.

2. Corinne McLaughlin and Gordon Davidson, *Spiritual Politics: Changing the World from the Inside Out,* (New York, NY: Ballantine Books, 1994), 116.

3. William Cohen and Janet Langhart, *Race and Reconciliation in America* (Lanham, MD: Lexington Books, 2009), 21.

4. Brené Brown, *I Thought It Was Just Me (But It Isn't): Making the Journey from "What will people think" to "I am enough,"* (New York, NY: Gotham Books, 2007), 74.

5. George Yancy, *Look, a White!: Philosophical Essays on Whiteness* (Philadelphia: Temple University Press, 2012), 156.

6. Brown, *I Thought It Was Just Me,* 74.

7. Eckhart Tolle, *A New Earth: Awakening to Your Life's Purpose* (New York, NY: Penguin Group, 2005), 121.

8. Abraham Maslow, "A theory of human motivation," *Psychological Review* 50, no. 4 (1943): 370–96. Retrieved from http://psychclassics.yorku.ca/Maslow/motivation.html.

9. Yancy, *Look, a White!,* 163.

10. Yancy, *Look, a White!*, 174.
11. Yancy, *Look, a White!*, 167.
12. Brown's research indicates that "there are tremendous differences when it comes to the social-community expectations that drive shame and the messages that reinforce those expectations. For men, the expectations and messages center around masculinity and what it means to 'be a man.' In other words — the 'how we experience shame' might be the same, but the 'why we experience shame' is very different." Further, "While women have the impossible task of balancing, negotiating and traversing expectations that are unattainable and often conflicting, men are suffocating under the tremendous pressure of always appearing 'strong, fearless and powerful', which is equally unattainable." Brown, *I Thought It Was Just Me*, 279–80.
13. Brown, *I Thought It Was Just Me*, xvii.
14. Brown, *I Thought It Was Just Me*, xxv.
15. Brown, *I Thought It Was Just Me*, xxvii.
16. Brown, *I Thought It Was Just Me*, 13.
17. Brown, *I Thought It Was Just Me*, 58–59.
18. Brown, *I Thought It Was Just Me*, 59.
19. Mary Watkins and Helene Shulman, Toward Psychologies of Liberation (New York: Palgrave Macmillan, 2008), 125.
20. Watkins and Shulman, *Toward Psychologies of Liberation*, 52.
21. Watkins and Shulman, *Toward Psychologies of Liberation*, 65
22. Watkins and Shulman, *Toward Psychologies of Liberation*, 66–74. The 12 bystander symptoms are described as the "psychic wounds" and they include: (1) the severing of the self, (2) preoccupation with personal survival and success, (3) comparative neurosis, (4) loneliness, (5) narcissism, (6) the degrading of others, (7) fear of oneself, of the abject, (8) the empty self, (9) the replacement of being with having, (10) greed and false feelings of entitlement, (11) psychic numbing, and (12) the obsessive-compulsive rehearsal of violence.
23. Watkins and Shulman, *Toward Psychologies of Liberation*, 66.
24. Watkins and Shulman, *Toward Psychologies of Liberation*, 70.
25. Watkins and Shulman, *Toward Psychologies of Liberation*, 70.
26. Watkins and Shulman, *Toward Psychologies of Liberation*, 71.
27. Watkins and Shulman, *Toward Psychologies of Liberation*, 73.
28. Watkins and Shulman, *Toward Psychologies of Liberation*, 73.
29. Watkins and Shulman, *Toward Psychologies of Liberation*, 74.
30. Cohen and Langhart, *Race and Reconciliation*, 163.
31. Dr. Brown's research focused on women's experiences. Although, I offer no assurance that men will necessarily relate to what is offered

here, I invite men to use this discussion to explore their own relationship to the issues presented.

32. Brené Brown, *The Gifts of Imperfection: Let Go of Who You Think You're Supposed to Be and Embrace Who You Are* (Center City, MN: Hazeldon, 2010), 46.

33. Mark Warren, *Fire in the Heart: How White Activists Embrace Racial Justice* (New York: Oxford University Press, 2010), 117–18.

34. Brown, *Gifts of Imperfection,* 46.

35. AnaLouise Keating takes a different angle to this issue. She challenges us to consider how the binary positioning inherent to identity politics, however well-intended, can backfire. The crux of the idea is that when we develop a certain attitude or ideal regarding how one is supposed to be, as part of a particular identity (in this case white ally), we can turn on one another as soon as differences are revealed. Keating writes, "The us-against-them stance we have employed in oppositional forms of consciousness seeps into all areas of our lives, infecting the way we perceive ourselves and each other. When we turn this lens against each other-as we so often do-we implode. Rather than work together to enact progressive social change, we battle each other, thus reproducing the status quo" AnaLouise Keating, "'I'm a citizen of the universe': Gloria Anzaldúa's Spiritual Activism as Catalyst for Social Change" *Feminist Studies* 34, nos. 1/2 (2008): 66.

36. Brown, *Gifts of Imperfection,* 46.

37. "The Destruction of Movement, Sinking into Privileged Despair," Accessed August 15, 2015, http://www.witnessingwhiteness.blogspot.com/2009/08/destruction-of-movement-sinking-into.html.

38. Brown, *I Thought It Was Just Me,* 11.

39. Brown, *I Thought It Was Just Me,* p. xxv.

40. Brown, *I Thought It Was Just Me,* p. 46.

41. Rick Carson, *Taming Your Gremlin: A Surprisingly Simple Method for Getting Out of Your Own Way* (New York: First Quill, 2003).

42. Michael Meade, *Fate and Destiny: The Two Agreements of the Soul* (Seattle: Greenfire Press), 202.

43. Meade, *Fate and Destiny,* 293.

44. Brown, *I Thought It Was Just Me,* 134.

45. Brown, *I Thought It Was Just Me,* 31.

46. Brown, *I Thought It Was Just Me,* xxv.

47. Brown, *I Thought It Was Just Me,* 49.

48. Brown, *Gifts of Imperfection.*

49. Brown, *Gifts of Imperfection,* p. 55.

50. Rebecca Parker, "Not Somewhere Else, But Here: The Struggle for Racial Justice as a Struggle to Inhabit My Country," in *Soul Work: Anti-racist Theologies in Dialogue,* edited by Marjorie Bowens-Wheatley and Nancy Palmer Jones (Boston: Skinner House, 2003), 171–98.

51. Marjorie Bowens-Wheatley and Nancy Palmer Jones, eds., *Soul Work: Anti-racist Theologies in Dialogue* (Boston: Skinner House, 2003), 188.

52. Brown, *Gifts of Imperfection,* 209.

53. Leonard Pitts, Jr., "Crazy Sometimes," in *When Race Becomes Real,* edited by Bernestine Singley (Chicago, IL: Lawrence Hill Books, 2002).

54. Brown, *I Thought It Was Just Me,* 11.

55. Brown, *I Thought It Was Just Me,* 15.

56. A more complete quote from Gloria Anzaldúa is worth reading. She writes, "By attending to what the other is not saying…and by looking for its opposite, unacknowledged emotion — the opposite of anger is fear, of self-righteousness is guilt, of hate is love — las nepantleras attempt to see through the other's situation to her underlying unconscious desire. Accepting doubts and ambiguity, they reframe the conflict and shift the point of view. Sitting face-to-face with all parties, they identify common bonds." According to Anzaldúa, this is what can allow for mediation between challenging polarities when they play out between people. Gloria Anzaldúa, "now let us shift…the path of conocimiento…inner work, public acts," in *this bridge we call home: radical visions for transformation* (New York: Routledge, 2002), 567.

57. Brown, *Gifts of Imperfection,* 53.

58. Brown, *I Thought It Was Just Me,* 281.

59. Tolle, *A New Earth,* 63.

60. Raúl Quiñones-Rosado, *Consciousness-in-Action: Toward an Integral Psychology of Liberation and Transformation* (Caguas, Puerto Rico: ile Publications, 2007), p. 117

61. Tolle, *A New Earth,* 78.

62. Bowens-Wheatley and Palmer Jones, *Soul Work,* 8.

63. Tolle, *A New Earth,* 214.

64. Tolle, *A New Earth,* 215.

65. Tolle, *A New Earth,* 62.

66. Gary Smith, "The Other Side of Route Two: Some Autobiographical Struggles with Theology, Race, and Class," in *Soul Work: Anti-racist Theologies in Dialogue,* edited by Marjorie Bowens-Wheatley and Nancy Palmer Jones, (Boston, MA: Skinner House, 2003), 68.

67. Yancy, *Look, a White!,* 5.

68. Yancy, *Look, a White!,* 5.

69. Yancy, *Look, a White!*, 10.
70. Meade, *Fate and Destiny*, 184.
71. Yancy, *Look, a White!*
72. Meade, *Fate and Destiny*, 162.

Chapter 3

1. Corinne McLaughlin and Gordon Davidson, *Spiritual Politics: Changing the World from the Inside Out* (New York: Ballantine Books, 1994), 25.
2. Marjorie Bowens-Wheatley and Nancy Palmer Jones, eds., *Soul Work: Anti-racist Theologies in Dialogue* (Boston: Skinner House, 2003), 17
3. Richard Tarnas, *The Passion of the Western Mind: Understanding the Ideas That Have Shaped Our World View* (New York: Ballantine Books, 1991).
4. Tarnas, *Passion of the Western Mind*, 417.
5. Tarnas, *Passion of the Western Mind*, 418.
6. Tarnas, *Passion of the Western Mind*, 312.
7. Tarnas, *Passion of the Western Mind*, 320.
8. Mary Watkins and Helene Shulman, *Toward Psychologies of Liberation* (New York: Palgrave Macmillan, 2008), 107.
9. Paul Rasor, "Reclaiming Our Prophetic Voice: Liberal Theology and the Challenge of Racism," in *Soul Work: Anti-racist Theologies in Dialogue*, eds. Marjorie Bowens-Wheatley and Nancy Palmer Jones (Boston, MA: Skinner House, 2003), 109.
10. Shelley Johnson Khadem, "Medicine Path: Spiritualist and New Age Representations of Native Americans." (PhD diss., The New School, 2010), 8.
11. Murphy Pizza and James Lewis, *Handbook of Contemporary Paganism* (Leiden, the Netherlands: Brill, 2009), 189.
12. Khadem, "Medicine Path," 177.
13. Michael York, *The Emerging Network: A Sociology of the New Age and Neo-Pagan Movements* (Landham, MA: Rowman & Littlefield, 1995) 34; McLaughlin and Davidson, *Spiritual Politics*.
14. Wouter Hanegraaff, "New Age Spiritualities as Secular Religion: a Historian's Perspective," *Social Compass* 46, no. 2 (1999): 146.
15. Khadem, "Medicine Path," 9.
16. Hanegraaff, "New Age Spiritualities," 153.
17. Khadem, "Medicine Path," 181.
18. Hanegraaff, "New Age Spiritualities," 154.
19. Hanegraaff, "New Age Spiritualities," 154–55.

20. Hanegraaff, "New Age Spiritualities," 157.

21. Hanegraaff, "New Age Spiritualities," 157.

22. Hanegraaff, "New Age Spiritualities," 155.

23. Hanegraaff, "New Age Spiritualities," 150, 155, and 158.

24. Michael York, "New Age Commodification and Appropriation of Spirituality," *Journal of Contemporary Religion* 16, no.3 (2001): 364.

25. Khadem, "Medicine Path," 216; Leela Fernandes, *Transforming Feminist Practice: Non-Violence, Social Justice and the Possibilities of a Spiritualized Feminism* (San Francisco: Aunt Lute Books, 2003), 16.

26. Khadem, "Medicine Path," 217.

27. Hanegraaff, "New Age Spiritualities," 158.

28. York, "New Age Commodification," 366–67.

29. Pizza and Lewis, *Handbook of Contemporary Paganism,* 181.

30. Pizza and Lewis, *Handbook of Contemporary Paganism,* 187.

31. Bowens-Wheatley and Palmer Jones, *Soul Work,* 108.

32. Bowens-Wheatley and Palmer Jones, *Soul Work,* 108.

33. The California chapter's National Association of Multicultural Education (NAME) regional conference, held in January 2014 in Fullerton, CA, included a workshop titled "Dispelling the Myth: Latinos Don't Care about Education," presented by Mike Madrid and Kimiya Maghzi. Despite persistent stereotypes, research suggests that Latino parents are very much invested in their children's education. See, for example, Alice M. Quiocho and Annette Daoud. "Dispelling Myths about Latino Parent Participation in Schools," *The Education Forum* 70 (2006): 255–67.

34. Fernandes, *Transforming Feminist Practice,* 12.

35. Fernandes, *Transforming Feminist Practice,* 17.

36. George Tinker, "Racism and Anti-racism in a Culture of Violence: Dreaming a New Dream," in *Soul Work: Anti-racist Theologies in Dialogue,* eds. Marjorie Bowens-Wheatley and Nancy Palmer Jones (Boston, MA: Skinner House, 2003), 89.

37. john a, powell suggests that "surplus suffering is caused by a lack of love. The fact that we fail to see the humanity in our brothers and sisters causes this surplus suffering. Then we have, starting to have, a merger of our spiritual challenge as well as our social justice challenges." What I take from this is that reclaiming my own humanity involves caring about ending others' suffering, as this would be a necessary part of seeing the full humanity in others. john a. powell, "Does Living a Spiritually Engaged Life Mandate Us to Be Actively Engaged in Issues of Social Justice?", *University of St. Thomas Law Review* 1, no. 1, (2003): 35.

38. Rebecca Parker, "Not Somewhere Else, But Here: The Struggle for Racial Justice as a Struggle to Inhabit My Country," in *Soul Work: Antiracist Theologies in Dialogue,* eds. Marjorie Bowens-Wheatley and Nancy Palmer Jones (Boston, MA: Skinner House, 2003), 171–98.

39. Parker, "Not Somewhere Else, But Here," 182.

40. Mark Warren, *Fire in the Heart: How White Activists Embrace Racial Justice* (New York: Oxford University Press, 2010), 87.

41. Michelle Alexander, *The New Jim Crow: Mass Incarceration in the Age of Colorblindness* (New York: The New Press, 2010).

42. Alexander, *New Jim Crow,* 96.

43. Eckhart Tolle, *A New Earth: Awakening to Your Life's Purpose* (New York: Penguin Group, 2005), 75.

44. Alexander, *New Jim Crow,* 235.

45. Alexander, *New Jim Crow,* 96.

46. Alexander, *New Jim Crow,* 103.

47. Alexander, *New Jim Crow,* 103.

48. Alexander, *New Jim Crow,* 115; Also see Michael Muskal, "Texas teen's probation for killing 4 while driving drunk stirs anger," *Los Angeles Times* December 12 2013. The defense used the term 'affluenza" to explain that the boy was not raised to see that there were consequences for his actions. Although, one can claim this case is about class, it is easily argued that white young kids are those who far more often have the chance to have parents pay for this kind of defense. Accessed August 16, 2015. http://www.latimes.com/nation/nationnow/la-na-nn-texas-teen-drunk-driving-probation-affluenza-20131212,0,61486.story#ixzz2ps64WWbK.

49. Alexander, *New Jim Crow,* 221.

50. Alexander, *New Jim Crow,* 211.

51. Alexander, *New Jim Crow,* 222.

52. Alexander, *New Jim Crow,* 218.

53. "Homeboy Industries," Accessed August 16, 2015, http://www.homeboyindustries.org/; McLaughlin and Davidson, *Spiritual Politics,* 93.

54. William Cohen and Janet Langhart Cohen, *Race and Reconciliation in America,* (Lanham, MD: Lexington Books, 2009), 22.

55. Alexander, *New Jim Crow,* 218.

56. Warren, *Fire in the Heart,* 217.

57. Parker, "Not Somewhere Else, But Here," 183.

Chapter 4

1. Joy, DeGruy, Post-Traumatic Slave Syndrome (Milwaukie, OR: Uptone Press, 2005).
2. The phrase "unity in diversity" is not new. From a historical point of view, the roots of the concept existed "in non-Western cultures such as indigenous peoples in North America and Taoist societies in 400–500 B.C.E. In premodern Western culture it has been implicit in the organic conceptions of the universe that have been manifest since the ancient Greek and Roman civilizations through medieval Europe and into the Romantic era." Roxanne Lalonde, "Unity in Diversity: Acceptance and Integration in an Era of Intolerance and Fragmentation" (MA thesis, Carleton University, Ottawa, Ontario: Department of Geography, 1994). More recently, it is a concept that was used by educational activist, Paulo Freire, in a way that highlights the need to ensure fairness and equity among all, regardless of difference. Paulo Friere, *Pedagogy of the Heart* (New York: Continuum, 1997).
3. The term "American" is troublesome, as it rightly describes not only those who live in North America, but also all those living in Central and South America as well. And yet, it is common for U.S. citizens, particularly those who are not attuned to issues of privilege, to follow the generally accepted use of the term "American" as referring exclusively to United States citizens. I recognize the problem with this and, for that reason, generally take pains to avoid the use of the term "American" when speaking of U.S. citizens. However, when describing the history of the culture generally described as "American" in this chapter, I follow the use of the term as used by the general population in order to provide information in a form least likely to confuse readers.
4. Shelly Tochluk, *Witnessing Whiteness: The Need to Talk About Race and How to Do It,* (Lanham, MD: Rowman & Littlefield-Education, 2010); Philip Cushman, *Constructing the Self, Constructing America: A Cultural History of Psychotherapy* (New York: Addison-Wesley, 1995).
5. Tochluk, *Witnessing Whiteness,* 53–81.
6. W.E.B. DuBois, *Darkwater: Voices from Within the Veil* (New York: Washington Square Press, 2004), 31.
7. DuBois, *Darkwater,* 25.
8. Mark Peffley and Jon Hurwitz, *Justice in America: The Separate Realities of Blacks and Whites* (Cambridge Studies in Public Opinion and Political Psychology, Cambridge University Press, 2010).
9. "Lead Facilitator" at The Indaba. Accessed August 16, 2015, http://www.theindaba.com/leadfacilitator.html.

10. Corinne McLaughlin and Gordon Davidson, *Spiritual Politics: Changing the World from the Inside Out* (New York: Ballantine Books, 1994), 213.

11. Eckhart Tolle, *A New Earth: Awakening to Your Life's Purpose* (New York: Penguin Group, 2005) 141.

12. Tolle, *A New Earth,* 142.

13. Tolle, *A New Earth,* 142.

14. Tolle, *A New Earth,* 159.

15. Mary Watkins and Helene Shulman, *Toward Psychologies of Liberation* (New York: Palgrave Macmillan, 2008), 125.

16. Interview conducted with Orland Bishop in July 2012.

17. Carol Lee Flinders, *At the Root of this Longing: Reconciling a Spiritual Hunger and a Feminist Thirst* (San Francisco: Harper Collins, 1998), 265.; also McLaughlin and Davidson, *Spiritual Politics,* 60).

18. DeGruy, *Post-Traumatic Slave Syndrome.*

19. Interview conducted with Orland Bishop in June 2012.

20. McLaughlin and Davidson, *Spiritual Politics,* 336–46.

21. William Cohen and Janet Langhart Cohen, *Race and Reconciliation in America* (Lanham, MD: Lexington Books, 2009), 24.

22. Gloria Anzaldúa, "now let us shift…the path of conocimiento…inner work, public acts," in *this bridge we can home: radical visions for transformation* (New York: Routledge, 2002), 572.

23. Leela Fernandes, *Transforming Feminist Practice: Non-Violence, Social Justice and the Possibilities of a Spiritualized Feminism* (San Francisco: Aunt Lute Books, 2003).

24. The word "indaba" is Zulu and refers to a group coming together to talk about something important. For many years, the Shade Tree community, a spiritually-oriented, youth mentoring non-profit based in Los Angeles, hosted indaba events that brought together an extended network of diverse individuals from throughout Southern California. "Lead Facilitator" at The Indaba. Accessed August 16, 2015, http://www.theindaba.com/leadfacilitator.html.

25. Rebecca Parker, "Not Somewhere Else, But Here: The Struggle for Racial Justice as a Struggle to Inhabit My Country," in *Soul Work: Antiracist Theologies in Dialogue,* ed. Marjorie Bowens-Wheatley and Nancy Palmer Jones (Boston, MA: Skinner House, 2003), 171–98.

26. Mary Watkins, "Seeding Liberation: A Dialogue Between Depth Psychology and Liberation Psychology," in *Depth Psychology: Meditations in the field,* ed. Dennis Patrick Slattery and Lionel Corbett (Einsiedlen: Diamon, 2001), 204–224.

27. Parker, "Not Somewhere Else, But Here," 176.

28. Parker, "Not Somewhere Else, But Here," 177.

29. Parker, "Not Somewhere Else, But Here," 177.

30. James Cone is clear that white theology is perceived by many as "a racist, theological justification of the status quo." It is only by deconstructing our treasured stories, myths, and belief structures that we will be able to see that racism may exist in places many of us (white people) failed to observe previously. James Cone, *A Black Theology of Liberation* (Maryknoll, NY: Orbis Books, 1986), xiv.

31. Gary Howard, *We Can't Teach What We Don't Know,* (New York: Teachers College, 2006).

32. As a professor in a teacher education program, I can attest to the fact that there are state standards that expect teachers to work to uncover personal bias in order to best educate diverse learners. All teacher candidates take diversity classes. And yet, purely anecdotally, I would suggest that there is only so much that can be accomplished within the time frame given, only so much peeling away of the layers of the racial unconscious that have been generated over a lifetime, only so much language that can be learned, only so much healing that can be attained. The fact of the matter is that teacher training alone will never fully prepare someone to navigate the nuances of racial difference. It takes personal dedication and effort outside of the teacher training program, and far too few teachers have colleagues and friends who support this conversation moving forward.

33. Bowens-Wheatley and Nancy Palmer Jones, eds., *Soul Work: Anti-racist Theologies in Dialogue* (Boston: Skinner House, 2003), 49.

34. Robert Jensen, *All My Bones Shake: Seeking a Progressive Path to the Prophetic Voice* (Brooklyn, NY: Soft Skull Press, 2009) 144.

Chapter 5

1. Kathy Obear, "Facilitating Workshops with Whites to Dismantle Racism" (unpublished handouts, 2013).

2. Bron Taylor, "Earthen Spirituality or Cultural Genocide?: Radical Environmentalism's Appropriation of Native American Spirituality," *Religion* 27 (1997): 183–215.

3. Homi Bhabha, *The Location of Culture* (New York: Routledge, 1994): 39, quoted in Sybille De La Rosa, "Appropriation or Approximation: The Emergence of Intermediate Horizons," *The International Journal of Diversity in Organisations, Communities and Nations* 8, No. 3 (2008): 235–39.

4. Taylor, "Earthen Spirituality."

5. De La Rosa, "Appropriation or Approximation," 235–39.

6. Karlyn Crowley, *Feminism's New Age: Gender, Appropriation, and the Afterlife of Essentialism* (New York: SUNY Press, 2011): 9.

7. Shelly Tochluk, *Witnessing Whiteness: The Need to Talk About Race and How to Do It* (Lanham, MD: Rowman & Littlefield-Education, 2010): 23.

8. George Tinker, *American Indian Liberation* (Maryknoll, NY: Orbis Books, 2008): 1.

9. Shelly Johnson Khadem, "Medicine Path: Spiritualist and New Age Representations of Native Americans," (PhD diss., The New School, 2010): 177.

10. Murphy Pizza and James Lewis, *Handbook of Contemporary Paganism* (Leiden, the Netherlands: Brill, 2009): 581.

11. Clara Sue Kidwell, Homer Noley, and George Tinker, *A Native American Theology* (Maryknoll, NY: Orbis Books, 2006) 171.

12. Khadem, "Medicine Path," 160.

13. David Waldron and Janice Newton, "Rethinking Appropriation of the Indigenous: A Critique of the Romanticist Approach," *The Journal of Alternative and Emergent Religions* 16, no. 2 (2012): 70.

14. Kidwell, Noley, and Tinker, *A Native American Theology,* 178. "Today, Indians remain indisputably an oppressed minority in the United States. 'The result,' writes sociologist Menno Boldt in his book *Surviving as Indians,* 'is a cultural crisis manifested by a breakdown of social order in Indian communities.' The often-repeated statistics are staggering. The average yearly income is less than half the poverty level, and over half of all Natives are unemployed. On some reservations, unemployment runs as high as 85–90%. Health statistics chronically rank Native Americans at or near the bottom. Male life expectancy is 44 years, female 47. Infant mortality is twice the national average. Diabetes runs six times the national average; heart disease at about five times the national average; alcoholism five times the national average; and cirrhosis of the liver 18 times the national average. Substance abuse, school dropout rates, suicide, crime, and violence are major problems among both urban and reservation populations. Increasingly, violence victimizes those with least power — women, children, the elderly. Though Native Americans may often be, to the untrained eye, indistinguishable from the population at large, they still go to jail in disproportionate numbers, earn less, and die younger."

15. Khadem, "Medicine Path," 180.

16. Susanne Owen, *The Appropriation of Native American Spirituality* (London: Bloomsbury Academic, 2011): 14.

17. James Young and Conrad Brunk, *The Ethics of Cultural Appropriation* (Malden, MA: Wiley-Blackwell, 2009): 109.

18. Young and Brunk, *Ethics of Cultural Appropriation,* 97–100.

19. David Howes, "Cultural Appropriation and Resistance in the American Southwest: 'Decomodifying Indianness'," in *Cross-Cultural Consumption: Global Markets, Local Realities,* ed. David Howes (New York: Routledge, 1996): 144

20. Young and Brunk, *Ethics of Cultural Appropriation,* 93.

21. Cynthia Kasee, "Identity, Recovery, and Religious Imperialism," *Women & Therapy* 16, nos. 2/3: 87

22. Kasee, "Identity, Recovery, and Religious Imperialism," 85.

23. Kasee, "Identity, Recovery, and Religious Imperialism," 85.

24. Kasee, "Identity, Recovery, and Religious Imperialism," 86.

25. Kasee, "Identity, Recovery, and Religious Imperialism," 87. Also see Tinker, *Native American Theology,* 175. "Though Native religious traditions have been subject to consumption by hungry non-Natives at the 'spiritual delicatessen' ('Give me a slice of sweat lodge and a piece of vision quest with mayonnaise on fry bread'), freedom of religion remains elusive for Native Americans themselves. Native religious traditions are threatened by the destruction of sacred sites due to development and by laws that make traditional ceremonies difficult."

26. Strong, Pauline Turner & Posner, Laurie, "Selves in play: Sports, scouts, and American cultural citizenship," International Review for the Sociology of Sport, 45, 390-409, 2010, p. 402

27. Pauline Turner Strong, "Cultural Appropriation and the Crafting of Racialized Selves in American Youth Organizations: Toward and Ethnographic Approach," *Critical Methodologies* 9 (2009): 209.

28. Khadem, "Medicine Path," 229.

29. Karlyn Crowley, "The Indian Way is What's Inside: Gender and the Appropriation of American Indian Religion in New Age Culture," in *Feminism's New Age: Gender, Appropriation, and the Afterlife of Essentialism* (New York: SUNY Press, 2011).

30. Khadem, "Medicine Path," x and 186.

31. For readers who are aware of questions related to some authors' heritage, I note that I recognize that Andrea Smith's heritage has been contested. However, it is inappropriate for me to offer any information that could be interpreted as holding a position on this issue. I have been advised to steer clear.

32. Andrea Smith, "For All Those Who Were Indian in a Former Life," *Cultural Survival Quarterly* 17, no. 4 (1994): 70–71.

33. Andrea Smith, "Spiritual Appropriation as Sexual Violence," *Wicazo Sa Review* 20, no. 1 (2005): 97–111.
34. Smith, "Sexual Violence," 101.
35. Khadem, "Medicine Path," 206.
36. Owen, *Appropriation of Native American Spirituality,* 89–90.
37. Khadem, "Medicine Path," 211.
38. Owen, *Appropriation of Native American Spirituality,* 63.
39. Owen, *Appropriation of Native American Spirituality,* 19; Tinker, *Spirit and Resistance,* 73.
40. Owen, *Appropriation of Native American Spirituality,* 89.
41. Young and Brunk, *Ethics of Cultural Appropriation,* 112.
42. Owen, *Appropriation of Native American Spirituality,* 63.
43. Young and Brunk, *Ethics of Cultural Appropriation,* 97–100.
44. Khadem, "Medicine Path," 211.
45. Ward Churchill, "Spiritual Hucksterism: The Rise of the Plastic Medicine Men," in *From a Native Son: Selected Essays in Indigenism, 1985–1995* (Boston: South End Press, 1996). I recognize that Ward Churchill's heritage has been contested. However, it is inappropriate for me to offer any information that could be interpreted as holding a position on this issue. I have been advised to steer clear.
46. Owen, *Appropriation of Native American Spirituality,* 2.
47. George Tinker, *Spirit and Resistance: Political Theology and American Indian Liberation* (Minneapolis, MN: Fortress Press, 2004): 64.
48. Owen, *Appropriation of Native American Spirituality,* 89.
49. Important works include, but are not limited to, Vine Deloria Jr., *For this Land: Writings on Religion in America,* (New York: Routledge, 1999); Andrea Smith, "Spiritual Appropriation as Sexual Violence," *Wicazo Sa Review* 20, no. 1 (2005): 97–111; Wendy Rose, "The Great Pretenders: Further Reflections on White Shamanism." in *The State of Native America: Genocide, Colonisation and Resistance,* ed. Annette Jaimes, (Boston: South End, 1992): 403–21; Geary Hobson, "The Rise of the White Shaman as a New Version of Cultural Imperialism," in *The Remembered Earth: An Anthology of Contemporary Native American Literature,* ed. Gary Hobson (Albuquerque, NM: Red Earth Press, 1978): 100–8; Philip Deloria, *Playing Indian* (New Haven: Yale University Press, 1998).
50. Taylor, "Earthen Spirituality," 200, summarizing George Tinker, *Missionary Conquest: the Gospel and Native American Genocide* (Minneapolis, MN: Fortress, 1993): 122–23.
51. Tinker, *Spirit and Resistance,* 70.
52. Tinker, *Spirit and Resistance,* 53

53. Tinker, *Native American Liberation,* 173–74.
54. Khadem, "Medicine Path," 185; Michael York, "New Age Commodification and Appropriation of Spirituality," *Journal of Contemporary Religion* 16, no.1 (2001): 368.
55. Pizza and Lewis, *Handbook of Contemporary Paganism,* 182.
56. York, "New Age Commodification," 366.
57. Khadem, "Medicine Path," 183.
58. Murphy and James, *Contemporary Paganism,* 581; Crowley, *Feminism's New Age,* 1.
59. Tinker, *Spirit and Resistance,* 62–63.
60. Tinker, *Spirit and Resistance,* 63
61. Tinker, *Spirit and Resistance,* 63
62. Tinker, *Spirit and Resistance,* 70
63. Tinker, *Spirit and Resistance,* 45
64. Tinker, *American Indian Liberation,* 159–62. This list is a still-abbreviated version of what appears in the text: 1. White Amer-europeans must courageously own their past — without guilt — but with great intentionality — to change the present and the future. 2. We must work together to identify the systemic structures of oppression and mark them for genuine deconstruction, that is, for dismantling. 3. We dare not undertake this task without understanding…there will be enormous personal risks for all of us — to our lifestyle and to our economic well-being. 4. We must get serious about reducing consumption. 5. We must learn to relate across cultural boundaries in ways that are predicated on genuine and mutual respect. 6. Each of us [must] gain a proper sense of one's own community in order to avoid new-age encroachment and misappropriation of what belongs to someone else, that is, to another community and its culture. 7. White relatives must begin to learn from indigenous peoples worldwide the importance of respecting all their own relatives in the created world, including trees and rivers, animals and flying things. 8. Find ways to deconstruct the dominance of individualism in our society and to replace individualism with broader ideas of community. 9. Dream a new vision of the world in which domination and privileging lose their seemingly natural prominence in structuring a world society.
65. Kidwell, Noley, and Tinker, *A Native American Theology,* 173–74.
66. Tinker, *Spirit and Resistance,* 56–57.
67. Tinker, *Spirit and Resistance,* 53.
68. Tinker, *American Indian Liberation,* 14.
69. Tinker, *Spirit and Resistance,* 56–57.

70. Owen, *Appropriation of Native American Spirituality*, 39.

71. Owen, *Appropriation of Native American Spirituality*, 40.

72. Tinker, *American Indian Liberation*, 138.

73. Tinker, *American Indian Liberation*, 93.

74. Tinker, *Spirit and Resistance*, 53.

75. At one point in an interview with Bill Moyers, Oren Lyons said, "Yet at a meeting that was held in Hopi back in 1969, when we sat there with many Indian leaders from around the country, spiritual leaders, and they talked about these young people who were sitting on our doorsteps every day when we got up and they had come from all over the country and they were coming to be an Indian or they were coming to learn something about us. And we said, 'This is a very strange phenomenon, that our white brother's children are now coming to our doorstep and wanting to be part of us. What do we do with this?' One of the Hopi elders said, 'Well we have a prophecy about that.' And he said that there was going to come a time when they're going to come and ask for direction. Maybe this is what's happening. So it came under discussion and it was agreed upon at that time that perhaps this may be true. And if it is, then we should be more responsive then, to the questions. And we should maybe try to help. To see what we can do. To pass on whatever we can, however we can." Public Affairs Television. "The Faithkeeper, Interview with Bill Moyers, 3 July 1991 Public Affairs Television." http://www.ratical.org/many_worlds/6Nations/OL070391.html.

76. Tinker, *Spirit and Resistance*, 66.

77. Taylor, "Earthen Spirituality," 187.

78. Oren Lyons is quoted as saying, "We can't afford, now, to have these national borders. We can't afford to have racism. We can't afford apartheid. We cannot — it's one of those luxuries that we can't have anymore as human beings. We've got to think now, in real terms, for that seventh generation. And we've got to move in concert. We've got to sing the same song. We've got to have the same ceremony. We've got to get back to spiritual law if we are to survive." Public Affairs Television. "The Faithkeeper, Interview with Bill Moyers, 3 July 1991 Public Affairs Television." http://www.ratical.org/many_worlds/6Nations/OL070391.html

79. Tinker, *Spirit and Resistance*, 66.

80. Owen, *Appropriation of Native American Spirituality*, 60.

81. Owen, *Appropriation of Native American Spirituality*, 61.

82. Owen, *Appropriation of Native American Spirituality*, 61.

83. Owen, *Appropriation of Native American Spirituality*, 61.

84. Owen, *Appropriation of Native American Spirituality,* 62.

85. Owen, *Appropriation of Native American Spirituality,* 62.

86. Owen, *Appropriation of Native American Spirituality,* 2.

87. Owen, *Appropriation of Native American Spirituality,* 80.

88. James, "Earthen Spirituality," 203.

89. Owen, *Appropriation of Native American Spirituality,* 56.

90. Tinker, *Spirit and Resistance,* 66.

91. Tinker, *Spirit and Resistance,* 67.

92. Owen, *Appropriation of Native American Spirituality,* 50.

93. Owen, *Appropriation of Native American Spirituality,* 1.

94. Tinker, *Spirit and Resistance,* 32. Tinker reflects to someone who learned about a biological connection to Indian heritage and wanted to connect with the tradition that "the cultural competency aspects of the connection have been lost long ago and replaced by the dominant cultural responses and values of North American White (or Black or Chicano) society and its cultural responses and values" as part of sending the message that the cultural competency necessary to participate in Indian life is not likely to be developed by someone raised outside of the Native context.

95. "Sonoma, Arizona Sweat Lodge," accessed August 19, 2015, http://witnessingwhiteness.blogspot.com/2010/01/sonoma-az-sweat-lodge-james-arthur-ray.html.

96. "Street Poets," accessed August 19, 2015, http://www.streetpoetsinc.com/.

97. Owen, *Appropriation of Native American Spirituality,* 58.

98. Owen, *Appropriation of Native American Spirituality,* 58.

99. I am grateful to have received critical feedback from George Tinker directly on two drafts of this chapter. He was highly critical about both drafts and his criticism resulted in many changes. He expressed concern that he would be perceived as endorsing this work, which he did not. I have attempted to address as many of the critical points he expressed, and I moved forward without receiving any message from him that he would consider this chapter useful. I take full responsibility for offering my perspective and story, knowing that it has raised concerns that likely have not been fully addressed.

100. Tinker, *American Indian Liberation,* 40, 47–50, 64–65, 69, 71; Tinker, *Spirit and Resistance,* 57–58.

101. Tinker, *Spirit and Resistance,* 53.

102. Tinker, *American Indian Liberation,* 159–62. See note 64 for list.

103. Tinker, *Spirit and Resistance,* 65.

104. According to George Tinker, via written feedback to a draft of this chapter in October 2015, simply following all the protocols "merely scratches the surface of the deep reality" of the ceremony and is considered "mere surface-structure mimicry." Thus, he finds it a meaningless argument regarding the lodge I attend having any resemblance to the Native ceremony.

105. Tinker, *Spirit and Resistance,* 71–72.

106. Crowley, *Feminism's New Age,* 8 and 18.

107. Crowley, *Feminism's New Age,* 8.

108. Crowley, *Feminism's New Age,* 8

109. Crowley, *Feminism's New Age,* 169.

110. Crowley, *Feminism's New Age,* 158; Gloria Anzaldúa, "now let us shift…the path of conocimiento…inner work, public acts," in *this bridge we can home: radical visions for transformation* (New York: Routledge, 2002).

111. Crowley, *Feminism's New Age,* 158.

112. This quote appears in Waldron and Newton, "Rethinking Appropriation," 76, but was originally published in Starhawk, *The Spiral Dance: a Rebirth of the Religion of the Ancient Goddess* (San Francisco: Harper Collins Press, 1989): 214.

113. Orland Bishop is the African-American founder of Shade Tree, Black Gnostic Studies teacher, and initiate of the Zulu tradition by High Sanusi Healer Vusamazulu Credo Mutwa. "Lead Facilitator" at The Indaba, accessed August 16, 2015 http://www.theindaba.com/leadfacilitator.html.

114. The reality of these metaphysical concepts is impossible to prove. They do, however, reflect the type of spiritual beliefs that are common among spiritual seekers today. These beliefs make a difference in how many spiritual seekers interact with the world. In other words, I name these concepts not to convince the reader that they reflect a metaphysical truth, but because they have psychological and behavioral consequences.

115. This is in line with the way AnaLouise Keating describes spiritual activism. She states that "although spiritual activism begins at the level of the personal, it is not solipsistic; nor does it result in egocentrism, self-glorification, or other types of possessive individualism." AnaLouise Keating, "I'm a citizen of the universe": Gloria Anzaldúa's Spiritual Activismas Catalyst for Social Change," *Feminist Studies* 34, nos. 1/2 (2008): 58.

116. Tinker, *Spirit and Resistance,* 26.

117. Tinker, *Spirit and Resistance,* 26.

118. Tinker, *American Indian Liberation,* 81.

119. Tinker, *Spirit and Resistance,* 21. Tinker writes, "I want to argue for a breaking down of the old borders, more or less artificially established after 1492. The small, locally autonomous communities I envision would constitute something of a reemergence of a smaller-scale, local autonomy similar to those that were more common in the world before the emergence of large, centralized authoritarian state structures…I fully understand that my vision introduces significant modern problems with respect to how the world might work with the existence of so many smaller economies, currencies, markets, all resulting from multitudes of communities claiming autonomy Yet it is critical that we envision other possibilities for social/political configurations."

120. This quote appears in Waldron and Newton , "Rethinking Appropriation," 76, but was originally published in *Starhawk, The Spiral Dance, a Rebirth of the Religion of the Ancient Goddess* (San Francisco: Harper Collins Press, 1989) 214.

121. Khadem, "Medicine Path," 40.

122. Owen, *Appropriation of Native American Spirituality,* 105.

123. Owen, *Appropriation of Native American Spirituality,* 105.

124. Owen, *Appropriation of Native American Spirituality,* 106.

125. Young and Brunk, *Ethics of Cultural Appropriation,* 108.

126. Young and Brunk, *Ethics of Cultural Appropriation,* 110.

127. Pizza and Lewis, *Handbook of Contemporary Paganism,* 580.

128. Pizza and Lewis, *Handbook of Contemporary Paganism,* 73–77. Also, the use of the term "essentialist" here refers to the idea that there are some necessary attributes or qualities inherent to being a woman. For example, women being considered fundamentally nurturing, peaceful, or caretaking. It is similar to the romantic notion of Native Americans as being naturally in tune with nature. I perceive this as boxing people in to a certain ideal that relies on stereotypes and leads to prejudicial judgment.

129. Pizza and Lewis, *Handbook of Contemporary Paganism,* 581.

130. Owen, *Appropriation of Native American Spirituality,* 1.

131. Kasee, "Identity, Recovery, and Religious Imperialism," 89–91.

132. Baris Buyukokutan, "Toward a Theory of Cultural Appropriation: Buddhism, the Vietnam War, and the Field of U.S. Poetry," *American Psychological Review* 76, no. 4: 620–39.

133. Tony Perry, "Judge finds yoga complaint a stretch," *Los Angeles Times,* July 2, 2013.

Chapter 6

1. Unidentified author, received April 23, 2013 as part of a newsletter sent to a listserv.

2. Corinne McLaughlin and Gordon Davidson, *Spiritual Politics: Changing the World from the Inside Out* (New York: Ballantine Books, 1994): 388.

3. Barry Johnson, *Polarity Management: Identifying and Managing Unsolvable Problems* (Middleville, MI: Polarity Management Associates, 1996): 65.

4. Shelly Tochluk and Cameron Levin, "Powerful Partnerships: Transformative Alliance Building" in *Accountability and White Anti-racist Organizing: Stories from Our Work,* ed. Bonnie Cushing et al. (Roselle, NJ: Crandall, Dostie, & Douglass Books, 2010): 190–219.

5. Marjorie Bowens-Wheatley and Nancy Palmer Jones, eds., S*oul Work: Anti-racist Theologies in Dialogue* (Boston, MA: Skinner House, 2003): 16.

6. Michael Meade, *Fate and Destiny: The Two Agreements of the Soul* (Seattle, WA: Greenfire Press): 123.

7. Gillian Burlingham, "Burning Deep Inside: Anti-racist Accountability in a Faith Community," in Accountability and White Anti-racist Organizing: Stories from Our Work, ed. Bonnie Cushing, et al. (Roselle, NJ: Crandall, Dostie & Douglass Books, 2010): 94.

8. Sharon Martinas, with Mickey Ellinger, "'Passing It On:' Reflections of a White Anti-racist Solidarity Organizer," in *Accountability and White Anti-racist Organizing: Stories from Our Work,* ed. Bonnie Cushing, et al. (Roselle, NJ: Crandall, Dostie & Douglass Books, 2010): 144.

9. Burlingham, "Burning Deep Inside," 92.

10. Burlingham, "Burning Deep Inside," 88.

11. McLaughlin and Davidson, *Spiritual Politics,* 208.

12. Burlingham, "Burning Deep Inside," p. 92.

13. European Dissent, "European Dissent Accountability Statement," in *Accountability and White Anti-racist Organizing: Stories from Our Work,* ed. Bonnie Cushing, et al. (Roselle, NJ: Crandall, Dostie & Douglass Books, 2010): 222–24.

14. European Dissent, "Accountability Statement," p. 223

15. Christine Schmidt, "From Within: Practicing White Antiracism in Public Schools," in *Accountability and White Anti-racist Organizing: Stories from Our Work,* ed. Bonnie Cushing, et al. (Roselle, NJ: Crandall, Dostie & Douglass Books, 2010): 51

16. Schmidt, "From Within," 52.

17. Mark Warren, *Fire in the Heart: How White Activists Embrace Racial Justice* (New York: Oxford University Press, 2010): 152–76.

18. Raúl Quiñones-Rosado, *Consciousness-in-Action: Toward an Integral Psychology of Liberation and Transformation* (Caguas, Puerto Rico: ile Publications, 2007): 132.

19. Warren, *Fire in the Heart,* 157.

20. Warren, *Fire in the Heart,* 227.

21. Paulo Freire, *Pedagogy of the Oppressed* (New York: Continuum, 1970).

22. This 2008 presentation was our second attempt at discussing AWARE's ideas about Transformational Alliance Building at WPC. The year before, my white colleague, myself, and another AWARE-LA member partnered with a man of color I knew well who was not affiliated with AWARE-LA. He and I had engaged in many conversations on accountability for years, and because of that, and his frequent attendance at WPC, we decided to set the stage with AWARE-LA presenting what we had learned through our investigation in accountability issues, and then inviting this colleague of color to offer reaction and commentary. We did not realize at the time that this set-up would create an adversarial tone within the workshop. Having realized our error afterwards, we decided that for the 2008 workshop we would raise funds so that we would have an AWARE-LA affiliated multiracial team present the information as a united body. It was in the context of planning for this workshop that the story told in this chapter took place.

23. Quiñones-Rosado, *Consciousness-in-Action,* 134.

24. Quiñones-Rosado, *Consciousness-in-Action,* 61.

25. Quiñones-Rosado, *Consciousness-in-Action,* 58.

26. Quiñones-Rosado, *Consciousness-in-Action,* 51.

27. Martinas and Ellinger, "'Passing It On,'" 158.

28. Robert Jensen, *All My Bones Shake: Seeking a Progressive Path to the Prophetic Voice* (Brooklyn, NY: Soft Skull Press, 2009): 130.

29. Eckhart Tolle, *A New Earth: Awakening to Your Life's Purpose* (New York: Penguin Group, 2005), 215.

30. Mary Watkins and Helene Shulman, *Toward Psychologies of Liberation* (New York: Palgrave Macmillan, 2008): 332.

31. Watkins and Shulman, *Psychologies of Liberation,* 333.

32. Watkins and Shulman, *Psychologies of Liberation,* 333.

33. Watkins and Shulman, *Psychologies of Liberation,* 333.

34. Quiñones-Rosado, *Consciousness-in-Action,* 109.

35. Quiñones-Rosado, *Consciousness-in-Action,* 110.

36. Quiñones-Rosado, *Consciousness-in-Action,* 114.

37. Quiñones-Rosado, *Consciousness-in-Action,* 118–20.

38. In addition to Quiñones-Rosado's process of moving through percep-

tual position, Gloria Anzaldúa also offers ideas regarding how to shift ones' perspective. She describes the ability to locate a neutral position as shifting one's perspective to "la naguala." This involves recognizing that each person has a "knower" who can act out of choice. The challenge is that the knower can often be "displaced by the ego." Anzaldúa then offers how a "connectionist" view allows one to see another's perspective, allowing for a reduction in defensiveness. She writes, "This shift occurs when you give up investment in your point of view and recognize the real situation free of projections — not filtered through your habitual defensive preoccupations. Moving back and forth from the situation to la naguala's view, you glean a new description of the world (reality) — a Toltec interpretation. When you're in the place between worldviews (nepantla) you're able to slip between realities to a neutral perception. A decision made in the in-between place becomes a turning point initiating psychological and spiritual transformations, making other kinds of experiences possible." Gloria Anzaldúa, "now let us shift…the path of conocimiento…inner work, public acts," in *this bridge we can home: radical visions for transformation* (New York: Routledge, 2002): 569.

39. Burlingham, "Burning Deep Inside," 94.

Works Cited

Adams, Marianne, Lee Anne Bell, and Pat Griffin. *Teaching for Diversity and Social Justice*. New York: Routledge, 2007.

Aizenstat, Steven. "Steven Aizenstat." Accessed August 16, 2015. http://www.dreamtending.com/about.html.

Alexander, Michelle. *The New Jim Crow: Mass Incarceration in the Age of Color-blindness*. New York: The New Press, 2010.

Anthony, Dick, Bruce Ecker, and Ken Wilber. *Spiritual Choices: The Problems of Recognizing Authentic Paths to Inner Transformation*. New York: Paragon House, 1987.

Anzaldúa, Gloria. "now let us shift...the path of conocimiento...inner work, public acts." In *this bridge we call home: radical visions for transformation*, edited by Gloria E. Anzaldúa and AnaLouise Keating, 540–578. New York: Routledge, 2002.

AWARE-LA. "Models." Accessed August 16, 2015. http://awarela.wordpress.com/models/.

Berman Cushing, Bonnie, Lila Cabbil, Margery Freeman, Jeff Hitchcock, and Kimberley Richards, eds. *Accountability and White Anti-racist Organizing: Stories from Our Work*. Roselle, NJ: Crandall, Dostie & Douglass Books, 2010.

Bertrand, Marianne and Sendhil Mullainathan. "Are Emily and Greg More Employable than Lakisha and Jamal? A Field Experiment on Labor Market Discrimination." Working Paper No. 9873, National Bureau of Economic Research: 2003.

Bowens-Wheatley, Marjorie and Nancy Palmer Jones, eds. *Soul Work: Anti-racist Theologies in Dialogue*. Boston: Skinner House, 2003.

Brown, Brené. *I Thought It Was Just Me (But It Isn't): Making the Journey from "What will people think" to "I am enough."* New York: Gotham Books, 2007.

Brown, Brené. *The Gifts of Imperfection: Let Go of Who You Think You're Supposed to Be and Embrace Who You Are.* Center City, MN: Hazeldon, 2010.

Burlingham, Gillian. "Burning Deep Inside: Anti-racist Accountability in a Faith Community." In *Accountability and White Anti-racist Organizing: Stories from Our Work,* edited by Bonnie Berman Cushing et al., 87–101. Roselle, NJ: Crandall, Dostie & Douglass Books, 2010.

Buyukokutan, Baris. "Toward a Theory of Cultural Appropriation: Buddhism, the Vietnam War, and the Field of U.S. Poetry." *American Psychological Review* 76, no. 4 (2011): 620–39.

Carson, Rick. *Taming Your Gremlin: A Surprisingly Simple Method for Getting Out of Your Own Way.* New York: First Quill, 2003.

Churchill, Ward. *From a Native Son: Selected Essays in Indigenism, 1985–1995.* Boston: South End Press, 1996.

Cohen, William and Janet Langhart Cohen. *Race and Reconciliation in America.* Lanham, MD: Lexington Books, 2009.

Cone, James. *A Black Theology of Liberation.* Maryknoll, NY: Orbis Books, 1986.

Crenshaw, Kimberlé. "Mapping the Margins: Intersectionality, Identity Politics, and Violence against Women of Color." *Stanford Law Review* 43, no. 6 (1991): 1241–99.

Crowley, Karlyn. *Feminism's New Age: Gender, Appropriation, and the Afterlife of Essentialism.* New York: SUNY Press, 2011.

Cushman, Philip. *Constructing the Self, Constructing America: A Cultural History of Psychotherapy.* New York: Addison-Wesley, 1995.

DeGruy, Joy. *Post-Traumatic Slave Syndrome.* Milwaukie, OR: Uptone Press, 2005.

De La Rosa, Sybille. "Appropriation or Approximation: The Emergence of Intermediate Horizons." *The International Journal of Diversity in Organisations, Communities and Nations* 8, no. 3 (2008): 235–39.

Deloria, Philip. *Playing Indian.* New Haven, CT: Yale University Press, 1998.

Deloria, Jr., Vine. *For this Land: Writings on Religion in America.* New York: Routledge, 1999.

De Souza Briggs, Xavier, ed. *The Geography of Opportunity: Race and Housing Choice in Metropolitan America.* The Brookings Institute, 2005.

DiAngelo, Robin. "Nothing to Add: A Challenge to White Silence in Racial Discussions." *Understanding & Dismantling Privilege* 2, no. 1 (2012).

DuBois, W.E.B. *Darkwater: Voices from Within the Veil.* New York: Washington Square Press, 2004.

European Dissent. "European Dissent Accountability Statement." In *Accountability and White Anti-racist Organizing: Stories from Our Work,* edited by Bonnie Berman Cushing, et al., 222–24. Roselle, NJ: Crandall, Dostie & Douglass Books, 2010.

Fernandes, Leela. *Transforming Feminist Practice: Non-Violence, Social Justice and the Possibilities of a Spiritualized Feminism.* San Francisco: Aunt Lute Books, 2003.

Flinders, Carol Lee. *At the Root of this Longing: Reconciling a Spiritual Hunger and a Feminist Thirst.* San Francisco: Harper Collins, 1998.

Francis, David. "Employers' Replies to Racial Names." National Bureau of Economic Research, http://www.nber.org/digest/sep03/w9873.html

Frankenberg, Ruth. *The Social Construction of Whiteness: White Women, Race Matters.* Minneapolis: University of Minnesota Press, 1993.

Freire, Paulo. *Pedagogy of the Oppressed.* New York: Continuum, 1970.

Friere, Paulo. *Pedagogy of the Heart.* New York: Continuum, 1997.

Global Oneness Project. "Sawubona." Accessed August 15, 2015. http://www.globalonenessproject.org/library/interviews/sawubona.

Grinde, Donald and Bruce Johansen, *Exemplar of Liberty: Native America and the Evolution of Democracy.* Native American Politics Series, no. 3, Los Angeles: UCLA American Indian Studies Center, 1991.

Hanegraaff, Wouter. "New Age Spiritualities as Secular Religion: a Historian's Perspective." *Social Compass* 46, no. 2 (1999): 145–60.

Hobson, Geary. "The Rise of the White Shaman as a New Version of Cultural Imperialism." In *The Remembered Earth,* edited by Geary Hobson, 100–8. Albuquerque, NM: Red Earth Press, 1978.

Homeboy Industries. Accessed August 16, 2015. http://www.homeboyindustries.org/.

Howard, Gary. *We Can't Teach What We Don't Know.* New York: Teachers College, 2006.

Howell, Benjamin. "Exploiting Race and Space: Concentrated Subprime Lending as Housing Discrimination." *California Law Review* 94, no. 1 (2006): 101–47.

Howes, David. "Cultural Appropriation and Resistance in the American Southwest: 'Decomodifying Indianness'." In *Cross-Cultural Consumption: Global Markets, Local Realities,* edited by David Howes, 138–160. New York: Routledge, 1996.

Jensen, Robert. *All My Bones Shake: Seeking a Progressive Path to the Prophetic Voice.* Brooklyn: Soft Skull Press, 2009.

Johansen, Bruce. *Forgotten Founders, Benjamin Franklin, the Iroquois and the Rationale for the American Revolution.* Ipswich, Mass: Gambit Inc., 1982.

Johnson, Barry. *Polarity Management: Identifying and Managing Unsolvable Problems.* Middleville, MI: Polarity Management Associates, 1996.

Kasee, Cynthia. "Identity, Recovery, and Religious Imperialism." *Women & Therapy* 16, nos. 2/3 (1995): 83–93.

Keating, AnaLouise. "'I'm a citizen of the universe': Gloria Anzaldúa's Spiritual Activism as Catalyst for Social Change." *Feminist Studies* 34, nos. 1/2 (2008): 53–69.

Khadem, Shelley Johnson. "Medicine Path: Spiritualist and New Age Representations of Native Americans." PhD diss., The New School, 2010.

Kidwell, C.S., Homer Noley, and George Tinker. A *Native American Theology.* Maryknoll,NY: Orbis Books, 2006.

Lalonde, Roxanne. "Unity in Diversity: Acceptance and Integration in an Era of Intolerance and Fragmentation." MA thesis, Carleton University, Ottawa, Ontario: Department of Geography, 1994.

Leonardo, Zeus. "The Souls of White Folk: Critical Pedagogy, Whiteness Studies, and Globalization Discourse." *Race, Ethnicity, and Education* 5 no. 1 (2002): 29–50.

Martinas, Sharon and Mickey Ellinger. "'Passing It On:' Reflections of a White Anti-racist Solidarity Organizer." In *Accountability and White Anti-racist Organizing: Stories from Our Work,* edited by Bonnie Berman Cushing et al., 141–69. Roselle, NJ: Crandall, Dostie & Douglass Books, 2010.

Maslow, Abraham. "A theory of human motivation." *Psychological Review* 50, no. 4 (1943): 370–96

McIntosh, Peggy. "White Privilege and Male Privilege: A Personal Account of Coming to See Correspondences through Work in Women's Studies." Working Paper 189. Wellesley, MA: Wellesley College Center for Research on Women, 1988.

McIntosh, Peggy. "Unpacking the Invisible Knapsack." Excerpted from Peggy McIntosh. "White Privilege and Male Privilege: A Personal Account of Coming to see Correspondences through Work in Women's Studies," Working Papcr 189. Wellesley, MA: Wellesley College Center for Research on Women, 1988.

McLaughlin, Corinne and Gordon Davidson. *Spiritual Politics: Changing the World from the Inside Out.* New York: Ballantine Books, 1994.

Meade, Michael. *Fate and Destiny: The Two Agreements of the Soul.* Seattle: Greenfire Press, 2012.

Muskal, Michael. "Texas teen's probation for killing 4 while driving drunk stirs anger." *Los Angeles Times* December 12 2013, accessed August 16, 2015. http://www.latimes.com/nation/nationnow/la-na-nn-texas-teen-drunk-driving-probation-affluenza-20131212,0,61486.story#ixzz2ps64WWbK.

Needleman, Jacob. *The American Soul: Rediscovering the Wisdom of the Founders.* New York: Putnam, 2003.

Obear, Kathy. "Facilitating Workshops with Whites to Dismantle Racism." Unpublished handouts, 2013.

Owen, Susanne. *The Appropriation of Native American Spirituality.* London: Bloomsbury Academic, 2011.

Parker, Rebecca. "Not Somewhere Else, But Here: The Struggle for Racial Justice as a Struggle to Inhabit My Country." In *Soul Work: Anti-racist Theologies in Dialogue,* edited by Marjorie Bowens-Wheatley and Nancy Palmer Jones, 171–198. Boston: Skinner House, 2003.

Peffley, Mark and Jon Hurwitz. *Justice in America: The Separate Realities of Blacks and Whites.* Cambridge Studies in Public Opinion and Political Psychology. Cambridge: Cambridge University Press, 2010.

Perry, Tony. "Judge finds yoga complaint a stretch." *Los Angeles Times,* July 2, 2013.

Pitts, Jr., Leonard. "Crazy Sometimes." In *When Race Becomes Real: Black and White Writers Confront Their Personal Histories,* edited by Bernestine Singley. Chicago, IL: Lawrence Hill Books, 2002.

Pizza, Murphy and James Lewis. *Handbook of Contemporary Paganism.* Leiden, the Netherlands: Brill, 2009.

powell, john a., "Does Living a Spiritually Engaged Life Mandate Us to Be Actively Engaged in Issues of Social Justice?" *University of St. Thomas Law Review* 1 no. 1 (2003): 30–38.

Public Affairs Television. "The Faithkeeper, Interview with Bill Moyers, 3 July 1991 Public Affairs Television." http://www.ratical.org/many_worlds/6Nations/OL070391.html.

Quiñones-Rosado, Raúl. *Consciousness-in-Action: Toward an Integral Psychology of Liberation and Transformation.* Caguas, Puerto Rico: ile Publications, 2007.

Quiocho, Alice M. and Annette Daoud. "Dispelling Myths about Latino Parent Participation in Schools." *The Education Forum* 70 (2006): 255–67.

Race Forward. "Our Mission." Accessed August 22, 2015. https://www.raceforward.org/about.

Rasor, Paul. "Reclaiming Our Prophetic Voice: Liberal Theology and the Challenge of Racism." In *Soul Work: Anti-racist Theologies in Dialogue,* edited by Marjorie Bowens-Wheatley and Nancy Palmer Jones, 105–25. Boston: Skinner House, 2003.

Rose, Wendy. "The Great Pretenders: Further Reflections on White Shamanism." In *The State of Native America: Genocide, Colonisation and Resistance,* edited by Annette Jaimes, 403–21. Boston: South End. 1992.

Schmidt, Christine. "From Within: Practicing White Antiracism in Public Schools." In *Accountability and White Anti-racist Organizing: Stories from Our Work,* edited by Bonnie Berman Cushing et al., 44–61. Roselle, NJ: Crandall, Dostie & Douglass Books, 2010.

Shorter, David. "'I'm not an Indian.'" Accessed August 22, 2015. http://indiancountrytodaymedianetwork.com/2015/07/01/four-words-andrea-smith-im-not-indian.

Smith, Andrea. "Spiritual Appropriation as Sexual Violence." *Wicazo Sa Review* 20, no. 1 (2005): 97–111.

Smith, Andrea. "For All Those Who Were Indian in a Former Life." *Cultural Survival Quarterly* 17, no. 4 (1994): 70–71.

Smith, Gary. "The Other Side of Route Two: Some Autobiographical Struggles with Theology, Race, and Class." In *Soul Work: Anti-racist Theologies in Dialogue,* edited by Marjorie Bowens-Wheatley and Nancy Palmer Jones, 63–78. Boston: Skinner House, 2003.

Starhawk. *The Spiral Dance, a Rebirth of the Religion of the Ancient Goddess.* San Francisco: Harper Collins Press, 1989.

Street Poets. Accessed August 19, 2015. http://www.streetpoetsinc.com/.

Strong, Pauline Turner. "Cultural Appropriation and the Crafting of Racialized Selves in American Youth Organizations: Toward and Ethnographic Approach." *Critical Methodologies* 9 (2009): 197–213.

Strong, Pauline Turner and Laurie Posner. "Selves in play: Sports, Scouts, and American Cultural Citizenship." *International Review for the Sociology of Sport* 45 (2010): 390–409.

Sue, Derald Wing, Christina Capodilupo, Gina Torino, Jennifer Bucceri, Aisha Holder, Kevin Nadal, and Marta Esquilin. "Racial Microaggressions in Everyday Life: Implications for Clinical Practice." *American Psychologist* 62, no. 4 (2007): 271–86.

Tarnas, Richard. *The Passion of the Western Mind: Understanding the Ideas That Have Shaped Our World View.* New York: Ballantine Books, 1991.

Taylor, Bron. "Earthen Spirituality or Cultural Genocide?: Radical Environmentalism's Appropriation of Native American Spirituality." *Religion* 27 (1997): 183–215.

The Indaba. "Lead Facilitator." Accessed August 16, 2015. http://www.theindaba.com/leadfacilitator.html.

Tinker, George. *Missionary Conquest: the Gospel and Native American Genocide.* Minneapolis, MN: Fortress Press, 1993.

Tinker, George. "Racism and Anti-racism in a Culture of Violence: Dreaming a New Dream." In *Soul Work: Anti-racist Theologies in Dialogue,* edited by Marjorie Bowens-Wheatley and Nancy Palmer Jones, 79–104. Boston: Skinner House, 2003.

Tinker, George. *Spirit and Resistance: Political Theology and American Indian Liberation.* Minneapolis, MN: Fortress Press, 2004.

Tinker, George. *American Indian Liberation*. Maryknoll, NY: Orbis Books, 2008.

Tochluk, Shelly & Cameron Levin. "Powerful Partnerships: Transformative Alliance Building." In *Accountability and White Anti-racist Organizing: Stories from Our Work*, edited by Bonnie Berman Cushing et al., 190–219. Roselle, NJ: Crandall, Dostie, and Douglass Books, 2010.

Tochluk, Shelly. *Witnessing Whiteness: The Need to Talk About Race and How to Do It*. Lanham, MD: Rowman & Littlefield-Education, 2010.

Tolle, Eckhart. *A New Earth: Awakening to Your Life's Purpose*. New York: Penguin Group, 2005.

Waldron, David & Janice Newton. "Rethinking Appropriation of the Indigenous: A Critique of the Romanticist Approach." *The Journal of Alternative and Emergent Religions* 16, no. 2 (2012): 64–85.

Wall, Vernon. "10 Myths of Social Justice." Accessed August 22, 2015. uncw.edu/sustainability/documents/10MythsSocialJustice.doc.

Warren, Mark. *Fire in the Heart: How White Activists Embrace Racial Justice*. New York: Oxford University Press, 2010.

Watkins, Mary. "Seeding Liberation: A Dialogue Between Depth Psychology and Liberation Psychology." In *Depth Psychology: Meditations in the field*, edited by Dennis Patrick Slattery and Lionel Corbett, 204–24. Einsiedlen: Diamon, 2001.

Watkins, Mary and Helene Shulman. *Toward Psychologies of Liberation*. New York: Palgrave Macmillan, 2008.

White Privilege Conference. "White Privilege Conference Recommended Resource List." Accessed August 22, 2015. http://www.whiteprivilegeconference.com/resources/WPC-Resource-List-July2012.pdf

Wing, Derald, Christina Capodilupo, Gina Torino, Jennifer Bucceri, Aisha Holder, Kevin Nadal, and Marta Esquilin. "Racial Microaggressions in Everyday Life: Implications for Clinical Practice." *American Psychologist* 62, no. 4 (2007): 271–86.

Witnessing Whiteness. "The Destruction of Movement, Sinking into Privileged Despair/." Accessed August 15, 2015. http://www.witnessingwhiteness.blogspot.com/2009/08/destruction-of-movement-sinking-into.html.

Witnessing Whiteness. "Sonoma, Arizona Sweat Lodge." Accessed August 19, 2015. http://witnessingwhiteness.blogspot.com/2010/01/sonoma-az-sweat-lodge-james-arthur-ray.html.

Yancy, George. *Look, a White!: Philosophical Essays on Whiteness.* Philadelphia: Temple University Press, 2012.

York, Michael. *The Emerging Network: A Sociology of the New Age and Neo-Pagan Movements.* Landham, MA: Rowman & Littlefield, 1995.

York, Michael. "New Age Commodification and Appropriation of Spirituality." *Journal of Contemporary Religion* 16, no. 3 (2001): 361–72.

Young, James and Conrad Brunk. *The Ethics of Cultural Appropriation.* Malden, MA: Wiley-Blackwell, 2009.

Index

A

About the author

Shelly Tochluk is the author of *Witnessing Whiteness: The Need to Talk About Race and How to Do It.* An educator, with a background in psychology, Shelly Tochluk spent ten years as a researcher, counselor, and teacher in California's public schools. She now trains teachers to work with Los Angeles' diverse school population as Professor of Education at Mount Saint Mary's University - Los Angeles. Her personal dedication to confront issues of race developed first through her participation with UCLA's NCAA Division-1 All-American Track and Field 4X400 meter relay team and later through her inner city teaching experiences. She currently volunteers with AWARE-LA (Alliance of White Anti-Racists Everywhere-Los Angeles). With this group, she co-created and produces the Unmasking Whiteness - Summer Institute that leads white people into a deeper understanding of their personal relationship to race, white privilege, and systemic racism.